A STUDY IN MORAL THEORY

GEORGE ALLEN
PUBLISHERS LONDON
& UNWIN LIMITED
RUSKIN HOUSE

A STUDY IN MORAL THEORY

BY

JOHN LAIRD, M.A.

REGIUS PROFESSOR OF MORAL PHILOSOPHY IN THE
UNIVERSITY OF ABERDEEN
Author of "Problems of the Self," and of "A Study in Realism"

LONDON: GEORGE ALLEN & UNWIN LTD.
RUSKIN HOUSE, 40 MUSEUM STREET, W.C.1

Printed in Great Britain by
UNWIN BROTHERS, LIMITED, LONDON AND WOKING

First published in 1926

TO

MY WIFE

PREFACE

THE argument of this study arranges itself naturally into four divisions, of which the first is analytical, the second psychological, the third occupied with certain questions in social theory, and the fourth more comprehensive or philosophical. It is probable, however, that I owe the reader something more than this terse and formal account of its plan, and that I should endeavour, here at the outset, to give him a rough outline of its attitude and purpose. So much in human nature is pertinent to moral theory that there is a greater danger here than in most other subjects of finding oneself rather in a maze than in a way. A writer in these matters can but try to avoid excessive complication in his exposition. If the effect of attempting this general survey in this place, however, should be to plunge the reader headlong into difficult questions which, in the text, are at any rate approached more gradually, all I can do is to express my regret to him, and advise him to skip the rest of the preface. I believe I can truly assure him that there is easier going ahead.

According to a very general opinion, moralists take upon themselves the really endless task of exploring and assessing the whole territory of that which is good, as well as the onerous problem of effectively examining the underlying principles in righteous and honourable conduct. If so, they have a twofold problem; and perhaps they need not expect to find a single answer. As Grote, for one, has shown, the analysis and description of that which may be *won* need not correspond precisely to the corresponding enquiry into that which should be *done*. The *bonum*, in certain respects, need not define the same field as the *faciendum*. To be more explicit, it is evident that the former problem may be treated, and with entire legitimacy, in many and most various fashions. Goodness and The Ideal may perhaps be most clearly discernible in the fair image of a City of God, or of a Republic where the seeds of spiritual excellence may be sowed without fear of any scathe arising from sourness of the soil or from vulgar frailty; or, again, may perhaps be extracted from certain large perspectives derived, quite generally, from the course of mundane history or from the play of social forces. In comparison with these methods any attempt, in the traditional Protestant vein, to investigate the character and implications of personal goodness may seem incredibly meagre and strigose.

The problems that are rooted in the facts of duty and of moral obligation, upon the other hand, seem at the first look (and in a sense truly *are*) distinctly more manageable. To be sure, these also are not simply personal, since peoples and associations have their corporate duties, and since the duty of any man to act in concert with his fellows raises all the issues that may be relevant to the most elaborate of public actions. And if they *were* simply personal, personality, in all soberness, is complicated enough. Nevertheless, it seems evident that the voice of duty speaks to individual men and women in the same authentic tones and with the same indefeasible authority as to any corporate (or, indeed, to any superhuman) entity. This would be impossible unless the voice could clearly be heard, and could also be obeyed by those who accept it—that is to say, by all of us during a portion, at least, of our lives.

If these two courses were alternative methods of surveying the same field, something, but not very much, might be gained from the relative simplicity of the latter. As we have seen, however, they need not define quite the same province, and in any case we should have some better method of deciding between them than any that has been mentioned hitherto. Upon reflection, however, despite so much that has often been assumed to the contrary, it seems abundantly plain that the second method, and not the first, directly delineates the moralist's province. For goodness or excellence in general is wider than morals, and is relevant to morals only when it is qualified in a very significant way. To choose a simple instance, happiness in its mere existence is good and valuable, and yet happiness is relevant to morals only when the pursuit or control or abandonment of it is in question. Suffering might exist in a world of lowly animals where moral questions could not arise. The infliction of this suffering by a being who knew he could prevent it, on the other hand, is emphatically a moral question.

Values and excellent pursuits, in short, may be, and very often are, entirely non-moral, and these non-moral excellences become relevant to morals only when we raise the question of promoting or renouncing them. I submit, therefore, that the second type of enquiry and not the first is the true and proper object of moral study.

This conviction (together with the explanation and defence of it at far greater length than is appropriate to this preface) determines the whole course of the first, or analytical, portion of this study. This analytical argument begins with the second chapter (the first chapter being a very general introduction) and extends to the end of the fifth.

The course of it is, briefly, as follows : Although a certain number of moralists have maintained that " duty for duty's sake " is the whole body of ethics, and although there is certainly a sense (which needs careful definition) in which duty is supreme and self-justifying, it seems impossible to deny that duty in any given case is in reality the best use that any moral being or set of moral beings can make of their capacities with respect to a given opportunity ; or, in other words, that the justification of duty must be in terms of the values it sustains and conserves. Into this (as the example of happiness has already shown) non-moral values may enter. The wickedness of torturing an animal, to keep to this simple example, is at least partly determined by the physical evil of mere animal suffering. There is no sense in maintaining that the animal's non-moral agony has nothing to do with the matter. Thus, beginning with personal duty, we reach very speedily a much larger thing, and have to distinguish, in a most catholic fashion and with a liberal aim, between superordinate or dominant goods, and subordinate and consequential ones. The variety of these goods, and the subtlety of their conflicts and confluences among the shifting sands of our existence in time, affords a problem which, if it is answered simply, cannot be answered truly. Despite this complexity, however, I venture to hope that, if we do not expect too much from it, a general but faithful conspectus may have genuinely significant results.

This general conspectus is attempted in the third chapter, and in the fourth its applicability to conduct is considered. The application is essential, since conduct consists of particular actions, and since there certainly is an art of wise living as well as a science of ethical principle. So much of this art, however, is rather the use of a wide discretion in the business of action than truly what Aristotle would have called a "practical syllogism," and so much of it is an affair of tact or of delicate sensitivity, that we may have to be careful lest this portion of the discussion, instead of removing difficulties, should aggravate and increase them. This problem in application, however, has to be faced, since the facts require it. Moreover, in view of the serious objections which doubters and sophists and perplexed persons have brought against the possibility of any genuine *knowledge* of good or of evil, it is necessary also to consider the chief of these objections, and, if they may be overcome, to enquire more freely and at the same time more exactly into the respects into which we may reasonably claim either certainty or strong probability in this important subject. This latter is the problem of the fifth chapter of the book, and concludes the analytical section.

Chapters VI, VII and VIII form the psychological section of the study, and the reader may reasonably ask why psychology, contrary to the practice of so many writers on these subjects, occupies the second place in the discussion instead of the first place, as well as the grounds for selecting for discussion those particular psychological topics which determine the constitution of the section itself.

The answer to the first of these questions, I think, is not very hard. I am a little doubtful, I confess, whether the usual way of stating this contrast is entirely adequate. It is easy to say, and not altogether difficult to believe, that psychology, being merely causal, positive and descriptive, must be ethically neutral and entirely un-ideal ; or that when psychological facts are used for a purpose (as in social reform, vocational guidance, or industrial efficiency) the science of psychology ceases, being replaced by something hortatory and given to taking sides.   But when this is said, something important seems to be forgotten.   In reality, our psychical lives are at least half ideal, since they are directed towards the future ; ideality can scarcely be described if ideals are left out of account, and vision and visionariness alike are authentic psychological forces.   Again, to choose the other side of the contrast, ethics is not a hortatory study, and in that sense does not take sides. If it shows the good and the just, it need not exhort us concerning them, for their authority is too fine a thing for praise or meddlesome urgings.   In a word, there is something overforward when a moralist begins to preach.   Despite these qualifications, however, the principal outlines of this contrast have manifestly to be accepted.   Psychology, we may say, has for its province the investigation into every possibility in the way of psychical development or of psychical control over the resources of our living.   It is not called upon to scrutinise the worth or the meanness of these, and this is just what ethics has to do.   Or, again, in so far as ethics is concerned, as it properly is, with what ought to be done, it cannot be the vassal of a purely factual science.   In its own affairs it must lead and not follow.   It is autonomous, not consequential.

Per contra, an ethic which sets out from the analysis of duty plainly runs upon psychology at every turn, for it can never be anyone's duty to perform that which he cannot perform, and if the *best* use of our lives is enjoined we must clearly have acquaintance with the *possible* uses of them.   For very urgent reasons, therefore, these psychological problems press vigorously upon every element in this discussion, and it seemed essential to attempt to vindicate the human possibility of the analytical section by an independent investigation into the control of conduct (such control being in the main psychological), as well as by considering the special points in moral psychology which had the closest bearing upon the earlier discussion. The truth is that we commonly employ an immensely over-simplified psychological theory in dealing with these matters, because we think in terms of the knowledge of good and evil, upon the one hand, and of the " will " upon the other. If, however, we mean by the " will " some faculty of responding immediately and with complete accuracy to any intention, admonition or principle which is expressly understood, it is plain that only a small part of our actions pertain to the " will " in this restricted sense, and that, as well as knowledge, many other psychological factors enter, among which emotion and sentiment, to say nothing of habit, are among the more considerable.

According to the view I am endeavouring to defend, this common opinion, although dangerously and often mischievously oversimplified, has grasped in effect the central feature of a very tangled situation, and if this be the truth, what is chiefly required of my argument is the retention of this central truth, its defence against objectors, and, at the same time, its modification in such a way as to make it capable, at least in outline, of dealing with the psychological realities with which it is concerned. To be frank, I am more doubtful of my success in this particular than in any other portion of the argument (and I think I am doubtful very often, although frequently, I suspect, in the wrong places). Nevertheless, it is surely exceedingly hard to deny that, however great the importance we attach to purity of heart or to other sub- or semi-conscious conditions, however frankly we may admit that there is a generous quality that cannot be voluntarily summoned in courage,

loving-kindness, and many other of the virtues, and
however indubitable it may be that habit and the
obscurer of the sentiments form a massive impulsive
background, always present in the actions which we call
voluntary, and on occasion predominating enormously
in the actual determination of action, it still remains
true that ultimately the supreme direction and control
of our conduct depends upon the intelligent and enlightened parts of us, and that these, in the last analysis,
have an authority, and even a power, that nothing else
can have, and that effectually discriminates between
moral beings and other creatures which, like the higher
animals, are moral only by the courtesy of a halting
analogy.   At any rate, this is the general spirit in which
the reflections of this psychological section are offered,
and if the seventh chapter, concerning unconscious
regulation, is unduly concerned with theories that have
an exaggerated vogue to-day, the eighth, which deals
with freedom, treats of matters as ancient as they are
cardinal.

The ninth chapter presents a retrospect of the argument of the first two sections, and is followed by a discussion, in two chapters, of certain social implications
pertaining to the theory of the book and of further
explanations in this regard.   The restriction of the topics
here dealt with forbid the ascription of such a title as
" the sociological section " to this part of the discussion ;
but although the problems of " Self and Others " and
of " Action in Concert " are only a small portion of
sociological debate, they are clearly of great importance,
despite their relatively abstract character.   In the eyes
of some of my readers, I know very well, the restricted
scope of these chapters must appear not only reprehen-
sible in itself, but a proof of the defective character of the
whole course of this study.   " The man," I hear them

saying, " has begun all wrong by attacking his problems from the standpoint of the individual agent. At long last he appears to make the discovery that human beings are social creatures, and he offers us a few beggarly observations by way of atoning for his unpardonable misconceptions."

It is hopeless, I know, to convince anyone who argues in this strain, but I should like to explain, for the benefit of the unconverted, why I do not consider that the charge is true. I think, indeed (for reasons which I endeavour to supply in their proper place), that there might be duties without reference to any social companions whatsoever. For the most part, however (and among actual human beings perhaps altogether), it is abundantly evident that every duty has a social aspect, and that the sociality of our existence has entered into the very substance of us. What I am endeavouring to explain is not a non-social ethic, but one in which duties and responsibilities actually do attach to individual men and women, and, so far as we can see, confront us and are accepted by us in our personal capacity with a clearness that is at least less evident in any other example of their incidence. I should add, perhaps, that it is frequently both possible and necessary to distinguish between the self-regarding and the other-regarding aspects and consequences of any course of conduct, just as, among the other-regarding aspects and consequences, it is possible, and often necessary, to distinguish between the effects of our conduct upon our next-door neighbours and upon the Emperor of Siam. Finally, I may, perhaps, be permitted to point out that I have attempted to defend the relevant conception of personality by argument, not by mere assertion, and consequently that the assertions of superior persons to the effect that selfhood is a sort of painful miasma, half-being or all illusion, are irrelevant unless *they* also can summon something in the guise of argument to their aid.

The twelfth and last chapter deals with some of the broader and therefore more philosophical aspects of this enquiry.

It remains to fulfil the pleasant obligation of acknowledging with gratitude the help I have received. A portion of this gratitude has to travel a great distance, for although during several years I have spent much of my time in these islands in attempting to put my ideas about moral theory upon paper and in tearing the paper up again, it was not until I was invited to become Mills Lecturer in the University of California that these opinions attained anything tangibly approaching their present substance. I hope that the form in which they now appear has avoided some of the crudities and inadequacies that I inflicted upon a very patient audience in California, and if any of my colleagues or pupils there should chance to read this book, I hope they will accept this expression of my gratitude. During the process of question and answer in California I found that the courteous American appearance of suffering *any* lecturer gladly did not interfere with a private criticism both sharp and apposite. I hope I have benefited from these stimulating discussions.

I am most grateful to Mr. A. J. Dorward, my former colleague in Belfast ; and to my colleague, Mr. O. de Selincourt, in this University, for the pains and skill they have shown in helping me in the correction of the proofs during a very busy time.

JOHN LAIRD.

KING'S COLLEGE, OLD ABERDEEN,
   November, 1925.

CONTENTS

Chapter IV

THE APPLICATION TO PRACTICE 62

Chapter V

THE KNOWLEDGE OF GOOD AND EVIL . . 88

CONTENTS xxi

CONTENTS

A Study in Moral Theory

CHAPTER I

INTRODUCTION

IT is notorious that of all the subjects men are moved
to write about, Ethics has been one of the first and chief
since the days when writing began. This circumstance
itself prompts many reflections, some of them pleasant,
others not so pleasant. It is gratifying, on the whole,
to remember that these discussions, even if they are
bookish, indicate a persistent and a very general interest
in moral matters. Curiosity, inquisitiveness even, and
a reflective bent of the mind are very general attributes
of human nature. Most of us believe that they ought
to be cultivated; and we should consider ourselves
very sadly placed if we did not, or could not, reflect
upon the values of things, the aim of the business of
living, the excellence of that which we are minded to
do. We suppose also (rashly, perhaps, but still not
wholly without reason) that there are the seeds of hope
and a certain nurture for it in this affair. Something
should be learned from so much scrutiny and debate,
something effective for our improvement in so far as
this improvement may be attained. It might be otherwise, indeed, if these voluminous discussions were the
work of sectaries or cloistered persons protesting

shrilly from behind learned walls. This, however, is not the fact. Moral problems confront us every hour ; and if we do not reflect upon them every day, we reflect at least very often. Moral discussions are mirrored in literature of every species ; and in the mirror they may be signals, not simple images.

The cynics, on the other hand, have another construction to offer. We may say, if we choose, that it is biased, but we cannot call it baseless. Indeed, we have the right to ignore these cynics when they say that moralizing is just a way of taking ourselves far too seriously, an excuse for meddling, a cloak for the vice of exhortation. Such criticisms, if they are pertinent at all, are themselves moral criticisms, and the makers of them are the companions of their opponents, smeared, if we care to put it so, with the same wallow. Much shrewder criticism, however, is possible here, with never a trace of self-stultifying. It is very reasonable to argue that the subjects most discussed are precisely those that are inconclusive. Prone as we are to discussion, we have also a certain prudence ; and the fear of ridicule is enough in itself to forbid any large number of chatterers and dabblers from airing their opinions where established evidence and rigorous expert mastery are ready to rebuke them. There are circle squarers and believers in a flat earth, but not very many. When a subject is known to be inconclusive, however, and at the same time excites general interest, we expect and find a great cloud of counsellors. Freedom, immortality, the standards of duty, and the ideal of human society are precisely in this position. There is nothing to prevent anyone from writing about them, and therefore many do. In a word, argument abounds ; and proof (we are told) is always absent.

So stated, this accusation is probably not inaccurate

and certainly it is pertinent. The sting of it, however, may perhaps be drawn.

In the first place, a certain degree of inconclusiveness need not imply futility. Indeed, there may be bigotry and intellectual rudeness in demanding conclusiveness where it is not to be had. Certainly we have every reason to be proud of the human intellect for devising conclusive arguments in mathematics, in logic, and in other places where it is admitted that such arguments are to be found. This is worth a hecatomb. What is more, even when this degree of conclusiveness is not to be expected (as in the more advanced of the experimental sciences), we may rightly venerate the luminous insight and the fruitful sagacity that have divined methods and principles which, if they are not wholly conclusive, have delivered us at least from aimlessness and from the stumbling that is incident to those who profess to walk by the light of nature. If moralists, then, were to emulate this sagacity, the rest of the world should, and probably would, admire them unstintedly. If, on the other hand, their art or their science is very slow to lend itself to conquests of this species, being too sinuous, too varied, too stubborn for any single plan or formula (at any rate so far as we can see), it is not, even then, to be inferred that reflection upon it is either useless or avoidable. The subject is not more elusive than our lives are, and even in our gropings we may learn.

In the second place, it is a fallacy to suppose that discussions must be worthless in which all and sundry are entitled to an opinion. If it were claimed, indeed, that any opinion is as good as any other upon these matters, that there is no such thing as delicate observation, subtle analysis, or orderly criticism of our ideas concerning them, then indeed we might expect futility, and we should have to do so unless we suspected revelation. For men certainly differ in their discernment, their persistence in sifting their ideas, their capacity for stating and appreciating what (as we say) they really mean; and these are the qualities which give substance and worth to an opinion. What may reasonably be claimed, however, is not this absurdity, but something entirely different. The sounder claim is, firstly, that every one of us has moral experience which, being what we are, we all do reflect upon—some more than others, but all in considerable measure; and, secondly, that there is a certain appreciable equality between all moral beings in this particular, since each has sufficient moral experience to yield the basis of an opinion that counts, and since each is capable of a degree of reflection that entitles his opinion to consideration.

Quite plainly, these contentions omit a great deal, at any rate in their first intention. They would be indisputable only if the basis of any man's moral opinions were his own personal moral experience, that which he himself has been called upon to do or to suffer when conscience and duty enter. That, however, is not the whole of the evidence. Indeed, it may plausibly be represented as a very small portion of the evidence. To inform ourselves properly of moral issues, it may be urged, we should explore the whole territory of human (if not of divine) endeavour and consider the development of all standards, the structure, growth, and aims of societies, and everything else that may be relevant to conduct, such as our command over nature, the sciences of medicine and politics, the laws of economics, the lessons (if there are any) that come from theology and metaphysics. It is not Puritan individualism (so the argument runs), but the older ideals of the Greeks, that are truly relevant. To discover the use of our faculties that is fitting and excellent we must investigate the whole diameter of our collective capacities and ideals, drawing freely upon history, biology, state-craft, psychology, and sociology. These sciences, in their turn, may not be conclusive, but they do require expert knowledge, and opinions which are ill-informed concerning them are not worth a hearing.

There is truth in this, much truth, and all of it chastening and salutary; yet the claims of moral philosophy in the personal, individualistic, tradition-ally Protestant vein should not be set aside on this account. Morality, if there is such a thing, is binding upon individual men and women. It is not a thing these individuals can renounce or delegate to experts, governments, or the trend of the times. In short, look at it as we may, it is hard to resist the conclusion that without his own personal experience no one is fitted to judge of these matters; and that, when all is said, the cardinal principles of ethics ought to reveal themselves when there is resolute analysis of anyone's personal experience. If so, this personal analysis and these personal reflections are emphatically worth a hearing. Indeed, they are always indispensable, and they may very well be decisive.

On the whole, then, I think we should conclude that the cynic's objections are not well founded. To inter-pret the value of life as we see it, to form opinions on duty, on conscience, on the meaning of what (as we believe) we ought to do, is something we may not avoid, and a thing which, if it is sincere, is very unlikely to be worthless. So far from deploring this immense volume of expression upon moral questions, we should, on the contrary, welcome it; and this in any form in which the opinion appears. It is a commonplace, and justly so, that the best reflections upon moral questions are to be found, not, for the most part, in the pages of professed or professional moralists (although much may be learned from the best of these), but in poetry, the drama, the novel, or in the biographies of surgeons, of priests, of administrators, or of plain people. That is as it should be; and those philosophers who, like Aristotle, have busied themselves with the opinions of the many as well as with the opinions of the wise, have treated their subject as it ought to be treated.

I have tried to explain why I think this should be so, but since the mere mention of " common sense " and of the " plain man " is open to the most various constructions, I could not be pardoned if I did not try to prevent some of the more palpable misconstructions. Common sense, I suppose, means the body of current opinion within a given community at a given time. Hence it is neither sacrosanct nor likely to be more than a rough approximation to anything that is true. It cannot be sacrosanct because we know as a matter of history that current opinion on every matter is better or worse informed in different communities at different times; and even if we consider ourselves better informed than any other people in any age we could not surely have the effrontery to argue that our current opinions are incapable of improvement. Again, it seems plain that within any given community the current general opinion is not likely to be the best-informed opinion on any given topic. From the nature of the case this current, general opinion cannot be expert opinion, unless it is supposed that in some matters every one is an expert and as good as any other expert.

In many ways, therefore, the hardest things that are said of common sense are among the most just. Since most of us are prejudiced, slovenly in our thinking,

vague guessers with very little appreciation of the
essentials of accuracy, or of the meaning of adequate
proof, it is unlikely that the current opinion on any
topic is anywhere near the best. To expect very much
from it is to expect miracles from compulsory school
education. The usual opinion is an opinion that is
led, not an opinion that leads, and by the time an idea
is generally grasped it is almost certain to be antiquated.
If not, it is grasped only in the way in which jaded
people pick up blatant discoveries from a newspaper.
And there is usually very great disingenuousness in the
appeal to common sense. If we really knew the honest
opinion of most of our neighbours, and could discriminate that in it which is truly theirs, not simply accepted
from indolence or imposed by hearsay, we might, to
be sure, have some respect for it. In general, however,
there is no such inventory and nothing of this discrimination. What a man sets forth as the opinion of
" common sense " is usually his own opinion, combined
with the belief that in expressing it he is sheltering
himself behind the herd. He presumes general agreement without any sufficient evidence, and in suggesting
that his opponent is eccentric reveals his own calibre
by assuming that he has said a hard thing about him.
In a word, the man is lazy and a coward.

All this is true, but it is not all the truth. The necessary corrective is careful discrimination between those
matters in which current opinion is likely to be important
and those in which it is not. Of the former we may
say that if there are any matters on which the generality
of mankind have first-hand experience, and on which
they have to think for themselves, it is extremely
probable that the general opinion is well worth considering in so far as it may be ascertained. For this there
are many reasons. However loose, and slipshod, and

disingenuous our ordinary thinking may be, it is at
the least extremely unlikely that any opinions widely
held and widely followed are hopelessly astray. The
test of practice is too stern for this, the pressure
of actuality far too considerable. What commonly
happens, indeed, is that the prevailing opinions are
bewildered and untidy fusions of blurred but cardinal
elements; and the besetting sin of most theorists upon
these general topics is that although they take a little
longer to contradict themselves than other people,
they are, on the whole, more likely to omit essential
points. A thinker, therefore, who ignores current
opinion does so at his peril. He may, indeed, be a
better thinker than his fellows, more apt in logical
reflection or in the expression of it, but he is likely
to forget some of the massive stubborn wisdom that
is at least half-articulated in the body of current beliefs.

For the reasons already given, I think it is a mistake
to suppose, as many do, that the whole of a moralist's
business is to clarify common opinion, and to compel
it to become systematic by a sort of Socratic self-
examination. This is because there may be a great
deal of relevant knowledge (derived, say, from history
and from the sciences) which could not possibly be
elicited from the resources of self-reflection upon
first-hand experience; and a moralist who would ape
the son of Sophroniscus in these modern days should
at least go to school with many famous sages before
he begins to set these limpid, direct, ingenuous,
leading questions. Yet it is not too much to say that
the principal evidence in these enquiries is, and must
always be, the analysis of that moral experience which
comes to everyone by the mere fact of responsible
behaviour. It is possible, indeed, that a trained
observer may be a better interpreter of man's actions

and of the ends that humanity pursues than most of the other actors, and even that such an one should be a shrewder judge of others than of himself. As Francis Bacon said : " The calling of a man's self to a strict account is a medicine sometimes too piercing and corrosive ; reading good books of morality is a little flat and dead ; observing our faults in others is sometimes improper for our case ; but the best receipt (best, I say, to work and best to take) is the admonition of a friend." [1] On the whole, however, it is the examined life that instructs us here, and its principles are elicited from individual searchings of the heart and of the conscience. For this there is a reason entirely sufficient. When a man finds himself faced with a moral alternative he knows that he is faced with a problem that in principle is general. To have moral experience at all is therefore to encounter some principle, and every moral act implies the use of principle and some knowledge of it. Since every responsible being has to train himself in moral matters, he has therefore to train himself in moral principles. Accordingly, in his degree he is a moralist and an expert. In short, anyone who takes account of his actions should also take account of his principles.

These observations indicate, and in a measure may serve to defend, the general standpoint occupied by this study. We have the right, indeed, to hope, and we may be wise to expect, highly important results, say, from the present ferment in the social sciences and in psychology, or from the liberating ideas now current in biology. Nevertheless, anyone who is tempted to look for a new, an alien, and an utterly unexpected ethic to arise from these sources is not even, I believe, " legitimately tempted," if I may be pardoned for

[1] Bacon's *Essays*: " Of friendship."

using Lord Haldane's phrase. However profoundly these mechanical, medical, and psychical discoveries may properly alter our outlook upon life, and the mode in which we set out to regulate it, it is scarcely to be supposed that they can do more than modulate the essentials of moral theory. For, as we have seen, if moral experience is truly what it claims to be, it must show, and must have shown itself (not too dimly), in all who assume moral responsibility—that is to say, in nearly all of us and for many ages past. The cardinal features of the moral domain present themselves, quite plainly, whenever a man is aware that he has a duty to do ; and therefore these cardinal features are relatively little at the mercy of fresh discoveries in science, or of new and strange problems arising out of the means which civilization affords for the instruction of our lives. The ultimate problems in morals, in a word, have presented themselves in the same essential fashion to a great multitude for a great while, however true it may be that the entanglements of living have perplexed, or the haze of local conditions has obscured, them.

The need for continuous discussion of these topics (apart from the fact that the dead speak only in the living, and are apt to make living minds a prey to their own corruption if living mouths are content to repeat dead words) is precisely the necessity for mastering principles (irrespective of their antiquity) in our own time, and for applying them to the needs of our own generation. Hence, while we should not strain after novelty, we dare not avoid dealing with much that is new. It is unlikely, however, that each generation, simply because it comes fresh to its problems, should consider itself bound to inaugurate a latter-day revolution in its principal findings. One of the signal advantages of philosophy, indeed, and one of the strongest reasons why moral *science* should still be accounted moral *philosophy*, is precisely that philosophers have usually been trained to keep their heads, in a measure at least, during all the whirling vicissitudes of the fashion in ideas.

Let us proceed, then (if the reader cares to put it so, in the good old-fashioned way), to consider the anatomy of fundamental moral conceptions.

CHAPTER II

THE CHARACTER OF MORAL ENQUIRY

OUR thinking is always an attempt to solve a problem. It is an endeavour to find an answer to the questions which some theme presents, to give a reason for the things which have a reason.

The problem which moral enquiry has to consider is a certain pertinent, inescapable question that is set by the fact of action. This question is whether any given action is what it ought to be. In other words, moral theory is concerned with the reasons that justify action; or else that condemn it. What is asked is whether there are any such reasons, and, if so, how and in what degree they justify.

Accordingly, one of the first things we have to do in this enquiry is to distinguish reasons which justify (or, at any rate, reasons of the kind which might conceivably justify), from reasons of every other sort. The essential contrast here is between reasons that are simply explanatory and reasons that justify or condemn. This contrast applies very sharply to actions. If, for example, we could show how an action came about, or the causes that sustain it in its present character, we should have answered certain relevant questions that might be asked about it; and therefore we should have explained it in these respects. We should not, however, have even begun to justify it. To justify it we should have to show, not that it *is* of a certain kind, or that it has come about in a certain way, but that it *ought to be* of this kind.

This distinction, I repeat, is entirely plain and quite fundamental. It is not even abstruse. When we speak, as Mr. Kipling does, of things for which there are "plenty of reasons but not a single excuse," we all recognize, and readily, what is meant, and we know that the difference is profound. Similarly, we all distinguish between a defence and an explanation, although sometimes, to be sure, we may be temporarily puzzled by spurious sagacities like *Tout comprendre c'est tout pardonner*. It would be permissible, therefore, to leave the distinction as it stands. Yet it is so momentous and so often forgotten that the leisurely survey of a few illustrations need not be dilatory, and may even repay. If we select instances in which the distinction may easily be clouded over by inadvertence, so much the better.

Let us consider, then, the account of President Wilson's actions at the Versailles Conference that Mr. Keynes gives us in his *Economic Consequences of the Peace*, and let us assume, purely for the argument's sake, that Mr. Keynes described in that work, not only what he thought he saw, but what actually was before his very penetrating eyes. His story, we may say, is in effect that the late President, having at the time a prestige, power, and moral opportunity unequalled in the world before, nevertheless let the opportunity slip for reasons readily explicable, but not of the type that justify. Insensitive to the *nuances* of his environment, he played a game of blind-man's buff in a party of nimbler spirits. Theological rather than intellectual in his outlook, he was better fitted to pray for a new dispensation than to organize one. " Thus, day after day, and week after week, he allowed himself to be

closeted, unsupported, unadvised, and alone with men
much sharper than himself, in situations of supreme
difficulty, where he needed for success every description of resource, fertility, and knowledge. He allowed
himself to be drugged by their atmosphere, to discuss
on the basis of their plans and of their data, and to be
led along their paths." [1]

What is here *explained*, then, is the calamitous but
not unexampled circumstance of a man of great station
and of high ideals, who nevertheless accomplished,
upon the whole, precisely the opposite of what initially
he set out to perform, and finally, in the name of
principle, succumbed to sophistry and dishonest patch-
work. This may, or may not, be the truth, and if it
is the truth, it may not be all of it; but if it is true, what
we have here presented is a *sufficient explanation* of an
unjustifiable event. Certainly these explanations may
incidentally have the effect, not indeed of justifying the
President, but of mitigating the severity with which
ignorant persons, moralizing freely from a station of
humble security, might be disposed to judge the man.
It is relevant here to remember (if the narrative is
correct in what it relates) that the President was, in
fact, the wrong man for the task, although from afar,
and before he left the decks of the *George Washington*,
he seemed pre-eminently the right one. For, if this
were so, he could not have succeeded, except by the
merest hazard, and in that measure explanatory reasons
circumscribe the moralist's province. This circum-
scription, however, does not in any way annul the
distinction between the moralist's questions and the
psychologist's.

Again, we may consider an instance less terribly
public, where the bitterness of our present discontents

[1] Pp. 41-2.

cannot perturb us, and time itself lends eyes to our judgment. In the *Farington Diary*, on the evidence of Carlyle the surgeon, certain interesting details are supplied concerning the state of mind of a certain notorious duellist who perished, in the end, shortly after a combat which he had wantonly and indefensibly provoked. Lord Camelford, a cousin of Pitt's, died on March 8, 1804, after a duel with a certain Mr. Best, and the duel itself aroused horror, partly on account of Camelford's persistent participation in such affairs, partly on account of his singular ferocity upon the occasion in question. For Camelford, although in the wrong, refused the most ample opportunities for avoiding the combat by tendering the mildest form of apology, tried to persuade his second to arrange that the shots should be exchanged at eight paces, and exclaimed " That won't do " when his opponent presented his pistol wide. In the common opinion of the world (that is to say, of polite society), the world was well rid of such a truculent ruffian ; yet (according to Carlyle's evidence) it appears that Camelford's truculence was self-enforced in the teeth of what he took to be a timid nature. He declared to Carlyle " that he had no animal courage, and laboured by any means to get the better of a weakness of nerves in this respect by attending cock-fightings, pugilism, etc. That in him Courage was a struggle of sentiment against constitution." [1]

Supposing, therefore, that Camelford was not mistaken in this estimate of his own character, we have here an explanation which certainly cannot justify and yet, in the psychological way, is a perfectly good explanation. As before, the explanation may be relevant to our estimate of Lord Camelford's character. If it

Farington Diary, vol. ii, p. 202.

were correct, he was not a mere bully or simply brutal ; and a courage so hard to come by, even if it were wofully misdirected, commands our sympathy in a certain degree. We cannot approve his actions, and we must condemn them ; but the explanation shows that certain forces that we commonly admire were potent in him, and that he was not actuated simply by those we unite in condemning. This is relevant, but, in its own way, cannot do more than give point to the distinction with which we are concerned.

As has been said, however, this distinction, cardinal and pellucid as it is, may be forgotten notwithstanding. Indeed, it has been forgotten very often, both by moralists and by other people, and I am inclined to think that a warning of Hume's written two centuries ago is thoroughly pertinent to-day. " In every system of morality which I have hitherto met with," Hume says, " I have always remarked that the author proceeds for some time in the ordinary way of reasoning, and establishes the being of a God, or makes observations concerning human affairs ; when of a sudden I am surprised to find, that instead of the usual copulation of propositions, *is* and *is not*, I meet with no proposition that is not connected with an *ought*, or an *ought not*. This change is imperceptible ; but is, however, of the last consequence. For as this *ought*, or *ought not*, expresses some new relation or affirmation, 'tis necessary that it should be observed and explained, and at the same time that a reason should be given, for what seems altogether inconceivable, how this new relation can be a deduction from others, which are entirely different from it.   But as authors do not commonly use this precaution, I shall presume to recommend it to the readers." [1]

[1] *Treatise of Human Nature*, Book III, Part I, section i, Selby-Bigge's edition, p. 469.

It is not true that Hume was the first to take this precaution, or that he has been the last to take it. What is still true, however, is that many, quite inexcusably, never take it, and that many others forget it.[1]

We have to ask, therefore, what this "new relation or affirmation" is that does not simply explain an action, but shows, or tends to show, that it is what it ought to be. Here, again, the answer in principle is not very difficult, for it is plain that the only consideration relevant to the justification or condemnation of an action is its value or lack of value, its goodness or badness. Wherever there is proof of well-being, there is at least a partial justification; and ill-being is always a damning circumstance. Where there is no question of good or ill there is also no question of justifying or condemning.

The truth of this, I think, can scarcely be disputed, although it may readily enough be concealed. Indeed, as Mr. Moore pointed out to a former generation in his *Principia Ethica*, it has been concealed very often. When actions are justified (say) because of their "conformity to nature" (whatever that may mean), because of their accordance with the course of "evolution," because of the extent of our self-realization in them, because they are "parts of happiness," or decreed by the Will of God, there may be no explicit mention of worth or its absence. Nevertheless, either worth is

---

[1] As an egregious example of the way in which a very wise man may neglect this precaution, the following passage from Mr. Havelock Ellis's *The Dance of Life* may be quoted (p. 245). "That morality is, *in the strict sense*, a matter of taste, of æsthetics, of what the Greeks called αἴσθησις, is *conclusively* shown by the fact that in the most widely separated tongues—possibly wherever the matter has been *carefully* investigated—moral goodness is *at the outset* expressed in terms of *taste*. What is good is what is *sweet*, and, sometimes, also, *salt*." [Italics mine, except the last three.]

implied or these arguments are irrelevant. If God is good and His purpose is the best, then His ways are justified and men ought to follow them. If not, there is no reason why men should.   Similarly, if the processes of evolution are good, or make for something better, then, *pro tanto*, we ought to go along with them. If they are bad, or have the seeds of decay in them, we ought to resist them so far as we can. In a word, there seems to be but one pretended justification that is ever offered other than a justification in terms of value. This is the plea of necessity—the tyrant's plea and the slave's—and necessity, pretty clearly, is not really a justification, but a denial of jurisdiction. What is urged is that necessity excuses because condemnation is out of place, and not that necessity either justifies or condemns.

Accordingly, we are bound to maintain that the only reason which can possibly justify or condemn is a reason based upon worth or its opposite. This being granted, however, certain further questions arise which are of the first importance for the ethical consideration of actions which ought, or ought not, to be performed. When there is choice (or the possibility of alternative action) it is not enough to say that an action which is good is (so far) justified, and that an action which is bad is (so far) condemned ; for the choice of a lesser good is wicked, although this lesser good really is a good, and the choice of the best is always justified, even when the best is very bad indeed.

Thus we have to say—

Firstly, that when we neglect alternative possibilities, an action is justified in so far as it is good, and condemned in so far as it is bad. (In the above statement it is assumed that the goodness of an action includes the goodness which the action entails, as well as the goodness which it possesses.)

Secondly, that when a question arises concerning two alternatives only, the choice of the better is always justified, the choice of the worse always to be condemned. (Here it is assumed that a bad thing is always worse than a good one, that a lesser good is always worse than a greater one, and that a bad thing, notwithstanding its badness, is better than another bad thing which is still worse.)

Thirdly, that when many alternatives are possible, the best should always be chosen, and that this law holds even when the best is bad.

Fourthly, that when alternatives are equal in respect of their goodness or badness, there is no valid reason for preferring any one of these to any other.

Fifthly, that if any alternative in itself is neutral (i.e. neither good nor bad) it is still better than a thing which is positively evil, and worse than a thing which is positively good.

In these statements it is assumed that we have some knowledge of good and evil, some power of comparing better with worse; that we may be able to choose between them; and that these principles apply to any choice in accordance with this knowledge. They may therefore be disputed on the ground that there is no such thing as a knowledge of good or evil (this is what the sceptics say), or, again, that choice is an illusion (as some have argued who deny the freedom of the will). The effect of these very radical objections would be that these so-called principles are vain and void because they apply to nothing. Even so, however, it is not denied that they would be true, and that they would justify or condemn, if they did apply to anything; and other, minor objections should not deny this either. Thus it is often alleged that no action (taken along with its consequences) can be neutral or indifferent, and many people appear to deny, with the utmost vigour, that the best possible action may nevertheless be bad. The first of these statements may possibly be true, although I cannot think it certain or even likely. The second, I think, can save itself only by a questionable and perhaps a desperate device. There are diseases that can never be cured, lives that can never be useful, calamities in the face of which nothing but alleviation can be hoped for, either from action or from inaction. In any ordinary sense, the best, in these cases, is very bad indeed, but it is possible to argue that the honest endeavour to do the best, even when there is little hope or none, dignifies and sweetens the action, and makes it both admirable and excellent. This may consistently be held.

A justifying reason, then (or a reason which shows that a given action *ought* to be performed), is a reason in terms of value ; and anything which ought to be done, ought to be done for a sufficient reason. The latter part of this statement, it is true, is sometimes disputed. There is no reason for duty, it is said, except duty itself. Duties are unconditional demands, categorical imperatives, self-justifying injunctions. To suppose that these injunctions are justified only because they are good *for* something *else*, is to smirch and to flout them ; for they are sovereign in their own right.

This complaint, however, is itself a misunderstanding. The *ought* of morality may very well justify itself ; but if we are right, it can do so only if it contains within itself the reason for its indefeasible authority. And this reason must be the supremacy of the value it enjoins, contains, or sustains. This, I submit, is entirely evident ; and there is neither accident nor inadvertence in the circumstance that Immanuel Kant, who might appear to be the most celebrated and the most formidable opponent of any such contention, himself assents to it implicitly. " Nothing," he says in the famous exordium to the first section of his *Fundamental Principles*, " can possibly be conceived in the world, or even out of it, which can be called good without qualification, except a Good Will " ; and he goes on to explain that even if the good will, exerting itself to its uttermost, could still bring nothing to effect in an intractable world, it would yet, like a jewel, " shine by its own light, as a thing which has its whole value in itself." This statement, if it means anything, means that the good will is self-justifying because of its intrinsic value, and that nothing except unconditional goodness can justify unconditionally.

Accordingly, in his own fashion, Kant himself assents to the view that an imperative of morality, a decree of what *ought* to be done, is justified by its value and by nothing else. The cardinal principle here is that the thing that ought to be done is the best thing that can be done ; and this principle implies, in its turn, that any man's duty, that which he ought to do, is, quite simply, the best that he can achieve. This assertion, indeed, may appear entirely trivial, since no one could possibly dispute it ; and I hope that no one will. It is one thing, however, to show that a statement is manifestly indisputable, quite another thing to show that it is trivial ; and even if our proposition really is trivial in certain of its senses, the discussion of it may serve at least to raise points of high importance. Manifestly, I think, it does. When we say, for short, that duty is the adoption of the best, we are not saying simply that duty is duty, or that the best is the best. We are asserting a necessary and a fundamental connection between value and obligation, excellence and authority, worth and duty. In the language of philosophers this

connection is a *synthetic* connection, a union of things
significantly different, not the empty iteration of that
which is eternally the same. We are saying, indeed,
that the character of excellence implies a command,
that excellent things, just because of their excellence,
ought to be sought and achieved. I cannot think that
this is trivial. On the contrary, it seems to me momentous, and very well worth investigating.

An imperative, we say, is a command addressed to
the will, and if it be argued in reply that the " will "
is not an entity, but only a name for some of the fondest
superstitions of an obsolescent psychology, it should
be conceded, at least, that commands are meaningless
unless they can be understood and responded to. The
imperatives of duty, then, enjoin a certain response to a
value that is comprehensible; and response and understanding are not the same. Indeed, the difference, and
at the same time the connection, between them is the
most significant, as it is perhaps the most perplexing,
circumstance in the whole of this enquiry.

Plainly, the knowledge of good or evil is not the
same thing as the response to these. All experience
shows that the first may occur without the second, and
it is very commonly argued that the second, in some
fashion, may occur without the first. Moral enquiry,
indeed, seems to be not simply an enquiry into the
principles of practice, but an enquiry into practical
principles. This is a hard saying, and in some respects
perhaps a misleading one. It may be urged, with very
great plausibility, that *any* enquiry must be speculative
and entirely theoretical, and so that moral enquiry must
be. Like other enquiries it is a knowing and not a
doing. On the other hand, it is clear that moral
principles are themselves active, and therefore are
different from many others. The principles of dynamics

describe forces without themselves being forcible. Moral principles are not mere descriptions of action but themselves active. In responsible agents they are the revelations of a moving and actuating principle which, by revealing itself, controls and commands.

The inference here may be more complicated than it seems. At the least, however, it is certain that morality, as it applies to human agents, deals with that which we ought to do, that is to say, with a certain appropriate response, not simply with the understanding of certain matters. Imperatives of action are its essence. As we shall see, indeed, it is a disputed question whether these imperatives are the whole of the subject-matter of ethical theory—whether, in other words, the justification of imperatives is all that a moralist should consider. It cannot be denied, however, that they define a significant and a most important part of the investigation which he undertakes. If the " ought " is something more than the imperatives we encounter in responsible action—and I am far from denying that it may be— at any rate it includes these imperatives. There is a certain promise, therefore, in beginning our adventure with an analysis of these imperatives in the form in which we seem to encounter them.

In our own case the " ought " presents itself as a command to action self-accepted and self-imposed. It is not a thing that can be forced upon us. Although it may be *told* us by others, we *ourselves* have to accept it when we act responsibly. In accepting it, however, we do not accept it as a thing without reason, but as something which has a reason. This is because we recognize that the knowledge of good and evil imposes an obligation to act in accordance with such knowledge. The knowledge is also a behest in so far as it relates to matters that may be achieved by the knower. Anyone,

in short, who believes that certain actions are the best
he can do, thereby admits that he ought to do them.
The knowledge is of the sort which should dominate
response, and the appropriateness of its hegemony,
when we have the knowledge, is not in dispute.

It is true that no further reason can be given here.
The ultimate analysis of moral experience in this matter
is simply that the best does command, although its
commands may not be obeyed. This is the dictate of
the best to a creature responsive to values in so far as
it appreciates them ; and we cannot believe, I think,
that this connection between the idea of value and the
actions which may be guided by that idea, is simply a
psychological fact that happens to have a place in the
constitution of the human species. On the contrary,
we believe it to be the implicate of insight and of right
reason. Our nature, it is true, accepts these commands,
but it does so because it has some knowledge of good
and of evil, and (in some measure) the power of acting
or forbearing to act in accordance with these instructions and intimations of value. It is not impossible,
indeed, that this knowledge and this capacity is confined
to creatures vertebrate, mammalian, lately begotten, and
erect in stature ; that there are no flint-men in Saturn,
no discarnate moral beings, no angels, no divinities,
and no demons. We all believe, however, that if there
were such beings, beings beyond the confines of
humanity, who yet could know the good and pursue
it, then they *ought* to pursue it. The connection, in a
phrase, is *not* " planetary and telluric," although it
holds of a certain species upon this planet, and
although we may not be able to prove that it holds
of any other. What is relevant to the " ought "
is not a mere human characteristic, peculiar to the
species like leprosy or nakedness, but the intrinsic

appropriateness of a certain response to the knowledge of good and evil.

Summing up, then, we may say that there is a necessary and synthetic connection between value and obligation in every instance in which the thought of value may be a guide to action.[1] This is the plain, straightforward meaning of the " ought " in morals, and the meaning which is usually contemplated in moral theory. It may be argued, however, that the " ought " in this sense is not peculiarly moral, since it applies to regions outside the province of morals; and again, that although the " ought " in this sense defines a wide, and perhaps the central, part of this moral province,

[1] Examining the question "Does Moral Philosophy rest on a Mistake ? " Mr. H. A. Prichard, of Trinity College, Oxford, in the course of an acute and exceptionally resolute argument in *Mind* of January 1912, points out the necessity for an " intermediate link " between " good " and " ought," viz. " the further thesis that what is good ought to be," and he proceeds : " The necessity of this link is obvious. An ' ought,' if it is to be derived at all, can only be derived from another ' ought.' Moreover, this link tacitly presupposes another, viz. that the apprehension that something good which is not an action ought to be, involves just the feeling of imperativeness or obligation which is to be aroused by the thought of the action which will originate it. Otherwise the argument will not lead us to feel the obligation to produce it by the action. And surely both this link and its implication are false. The word ' ought ' refers to actions, and to actions alone " (p. 24).

If there were no link, or no link expressly related to an agent's choice, I should agree that moral philosophy may truly " rest on a mistake," and might even be driven to Mr. Prichard's own conclusion that " the sense of obligation to do, or the rightness of, an action of a particular kind is absolutely underivative or immediate " (p. 27). I suggest, however, that the link is quite peculiarly obvious, and am only concerned to state it firmly and with precision. While the point (for the most cogent reasons) is very often discussed, there is apt, I think, to be a certain hesitance in the discussion. I seem to find this, for example, in what the late Dr. Rashdall said (*The Theory of Good and Evil*, vol. i, p. 135 *sqq.*), although I am generally in agreement with his statements in this passage.

it cannot define the whole of it.   We must turn, therefore, to these objections.

When the possibility of an " ought " that is not a moral " ought " is considered, it may be contended, firstly, that there are legal imperatives as well as moral ones, and secondly that all the " normative " sciences, as they are called, contain and have to do with imperatives, although only one of these sciences is the science of ethics.   I have to show, therefore, that neither of these apparent objections is sufficient.

First, then, the legal point.

The ordinary citizen in these islands, when he hears or reads of what is said in courts of law, may well have a sense of bewilderment.   On the one hand, he hears, time and again, that " this is not a court of morals." On the other hand, he will see a great deal about " evidence as to character," read a great deal that cannot possibly be supposed to prove anything except that some suspected person is dissolute and disreputable, and note a multitude of sentences which are offensively moral on the part of the judge, since this official, having to condemn a legal offence, takes occasion to inform the prisoner that he is wicked and worthless in general. This is puzzling, and our bewildered citizen, seeking enlightenment from writers on jurisprudence, may be told, in effect, that the business of the law " is not to give lessons in conduct, but to keep the peace and settle or prevent disputes " [1]—although lawyers (and more particularly magistrates) very often forget this.   Pursuing the question further, he very naturally asks how the compulsion to educate his children, for example, can be plausibly represented as an instance of keeping the peace, or of settling any dispute except a dispute

[1] Sir F. Pollock, *Essays in the Law*, p. 266.

which the law itself creates.   And then he is told something a little more adequate and a little more enlightening.
The law, he is told, is a social contrivance, since it is
simply the body of regulations which any given society
has declared its intention of enforcing upon its members,
or upon any group of them.   Such is the enacted law
of developed communities.   In less developed ones the
declaration of it must be supposed to be understood
rather than formulated, and there is always a possible
difficulty concerning the manner of the declaration,
and the body which *de facto* makes or enforces it.   The
principle, however, is tolerably plain.   The business
of any administrative legal body is to follow its instructions, using its judgment and discretion only in so far
as these instructions permit.   Law-making, similarly,
may be regarded simply as a social arrangement, the
regularizing of regulations in whatever fashion is
currently recognized and accepted in any given society
at any particular time.

Clearly, however, as soon as we ask, not what this
social contrivance is, or how it conducts itself in accordance with its professions, but whether or not it is
justified, we are asking a relevant question which is
wholly and exclusively a moral one.   A law, we may
grant, is not a law unless it is the regulation of some
society over itself or its members, and unless it is something which may be, and is intended to be, enforced.
This does not tell us, however, whether any society
ought to make any such regulations ; or, if it should,
in what cases or upon what principles : yet these questions are moral questions and nothing else.   The truth
of this (which is entirely obvious) is frequently obscured
by definitions which purport to state what the function
of the law ought to be on the basis of simple descriptions of actual legal practice.   Thus, the law may be

defined, in Ihering's fashion, as something exclusively concerned with the delimitation of interests, or, again, as a thing occupied with the protection, not with the improvement of its subjects ; and in other similar ways. These contentions, certainly, are relevant to the problem of the justification of laws, in so far as they show, or attempt to show, that social regulations of any other kind (as sumptuary edicts, compulsory improvements, or laws of the type found in the Canon Law, or in a theocracy like Geneva) either cannot be enforced or, if they are enforced, are dangerous and mischievous. This, if it were true, would prove that only a certain kind of good can be achieved by legal regulation, and that the law, consequently, should confine itself to this province. The governing consideration, however, is always that law itself (and any particular law) is justified only by the good it achieves. If it were better for a community to have no laws at all than to have laws, then it ought not to have any. If it is best for it to have as few laws as possible, and these only for " keeping the peace," then it should have as few as possible, and these for the sole purpose of peace-keeping. If it is best and feasible for the community to legislate itself into excellence (making itself fit for heroes or saints to live in) then it ought to do so. In other words, the duty of the community, in this affair, is to do as much good as can be done by legal regulation.

I conclude, then, that the existence of legal imperatives by the side of moral ones does not in any way conflict with the doctrine that the justification of every imperative is entirely a moral question. The very existence of law, as well as the scope of its expediency, are to be justified, if at all, upon the strictly moral grounds of its use and worth ; and this is true of all the intricate questions that may be raised on this important matter. Thus, it is said that laws could never be justified (or even accepted) unless they conformed generally to the ethical ideas and the moral practice of the community they affect; that lawyer's justice is a monstrous thing unless it approaches moral justice as nearly as legal practice permits; that both the making and the enforcing of laws should be governed by certain special moral principles which forbid, for example, any attempt to raise revenue from iniquitous sources (as the slave trade, or opium, or saloons); that above statute laws there are higher or " unwritten " ones; and so forth. These questions, however they should be decided, should certainly be decided on moral grounds; and so should a host of other questions, such as the limits within which force can rightly be applied, or the circumstances, if any, in which it is a man's duty (or the duty of any group of men) to rebel against the laws or the customs of the community for conscience' sake.

Next, the second objection.

The existence of normative sciences, sciences which prescribe an " ought," and yet are other than ethics, may seem to establish a more formidable difficulty. Among such sciences, the two that are usually mentioned in this connection are logic and æsthetics— logic prescribing how we ought to think, and æsthetics endeavouring to ascertain the loveliness which ought to be sought and admired. It is not unlikely, however, that this list should be considerably extended, and that *all* the sciences which, as we say, have a practical side, are in their own way normative. Thus medicine, economics, and psychology do in fact admonish and guide us, no doubt from a restricted angle, but still effectively; and it is possible, at least, that the regulative, admonitory aspects of these sciences are integral to them, not an interesting but irrelevant appendage. We may pass over the point here, however, since the usual examples of logic and æsthetics are amply sufficient for defining and explaining the issue.

Mr. Johnson's statement of this question in the introduction to his *Logic* [1] is the clearest and the most concise I have seen. " Each of the normative studies," he says, " may be said to be based on a standard of value, the precise determination of which it is their function to formulate ; in each, imperatives are laid down which are acknowledged by the individual, not on any external authority, but as self-imposed; and, in each, the ultimate appeal is to the individual's intuitive judgment." To this, I think, speaking broadly, all of us ought to assent. What I have to maintain is that the normative character of these studies is quite precisely their moral character.

It will be agreed, I suppose, that when logic is regarded normatively as an injunction to truth-seeking, the language which is appropriate to this normative aspect of it is altogether a moral language. What is enjoined in this case is a certain discipline of the soul, fidelity to the subject studied, fairness of judgment, steadfastness and devotion to the truth. In a word, what is treated is the scientific conscience, the obligation that is admitted when truth is sought for truth's sake. To think at all is to commit ourselves to truth's keeping, to accept its authority and its commands ; and this authority is self-justifying because of its proper excellence. The same conclusion follows when we admit the authority of beauty, and seek beauty for beauty's sake.

The reply, I suppose, is that a scientific or an artistic

[1] Part I, p. xx.

conscience need not be a moral one. A man may think and think and be a rascal. He may be a great painter and a great villain. There is a suspicion, indeed, in many quarters that intellectual and moral excellence very seldom go together, and that artistry and morality touch very shyly if at all. This may, or may not, be a prejudice. What is important for our purposes is to notice (despite the paradox) that this rejoinder, even if it were true, may nevertheless be irrelevant. What beauty decrees for its own sake it decrees morally, and the behests of truth are moral behests. They are moral although they are not the whole of morals. The artist or the scientist who is vain or cruel or selfish or unscrupulous in matters outside his art or his science may be a very proper subject for moral censure, having regard to the conduct of his life as a whole, and yet he may think as a thinker should ponder, or enjoy as a lover of beauty should enjoy. If he does, he is, so far, virtuous and indisputably so.

In short, we are bound to maintain that every imperative, every normative injunction, is in reality moral. The artistic or the scientific conscience, as we call them, really are instances of conscience in a literal, straightforward, and therefore in an entirely moral sense. When we contrast these varieties of conscience with the ordinary moral conscience, the authentic quarrel is between the claims of art or of knowledge on the one hand, and the moral demands of a complete regulation of our lives on the other. This sterner quarrel, to be sure, must itself be considered with some nicety ; and I mean to return to it. For the moment, however, I hope the reader will concede the point and admit that the objection has been answered.

Our conclusion, therefore, is that the central theme which moral theory sets out to investigate is the problem of the justification of imperatives. The proper employment of analytical morals is in the search for the *reasons* for what ought to be done; and this is the theme of our next few chapters. In the present chapter, however, it is advisable to make certain other explanations before advancing in our study in ethical anatomy.

Most so-called theories of morals, despite their claims, are, in the last analysis, either sceptical or irrelevant. They are so framed that they cannot even begin to justify anything, for they are content with a mere explanation to the effect that our acceptance of what we call right is a product of fear, or custom, or social evolution, or the " life-force." By these pathways we might certainly attain a descriptive survey of cultural histories and of their origins, or an inventory of what men have been accustomed to call just and good, but we should have said nothing at all about the critical investigation of any of these standards. In the language formerly used, we might have explained something, but we could not have justified anything.

Accordingly, we have no proper concern with theories and moral systems of this type. Scepticism, indeed, unless it takes itself (which is false) to be the end, and not the beginning, of wisdom in these affairs, is, philosophically speaking, a fine and an indispensable thing; and every moralist should set himself to consider, and, if possible, to answer, any objections to his beliefs that are based upon a grounded suspicion that there is a lurking superstition at the heart of them. This is no reason, however, for doing obeisance to conscious or unconscious scepticisms that are based upon negligence or avoidable misunderstanding. Certainly the description of customs and cultures is of the greatest importance, for these cultures and customs often show within themselves those very standards in human practice which are the result of humanity's attempt to take morality as it should be taken—that is, to find in it a direction for the conduct of human lives in such a fashion that they may yield the best they have to give. Mere description, however, which remains but description, is a gathering of material for moral scrutiny, and nothing on earth besides.

I shall therefore ignore all such " theories " in this preliminary investigation and treat only of principles which really do attempt an answer to the moral question. Of these one at least requires very special consideration. Moral theories proper deal either with the conception of value or with the conception of obligation. We have chosen the latter because it seemed to be the truth. But now we must defend it expressly against the former.

According to this notable school of opinion, the subject-matter of ethics is goodness, or The Good, with the corollary, perhaps, that the subject-matter of human ethics is the good for man. By " good " in this reference value of every species seems to be meant; and this, in its turn, may even be defined as a simple, unanalysable predicate. If this were so ethics would be identical with pure axiology, the science of values of every species, and the conduct of life in accordance with values would be only a special application of this general enquiry. I cannot, however, believe that this is what we mean by it. This definite application to life and conduct is precisely the thing that we study, and although right conduct must be justified by its value, it is *conduct* with which we have to do. To confirm this statement, I think, we have only to consider what we mean when we distinguish moral excellence from excellence of other kinds. If happiness, for example, is a good, then there is goodness wherever there is happiness. Something good is occurring when a lizard enjoys the sun, or a kitten frisks with its tail, but there is surely no moral excellence in these cases unless we suppose that some benign agency has purposely brought the happiness about.   Similarly, wherever beauty occurs, there is an instance of a certain variety of excellence.   A good thing is present ; but although we might praise the moral excellence of a demiurge who had given us sunsets for our delight, the mere existence of a beautiful thing could scarcely be said to be a moral matter.   Moral excellence, in short, consists in the *use* of opportunities for bringing values about. The analysis of excellence and the description of excellent things, while implied in ethical study, is not that study.

A reply, seemingly possible, cannot, I think, be sustained.   In terms of our own argument, it may be contended, there is an ethical question in the straitest sense wherever there is any question of what ought to be or of what ought to exist.   Now anything which is good is such that it ought to exist.   Hence there can be no final distinction, or even any real one, between axiology and morals.

This seems incorrect.   Since the " ought " is justified by the value it subserves, it must indeed be true that the value of any possible thing is a reason which (so far) would justify the bringing of it into existence, although the only sufficient justification for bringing it to pass would be, not that the thing would be good, but that it would be the best.   When we affirm, however, as we sometimes do, that anything which is good is a thing which ought to be, we do not, I think, intend to make a statement which is true without any qualification ; and I am sure that, if we do, we conceal some of the links in a chain of argument.   What we mean, I believe, is that these excellent things ought to exist *if* considerations of value were relevant to their existence. They are the things that would be appropriate to a righteous universe, or to a scheme of things divinely devised. Without some such implication I cannot see that the " ought " in any intelligible sense enters into the question at all. When we say that the world contains happiness here, and beauty there, and that beauty and happiness are excellent, we are making statements about values and their incidence, but are saying nothing whatever about what ought to exist. When, inferring from this, we say (if we do) that the world, in these respects, is what it ought to be, we imply that there is a sense in which values may determine existence, in which the worth of things sustains and produces them, or at least tends to do so. In short, the " ought " implies agency ; and although we need not expect a merely general analysis to tell us precisely what this agency must be, we may suspect that all such statements derive a part at least of their verisimilitude from analogy with a type of agency with which we are quite familiar, that is to say, from analogy with choice, contrivance and design which are guided by the idea of the best.

I submit, then, that ethics, while it is justified by value and by nothing else, is not in itself the study of pure axiology, although it requires and indeed presupposes this. The relation, in short, between value and obligation is precisely that synthetic connection previously referred to, whereby a principle applicable to practice also becomes a practical principle. It may still be objected, however, that our reference to *imperatives* was altogether too narrow, since morality has, in fact, a very much ampler range. This is the problem that was broached, and then relinquished, a few pages back.

As we have seen, an imperative is a command, and it is essential to any command, whether it be self-imposed or imposed by some other, that it should be capable of being understood and obeyed. In general we scent no difficulties here, since we assume, *tout court*, that we have to deal with voluntary assent and compliance, that is to say, with the " will." It seems to be clear, however, that common sense, at least, is not prepared to restrict good conduct to voluntary decision, or even to conscious intent. The plain man is fully convinced that love and generosity and many others of the virtues cannot be attained by express resolution ; and, according to a very usual opinion, moral excellence applies to every quality of the soul that is either worth seeking in its own right, or involved in the pursuit of the good. As Aristotle said, " Conditions of the soul which are praised are just what we mean by goodness." [1] These virtues, dispositions, habits, and sentiments need not belong to definitive volition, although in part they may. Again, if " will and volition " are taken to connote fully conscious choice, the " purity of heart " and other such excellences enjoined in Christian morality seem frequently to be of the class that we call " sub-conscious." It may appear, indeed, to many that nothing is more amazing and more perturbing in all these disputes than the utter disparity between the current expression of principle, and our actual current meaning, in this very matter. The current expression of principle refers exclusively to the will and to a voluntary, full, and indeed forensic, " responsibility." Surreptitiously, however, or in flagrant conflict with his expressed beliefs, the plain man thinks of not a little that is very far from being voluntary in the accepted sense.

[1] *Nicomachean Ethics*, concluding sentence of Book I.

Even these surreptitious or inconsistent qualifications and dubieties, however, are all of them concerned with the life and capacities of a moral agent, and all have to do with the ordering of life in terms of experienced value. We shall be greatly occupied with them in the sequel, but it may be sufficient in the meanwhile if I suggest that moral principles, if they are not always imperatives addressed to the will, are at least directions addressed to the life, and addressed to beings whose consciousness and ideal capacities play a fundamental part in the acceptance of them. In terms of this governing consideration, even the sufficiency or the insufficiency of the "will" for the burdens that legal, moral, and everyday theory are often disposed to put upon it, is of lesser import.

The cardinal significance of action for moral theory was asserted at the beginning of this discussion, and our argument has now returned to it. I shall conclude this chapter by considering some further points that arise in this connection.

When we say that morals have to do with action, we do not, of course, mean to assert that every action is moral, or imply, for example, that the action of arsenic upon the tissues is a moral occurrence; and although it may be impossible at the present stage of our argument to define with complete precision what species of action is peculiarly and distinctively moral, we may say, provisionally, that responsible action is what is meant. Such action is not merely accountable (i.e. caused by a certain agent), but caused by an agent who is under an obligation to pursue what is good. The moral responsibility of any such agent may not be exhausted by his intentional pursuit of what he takes to be good, but it includes at least the possibility of this intentional action.

There is a sense, again, in which action may be taken to mean the mere utterance and outward garment of some purpose and condition of the soul. If so, it might appear reasonable to argue that the soul's purpose and intention are enormously more important than the mere shell and husk of their expression. Morality, it is urged, has to do with men's thoughts and desires as well as with outward behaviour, and in the last analysis outward behaviour is of small account in comparison with inward being. The fallacy here is surely sufficiently plain. Inward behaviour is just as much action as outward behaviour; and when behaviour which might be outward as well as inward is *kept* inward, the difference, in a moral regard, is most momentous. It is a bad thing, no doubt, to think murderously of one's enemy, but it is a worse thing to murder him. An intention, in short, is always an *intention to act* either outwardly or by inward regulation; and the intention itself is an (inward) action. Accordingly, there is *no* objection here.

Again, it is sometimes argued that character, not conduct, living not doing, are the true and proper subject of moral investigation. The ultimate moral imperative (we are told) is " Be thus and thus," not " Do this or that ! " In this there is the same fallacy as before. In so far as the distinction between what we ought to *be* and what we ought to *do* may be sustained, the command to *be* thus and thus is an injunction towards inward behaviour, a command for the ordering of a life which itself is a doing. What is enjoined is the active control and direction of an active thing. It would be foolish, however, to suppose that this active thing can or should withdraw wholly within itself and cultivate its enclosed perfections. It lives by adapting itself to its spiritual and material environment, and actions of this kind, adaptations to something not itself, are profoundly important for any sane ethic. Character differs indeed from actual conduct, since it is a disposition not an occurrence, and it is related not merely to actions that have occurred or that will occur, but also to actions that might occur although they do not happen in fact. When we say, for example, that a man is a liar or untrustworthy we mean that he is a person who would be treacherous or untruthful (very often at least) when the temptation or the opportunity occurs. If the description is just, we must suppose that the man has supplied sufficient evidence for it in certain of his past actions, and that in all probability he will continue to supply more. The name for the disposition, accordingly, implies the legitimacy of inference to *possible* actions of a certain kind, not simply to the actions which have been or will be part of the man's life-history. The man would still be a liar if we gave him no further opportunities for his duplicity.

All this, however, is not an objection. In so far as " character " is more than a name it designates an active disposition, fashioned in action and making for action. Our knowledge of it is derived from action, our beliefs concerning it are beliefs concerning actions inward or outward, actual or possible. And I do not think that further argument is needed.

CHAPTER III

OF IMPERATIVES AND OF THEIR JUSTIFICATION

THE pith of the last chapter was that imperatives, if they do not define the whole field of moral study, define a most essential and indeed the principal part of it ; and that the moral question proper is the justification of such imperatives. The intention of the present chapter, accordingly, is to consider the main divisions of these imperatives, and the general character of their justification.

Here we hàve the assistance of a very great philosopher, for the most celebrated division of imperatives is Immanuel Kant's where he distinguished categorical imperatives from hypothetical ones. *More suo*, the sage of Königsberg here employed certain current distinctions in formal logic for an extended purpose. In the language of the schools, a categorical proposition is a statement asserted directly and without conditions or governing conjectures, while a hypothetical proposition is one in which the apodosis is expressly contingent upon, and governed by, a ruling protasis (or assumption or hypothesis). Extending this usage by analogy, Kant meant by a categorical imperative one that is not subject to conditions or qualifications, but on the contrary " shines like a jewel by its own light," while a hypothetical imperative is borrowed and contingent. The latter class Kant subdivided into rules of skill and counsels of prudence, remarking that " the precepts for the physician to *cure* his patient and for a poisoner to *kill* him " are equally matters of skill, and that prudence can never yield us certainty. We need not, however, follow him into this further subdivision (for it is disputable), and may content ourselves for the moment with seizing and retaining his fundamental distinction between a command of morality, subject to no governing clause (since it is its own governor and its own vindicator) on the one hand, and, on the other hand, those derivative counsels, which merely inform us that we must employ certain means *if* we desire certain ends.

From this general standpoint, it is plain, we have innumerable examples to choose from. Thus, for many (although not for Kant himself) the injunction to seek peace and pensue it would be categorical, and it *is* categorical in form. The deplorably mischievous adage " Si *vis pacem*, para *bellum*," on the other hand, is on any showing hypothetical. And so on without end.

Nevertheless, distinctive as this division is, and readily intelligible as it may seem, there may still be a doubt whether the precise form in which Kant lays it down is either felicitous or as simple and instructive as it might be. To show this, I think, two observations should suffice. In the first place, Kant's hypothetical imperatives frequently do not seem to be imperatives at all. In the second place, his categorical imperatives have to be justified in some other fashion than the fashion he himself selects.

An imperative is at least a command, and it is surely unnecessary to suppose that a statement to the effect that, if a certain end is *desired* certain means are essential to its attainment, is a command at all. This would be correct only if the end were commanded, and an end which is desired need not be commanded in any way. When a man is tempted, as we say, his will is solicited, but he is surely not commanded to sin. The important contrast, in other words, is between governing and subordinate imperatives; and Kant confuses the question by speaking as if an attraction were the same thing as a governing imperative.

Again, if a "categorical" imperative means quite simply a governing one, there is no objection to it except that it is oddly named. Kant seems to hold, however, that an imperative is "categorical" when it is good in itself by virtue of its pure form without any relation to the conditions within which it governs, or the things which it governs, or the effects which are controlled by its government. If this be so, it may be pardonable to believe that such "categorical" government describes a government that does not govern.

Accordingly, some other division of imperatives seems to be needed, and I propose the following: Instead of hypothetical imperatives, I shall speak of subordinate ones. Such imperatives are commands, but they are commanded, not in their own right, but derivatively because something else is commanded. Accepting an obligation, I accept all consequential obligations. It need not be my duty to live in such and such a town; but if it is my duty to work there, it is therefore my duty to live there.

The correlative term to subordinate is superordinate, and the complexity of the business of living makes it probable that, in general, there is a very lengthy chain of sub- and superordinates relating to our duties, or a very subtle pattern of their interlacements. Since every superordinate, however, governs its due subordinate, the important question is whether the chain is fixed at the top, or the theme dominated by a supreme and dominating note. In other words, we have to ask whether there are many imperatives, not merely super-ordinate in a relative sense, but literally and authentically supreme, or only one of these, or none at all.

As we have seen, the authority of any imperative depends upon its worth or excellence. It is probable, therefore, that any hierarchy of imperatives must follow the divisions of excellence very closely, provided that the excellence is such that it may be commanded. The general divisions of such excellence as is supposed to be attainable would seem, therefore, to offer a promising clue. If so, our question is whether there are any supreme and dominating goods, each imposing its own authority, or only one such good, or a welter and confusion of them.

It is usual to distinguish goods or values according as they are " intrinsic " or " instrumental," and this distinction, upon the surface of it, seems of quite peculiar clarity. An " intrinsic " good, we are told, is good in and of itself, or for its own sake, and, if need be, good-for nothing else, nothing outside itself. An " instru-mental " good, on the other hand, is *only* " good-for." It is merely a tool for obtaining something *else*. Surgical operations, for example, or a dentist's excavations, are *not* intrinsic goods, and, if they are good at all, they are good but as the means or instruments for obtaining certain results that lie altogether beyond themselves. No one would choose them except for these extraneous reasons. It may sometimes be disputed, to be sure, whether (or how far) any given mode of action or employment of life which is accounted good, is taken to be *intrinsically* or *instrumentally* so. Some, for example, speak of their " work " (or labour or occupation or profession) as a thing having value in itself, as if it were good, quite simply, for its own sake; but it may be doubted whether these persons would really maintain, under cross-examination, that it is in itself a good thing merely to be busy, or occupied, or saved from thought and worry by the utter tyranny of one's job. Others, again, would maintain that all labour, however necessary, is in itself a bad thing, and a curse from Eden more burdensome than death itself; while a third party, somewhat more sagely, would begin to draw the plain distinctions that seem to be needed. All three, however, while drawing their lines in different places, would probably agree on the essential character of the line they meant to draw.

Notwithstanding this surface clarity, however, I am disposed to believe, and should like to suggest, that this distinction is maladroit, in reality, and that frequently it is downright confused. When anything is a means or an instrument towards that which is good, there are two alternatives. In the first of these the instrument is not good at all, although it has good effects; in the second the instrument acquires a virtue which it would not have if it were idle, or employed for some other purpose. If it does acquire this virtue, it does acquire it; and therefore it *is* good as long as it is effectively employed in this fashion. The genuine distinction, in short, is between things which are good in certain employments *only*, and things which are either always good and in all employments, or at any rate are good in some other fashion than simply in this limited one. To hold, as so many do, that " good " and " good-for " are different species of " good " and that the word " good " is ambiguous when applied to both of them, I believe to be a complete mistake. " Good-for " is either not " good " but " for," or else " good " in so far as " for." There are *not* two species, and there is *no* ambiguity.

So much, then, for "instrumental" goods. Let us turn to "intrinsic" ones. According to the concurrent testimony of the great majority of moralists, the intrinsic goodness of anything is the goodness which that thing has in itself, a goodness for which it is not beholden to anything else, not dependent upon context or surroundings or opportunities, but a goodness absolute, inalienable, and indeed imperturbable. This notion (as we must admit) seems very clear; and it is usual to argue that anything not "intrinsically" good borrows its goodness from some "intrinsic" good.

I shall try to show that the prominence (indeed, the pre-eminence) given to these "intrinsic" goods (if there are any) in most ethical systems is very ill-grounded.

As we have seen, the goods that are not intrinsic are supposed to derive their goodness from some particular circumstance, function or relation, and otherwise to be without any goodness at all. Our criticism was that if these good things acquire their goodness in these special connections, then, in these special connections, they really do acquire it. Indeed (as has been said), the most significant and the most important contrast here is between the things that are good in certain connections only, and those (if there are any) that are good in all possible connections. This, at least, is one important contrast; and I shall try to show that the intrinsic goodness of anything would not guarantee its goodness in all circumstances, and that the latter type of conception, not the former, is the important one in most ethical arguments.

This is easy to prove. Adopting a phrase of Mr. Moore's in his *Philosophical Studies*, we may define an intrinsic good as the goodness which would characterize a thing " if it existed quite alone, and if nothing further were to come of it." [1]   Since nothing, in fact, exists quite alone, and since everything in nature has consequences, it may be doubted whether this perfectly clear conception is likely to help us very much.   But let that pass.   What is more important to notice is that it does not at all follow that because something or other would be good quite alone, it is therefore good when it is not alone. Things that are excellent apart may mix very badly, and if anyone urges in reply that these things become different in the mixture he is throwing his case away with both hands.   For the confluence and intermixture of many desirable and of many undesirable things in their compulsory entanglement in a single life is precisely the most pressing question in moral philosophy. What we seek, in a word, is not something which " would be good quite alone," but a dominant good— one which, irradiating its surroundings, dignifies whatever it touches.   Such a good might or might not be good " quite alone."   If it is a dominating good, its intrinsic goodness matters very little.

I would not deny, indeed, that there *are* intrinsic goods.   A moment of happiness, for example, may be regarded as a sporadic excellence and fleeting value, good in its mere existence irrespective of the rest of the universe.   Every work of art, again, sonnet, or fugue, or Doric column, is held to be self-complete and self-detached ; for beautiful things are selflessly selfish. What I am concerned to deny is that this detachment or isolation, if it were possible, would normally be the determining consideration in moral affairs.   To appreciate this, we have only to notice, I think, how attenuated and how misleading the distinction between " means " and " end " commonly is.

It must be conceded, indeed, that certain actions are

[1] P. 326.

only means—a piece of simple machinery or of mere scaffolding, entirely effaced or discarded in the finished product—and that when the end of the series is taken to be intrinsically self-complete (as a thing of beauty is) the means, by definition, is sundered from it. Thus, if the end be the vision of sunrise upon a mountain lake, the journey before the dawn must be regarded (æsthetically at least) as a simple means. On the other hand, the mere coupling of means with their end, implies that the two form a single series; and it is plain that the very attempt to achieve an end by the employment of appropriate means should be judged according to the whole plan of it by any rational creature. It is not the end which justifies the means. The whole series must be justified; and when end and means are distinct, the end justifies the whole series only in the case in which the value of the end outweighs the disvalue or the neutrality of the means. Similarly, a series which has an end may be justified principally by the means. In a contest of skill, for example, the end is victory, but victory in itself is barren. It is the quality of the contest that is excellent.

The end of a series, in other words, is properly its completion and fulfilment, and it is a fallacy to suppose that the later stages of any process are necessarily more of a fulfilment than the earlier. Certainly we are prospective beings, and the future is always uncertain. In any pursuit, therefore, we direct our thoughts towards that which is still to come, and rightly so, since retrospect is a luxury unless it is used for instruction, and since there is always a chance that the future may annul whatever has gone before. This peculiar importance of the future (or unfinished) portion of a pursuit, however, while manifestly incident to our situation, does not even suggest that the later part must be a *fulfilment* in a way the earlier is not. On the contrary, *every* part is needed for the completing of the whole, and when the process is viewed in its completeness it may be entirely plain that the crucial values in it occurred long before the closing stages, or evenly throughout, or very near the beginning. In a sudden attack, for example, the surprise at the beginning may be three-quarters of the battle. And who can say what the critical moment is in the writing of a book ?

Accordingly, while it is possible to construct instances in which the end comes after the means, is distinct from them, and is that for the sake of which the means are undertaken, it is highly artificial and misleading, in general, to proceed in this fashion. The series of end-and-means must be judged as a whole (as everyone admits who remembers, let us say, that, although the death of a ruler may be desirable, his assassination need not be), and the series as a whole is commonly integrated very closely, or at any rate after a different fashion from the one that is contemplated in this distinction. This is particularly so as regards the point of time. It is the exception, not the rule, when the later stages of a process confer upon it the whole of its worth. To forget this is to assert by inadvertence that books are written for the sake of writing *Finis*, or dinners enjoyed only when the coffee comes. *Respice finem* is very true, but it is not the whole truth. If no one should be called fortunate until he is dead, it does not follow that a felicitous departure is the object of living.

What we seek, then, is a dominating rather than an intrinsic good, and I do not think we can argue that a dominating good must at any rate have intrinsic worth. There are at least two reasons which forbid. In the first place, while the distinction between a thing (in itself) and its influences may frequently be drawn, it also, very frequently, cannot be drawn at all. Thus, if we were to say that fidelity is a dominant good, I do not see how we could distinguish between intrinsic and extrinsic fidelity, or what fidelity would be except when applied and in use. Equity, again, which (if not too harsh) is a dominant good, seems to be a relation, and therefore non-existent if it does not, in fact, relate. And in general any organizing principle owes its very existence as well as its excellence to its integrative efficacy. In the second place, the composition and concurrence of values is so intricate a question that propositions like the one we are considering seem rather simple-minded. It seems plain that two bad things may together be good (as two poisons, to choose a trivial example, may unite into a beneficent salt), and that the values of any organized pattern bear no simple relation to its component values. I believe, indeed, that we may learn much in this matter by a cautious survey of the values we encounter, but we are not in a position to legislate *à priori*, and it is not at all certain that good must be born of good, or that excellent things in combination may not wreck one another.

It is our business, then, to look for the dominant goods that give a reason for all imperatives ; and I suggest that a survey, as general as may be, but still, in the end, drawn wholly from experience, is the most that philosophy can hope to undertake in the present state of our knowledge. It is clear, however, that anything approaching a complete inventory, even of human goods, if it is not entirely impossible, is at least intolerably prolix. To avoid this inconvenience, it is usual to classify goods, somewhat arbitrarily, but at any rate serviceably, under the rubrics of truth, beauty, moral excellence, and happiness. This division is drawn without prejudice to other views, as for example that the supreme commandment for any man is to love his kind and his world, or that there may be some high metaphysical sense (if we only knew it) in which a unitary and harmonious good is decreed for all existence. It is a division to be taken provisionally, but with some confidence. At the same time it launches us upon a troubled course.

One manifest difficulty is the extreme variety of the values and disvalues included in each of these general divisions. This variety, to be sure, is inevitable in a complicated and untidy field, but our divisions should help us at least to compare the better with the worse within each class, and indicate how we should set about to make comparisons. It would appear, however, that when we begin to make comparisons in point of happiness, say, the class called " happiness " is so wide and so little organized that we can scarcely avoid a great deal of fumbling. Even if by happiness we mean pleasure (which appears to be a more exact designation, although perhaps it is not), who is to compare the pleasures of tranquillity with the pleasures of excitement, the pleasures of the body with the pleasures of the mind, the pleasures which are due to relief from unrest with free and joyful pleasures where there is no torture of antecedent craving ? If pleasure-getting is a command, or even a direction, pleasure should afford some principle for our looking, but pleasures (as Mr. Johnson says of colours) seem to be marked by a peculiar kind of difference rather than by any nameable positive principle of unity.

The same thing holds of beauty. Granting that beauty should be sought, who is to compare the beauties of music, sculpture, literature, or nature ? All these may be beautiful, yet their beauties seem utterly diverse

If so, beauty splits into many beauties, and this bodes very ill for any system of rational preference in respect of beauty.

A second obvious difficulty is that values of these different classes, while distinguishable, may commingle in their incidence and interpenetrate one another. Thus happiness is allied with beauty, for beauty inspires delight, and is indeed so closely allied with its appropriate delight that many have supposed these two to be one and the same. In the same way, granting that virtue and happiness are different, and that many virtuous persons, taking the world to be an unrighteous place, have been profoundly miserable, it is still (in general) true that virtuous actions have a very poignant satisfaction, and that vice often entails its own peculiar misery. The attainment of truth, again (or, if the reader prefers, the belief in this attainment), may also be a joyful thing. We are told by many who have a claim to be heard (and by some others) that there is nothing so precious as the satisfaction of intellectual achievement. More-over, truth may be beautiful and happiness also.

In itself this type of circumstance is only a complica-tion, proving that values of different sorts may apply to the same things, and proving nothing at all besides. The point is important, however, and it has quite special importance for moral values, for it affects them in two ways. In the first place, every kind of value entails an injunction which plainly is moral. In the second place moral values seem to have authority over all others.

The moral aspect of the values of truth and of beauty has already been discussed when we considered the normative character of logic and of æsthetics, and there is no need to return to the point. We should note, however, that there is also a normative or manda-

tory side to "hedonics," or the study of happiness.
This is sometimes forgotten. As everyone knows,
hedonism, or the doctrine that pleasure [1] is the only
good, has been one of the great historical tendencies
of ethical opinion; but hedonists have usually dwelt
so fondly upon the attractions of their ideal that they
have tended to neglect its obligations; and their opponents have disputed the hedonist creed so hotly that,
often, they seem to have left no place at all for the
duties of seeking happiness. In this, however, both
sides are plainly wrong. The mere fact that all want
happiness neither denies nor affirms that we ought to
seek happiness, and no moral theory can afford to
neglect this question. On the other hand, when we
consider, not our own happiness only, but the happiness
of other creatures, it is utterly monstrous to deny that
there are hedonic imperatives enjoining happiness for
happiness' sake. To deny this would be to hold that
it is all one whether we torture an animal or make it
contented, that the mere physical comfort of a dying
person is not to be considered, that it is not our duty
to make little children happy if we can. We need not
trouble ourselves with this wicked nonsense.

Logic and æsthetics, then, together with the art of
devising happiness, enjoin and direct the quest for their
appropriate values, and so have a moral implication.
What is more, each of these classes of imperatives
appears to be self-justifying, and each of them to be
unconditioned within its own sphere. This, to be sure,
is not always recognized, and attempts are made, for
example, to show that truth and beauty ought to be
pursued for some other reason than verity or loveliness,
and have in fact to be justified on account of their
utility (let us say), or because certain persons have an

[1] For hedonists equate happiness with pleasure.

insatiable impulse towards pursuing them, which may not be thwarted without disaster. It is clear, however, that even if these additional justifications are relevant, they are nevertheless supererogatory in principle. To say, when we can, that we ought to believe this or that "simply because it is true" is a statement entirely sufficient. The utility of the belief may guide us, indeed, in the choice of what is most useful to study; but it is truth itself that justifies. This holds, no less, when some higher utility is claimed for the truth than mere material gain or social convenience. Truth, it is argued, is a universal healer and always clean; it purges the soul from its meanness and pettiness; and the discipline of strenuous thought, despite superficial objections, dignifies a man's whole character. This need not be denied, but the imperatives of truth-seeking do not require it, since their authority is complete without it. The same holds of beauty. When beauty for beauty's sake is the commandment, it is strictly speaking irrelevant to refer to its utility, its tendency to adorn a man's character, its truth (if it have any) or its comforting qualities.

These divisions of value, in short, do not only differ in kind, but legislate unconditionally within their kinds. They are dominant goods each of which has its own and a sufficient authority. It is this self-governing authority, I believe, which is awkwardly (and in many ways mistakenly) invoked in the concept of "intrinsic good." The authority here is, in fact, "intrinsic" because extrinsic considerations are plainly irrelevant to it; and although, as we have seen, the mere assignment of this authority to its appropriate class does not and cannot tell us what is enjoined within the class (as if an instruction to be logical were itself a complete system and art of logic), the admission of appropriate authority is not an idle thing.

Here, then, is one side of the question; but there is another side, and perhaps a still more important one. The kinds of these imperatives may conflict; and morality which, on the one hand, admits their authority, claims, on the other hand, to override the authority of any one of them (except its own) for sufficient reason. The scientific or the artistic conscience, as we have seen, *is* a conscience; yet the general or moral conscience asserts its claim to be suzerain over both.

Braving the charge of repetition, we may put the point most simply, perhaps, in the following way: As we have seen, the imperatives of truth or of beauty are unconditional each in its own kind. To say that a truth is ugly or noxious (if this could be said with justice) cannot affect the truth of it, and should not weigh with the intellectual conscience; and similar statements hold of beauty and of the artistic conscience. The moral qualities, again—moral in the most general sense—which are implied in these pursuits, the candour, fidelity, disinterestedness, and devotion which they enjoin, are in these cases subordinate to their governing goods. Even the effects of these disciplines upon the character of a man are, from the standpoint of these justifications, irrelevant by-products, however worthy of esteem they may be.

Yet in another way morality seems to condition these unconditionals, and to rule these sovereigns. This is easily proved, as a simple illustration shows. In a recent trial for murder at Chicago it was alleged that a pair of would-be intellectuals had done a boy to death in order to see how he would react to the ordeal. It is nothing to the point to say that the murderers were mad, or degenerate, or that they may have had some other motive. The plain truth is that if their motive had been the one alleged, it would have been a scientific motive, and their experiment would have been designed to discover a truth. This would not defend or excuse it, to say nothing of justifying it. To be brief, there are many things that may not be done even for the sake of truth. I will not speak of vivisection, but there should be limits at least to the brilliant surgical experiments that may be attempted in a public hospital, or to political experiments designed for the benefit of sociologists. Indeed, there are limits to the extent in which a man may experiment with himself for the sake of any science.[1] It may be permissible to cut a nerve in order to discover the order of sensations that accompany recovery—but not any nerve ; and if a doctor risks his life in investigating the causes of some fever, or the possibility of immunization from cancer, he is justified in doing so, not primarily because the discoveries he may make would be true, but because the results of these discoveries might prevent the loss of many other lives. The less signal the achievement, to be sure, the more disputable the example. We encounter the argument, even, that when there are no wars, men ought to risk their lives for mere adventure's sake, in the climbing of some high mountain, or in exploring the poles ; and in any profession serious risks may have to be taken for an end which may be trivial enough in some given case. What I have shown is only that certain actions should never be performed for the sake of truth alone.

" Art for art's sake " may similarly be overridden, although this maxim is usually the " last superstition " of enlightened cynics. It is very often contended, indeed, and perhaps correctly, that the artist, to gain experience, must taste and savour " life " in ways not permitted to other men, and that this imperative should banish his conscientious scruples and his moral

[1] Cf. Mr. Shaw's remarks in his preface to *The Doctor's Dilemma*.

squeamishness where such banishment is necessary. This need not be denied, but there are few who would maintain that there are no restrictions to this species of apologia; and these few are plainly wrong. If the murder before mentioned had been committed for an artistic, not for a scientific, purpose (as was also stated), it would have been none the less despicable. De Quincey's fantasy would not redeem it; and although in this country we may be far too apt to speak of " decadence " without a meaning, or to condemn a splendid spectacle for very little cause, although we may be still in Philistia through our denial of subsistence to the arts or on account of the ease with which we devastate natural beauty for the benefit of industry, it is not to be argued that any theme may be treated that might conceivably be beautified, that every splendid spectacle or fine adornment should be permitted irrespective of its cruelty, that the body politic is nothing but a minister to the arts, or that every kiln and pit and chimney is wholly and quite simply an offence against good taste. (*Cf.* Appendix II.)

The solution, however, is not very difficult. The ultimate moral question for any of us is the best use of the whole of our resources, capacities, and opportunities. Accordingly, although the search for truth, let us say, must be guided by the canons of truth and by these alone (since nothing but truth has any bearing upon truth), the values of truth cannot prescribe of themselves how large a proportion of our lives should be spent in the search after verities. Other employments are open to us, other commands should be obeyed; and if the values of some particular investigation, notwithstanding the truth of it, are plainly insignificant in comparison with the evils the investigation entails, then an investigation of this particular sort should never be undertaken.

The very conditions of our living prescribe an alternation of governing values. There are claims of ease as
well as labour ; and if sloth is a deadly sin, incessant
drudgery is a very great evil. When conflicts arise
they need not arise from artifice or mere perversity.
They are due, in the main, to the many-sidedness of our
station and to the necessary alternations of our temporal
existence. We need not expect a perfect solution, and
we need not despair of a tolerable one. If a married
clergyman feels that family ties hinder his undivided
devotion to his calling, or if a writer (as in the professional
imaginations of so many of our novelists) is irritated
at the claims of domesticity, is anyone to say that art
or religion prescribes celibacy for all who are devoted
to either, or that the most intimate companionship is
simply an artistic asset, or that compromise in these
affairs is never inevitable ? Our lives are *not* undivided
things ; for we have many allegiances and many
loyalties.

Summing up, then, we have to say that the moral
life enjoins the best use of all our opportunities, and
that moral conduct is therefore both a servant and a
leader. In seeking the best we have to choose between
different dominant goods at different times, and sometimes may have to reject a whole class of them, since
this class, although it is good, is for us not the best.
This is the obligation to a real sacrifice for a just and
sufficient reason ; and it governs the extent to which
we should devote ourselves to any dominant good. On
the other hand, in so far as we devote ourselves to art
or science, or the securing of happiness, we submit
ourselves to the guidance of truth or beauty or happiness
within the sphere of each ; for each of these legislates
for itself, and forbids us to tamper with its own proper
ends.

In its general outline, this conclusion gives the answer to the question which we set ourselves in this chapter. Every imperative, we argued, is a moral imperative, and each imperative is justified by its worth in so far as it is justified at all.   Now certain imperatives are consequential and subordinate, and in their case the problem is transferred to their governing super-ordinates.   Apart from experience there is no royal road to these supreme commandments, but a survey of our experience indicates that there are certain broad divisions of values attainable by human beings, and that each of these (for they differ in kind) are in their own way self-governing and self-justifying.   The chief of these divisions are respectively happiness, truth, beauty, and moral excellence.   The claims of happiness, despite the strictures of ascetic moralists, may not be set aside, and the claims of beauty or of science are not in dispute.   Moral values, however, raise a problem of some intricacy.   It is a moral duty to seek beauty, to think truly, to promote happiness ; and, when this is so, beauty, truth, or happiness are themselves the judges and the leaders.   On the other hand, we have to arbitrate between the claims of all dominant values, and to regulate both the degree of our subjection to any one of them and the preferring of any one of them to some other in accordance with our gifts and opportunities.   The qualities implied in this general regulation and in this reasonable subjection (both as they initiate and as they sustain) are what we mean by moral qualities.

Within each of these broad divisions (or *species*) of value there are, of course, many *varieties*, and these may yield discordant injunctions. Beauty is of so many sorts that nothing but aimless versatility is to be expected if a man tries to cultivate them all. Rigid specialization is an unfortunate condition of most of the sciences. The sources of happiness are protean and often conflicting. It is not to be supposed, therefore, that there is perfect or unquestioned organization within any one of these divisions; and morality, having to encounter these difficulties as well as the general difficulties of its œcumenical regulation, is therefore the more perplexed. It is not left, however, in a maelstrom and mere flux of things good and evil, but has much to guide it.

On the other hand, the view that there is but one supreme end, a perfect union of all these divisions of excellence, cannot, I think, be sustained. This is not because these divisions of excellence are in principle inharmonious. On the contrary, as we have seen, they tend to go together and may even be intrinsically allied. The reason is that in human beings at any rate the regulation of life cannot demand a greater degree or a different kind of unity than life itself permits. Life in any actual society is a wayward, fluctuating thing, subject to accident, demanding special concentration on points of relative detail at any given time, demanding growth and rest and play, a variable intermittent adjustment towards different things at different times. It is not a conspiracy of beauty and science, health and happiness, to form an ideal harmony altogether and all at once. On the contrary, it must always be a thing of alternating quests and of claims that compete in their kinds. This would be true even if accident could be done away, and if evil, gross and unqualified, were never found. In the real world, evil and accident remain.

I shall conclude this chapter by considering a possible objection. The account of morality I have given, it may be contended, bears no ordinary relation to morality in the current sense. These duties of science, or of art, or of happiness may be duties in a certain sense, but not in the usual one. Morality as we mean and intend it has a narrower, more conventional meaning. It is an affair of the virtues : of justice, courage, temperance, and prudence; of magnanimity, promise-keeping, and the avoidance of lies ; of benevolence, the family, and civic service ; of chastity and dignified living. To reduce these to any single principle may not be easy, but at any rate other qualities have nothing to do with morals, and the difficulty, perhaps, is not so very great. What has happened, we are told, is that the experience of mankind has discovered certain salient aspects of a man's duty towards himself or towards others, urged by the stress of fact rather than by any logical principle, and that these duties are the subject-matter of morality. From this department art and the sciences, to say nothing of ease and of play, are rigidly excluded.

This objection, I believe, is spurious. What anyone ought to do is surely the best that he can.[1] Accordingly, the achievement of *any* possible good and the regulation of our lives in the pursuit of it cannot possibly be irrelevant to morals. This consequence depends upon argument, not upon definition ; and the purpose of this chapter has been to supply an argument. If it be true that the majority of moralists—those, in fact, who are called traditional or conventional—have spent their powers in debating certain specified departments of social or of personal conduct, or certain qualities peculiarly important for *any* effective action, the fact

[1] This is verbally denied, to be sure, in a paradox like " *le mieux est l'ennemi du bien.*" This paradox, however, is defensible only if it is taken to mean that, despite hot-headed enthusiasts, it is often better to leave well enough alone than to meddle overmuch in the service of what may seem a finer cause. If so, the paradox disappears, as every paradox does when it attempts to overthrow what is entirely self-evident.

need not disturb us. It is legitimate to proceed so, and the field of ethics is broad enough for all such enquiries. Ultimately, however, this science must be based upon the values that justify action; for morality is the study which explores these values with a view to discovering the duties they determine. Even the idolatry of mere living, mistaken as its worship may be, is a relevant attitude in this regard. To be sure, it is the traditional objection to tradition, the conventional way of being unconventional; but it is no less moral than its enemy. The ideal which Pater ascribes to his Marius, whether it be true or false, is certainly, in its own way, a moral ideal. " Not pleasure," he says, " but fulness of life, and ' insight ' as conducting to that fulness—energy, variety, and choice of experience, including noble pain and sorrow even, loves such as those in the excellent old story of Apuleius, sincere and strenuous forms of the moral life, such as Seneca and Epictetus—whatever form of human life, in short, might be heroic, impassioned, ideal; from these the ' new Cyrenaicism ' of Marius took its criterion of values." This new Cyrenaicism, as we know, is with us to-day, and it loudly proclaims itself up to date. Traditional or untraditional, however, it is always a moral theory.

CHAPTER IV

THE APPLICATION TO PRACTICE

THE object of the previous chapter was to refer our imperatives, for their justification, to certain broad classes of dominant goods. These dominant goods, for the most part, are themselves non-moral; but the use of ourselves in pursuing them or in deciding between them, either for long periods or for short ones, *is* moral, and is the body of action that moral enquiry sets out to examine and assess.

This general reference to superordinate values, however, while necessary, is not sufficient. What has to be justified in any given case is action, and actions are always particular events, actual particulars when they are actual, possible particulars when we consider only what might be done. To be sure, the detail of all practice is as good as infinite, and there is multitudinous variety between particular actions of the same general type. Despite this, it is essential for us to consider the manner, extent, and security of moral guidance in respect to particular deeds.

This is the subject sometimes called casuistry, an art which, according to Mr. Bradley,[1] is "unlovely in life and unpleasant in decay, from which I myself should be loath to divide it," and, according to Mr. Moore,[2] is "the goal of ethical investigation." The

[1] *Principles of Logic*, p. 247.   [2] *Principia Ethica*, p. 5.

first of these judgments appears to be rather a condemnation of certain casuists than a reflection upon their art, and the second to applaud a goal that can seldom, perhaps, be reached. Even if our ethical studies, however, have to remain imperfectly casuistical (either from the nature of things, or on account of our invincible ignorance) they might still give important instruction concerning actual doing, and there does not seem to be the slightest reason why the scrutiny of particular actions should necessarily suggest evasion, or have to peer into matters which a healthy, blunt, ignorant reaction is content to ignore. In short, Mr. Bradley seems to be wrong—or merely a-weary of the *Ductor Dubitantium* and its fellows. It is surely neither offensive nor peculiar to suppose that Omniscience Itself knows the right in its very letters and in its commas, or that certain duties (such as the " perfect obligation " of paying one's debts) may be precise to a farthing. In any case, vituperation is needless. Casuistry may, indeed, be dull ; but in principle it is void of offence. There *is* an art of morals, for morality includes wise living ; and this is an art. This art, moreover, must apply to particular actions.

Accordingly, unless special reasons can be shown to the contrary, it must be assumed that any particular action might theoretically be justified even in its minutest details. This would be a justification of the action in terms of its maximum value, and it plainly involves all the implicates of the action as well as the action itself. Such implicates might even be retrospective, or contemporary, and yet different from the action. For the most part, however, we may regard any given action as a fresh beginning, and so have to consider only its *own* character and intention, together with its *own* effects. Granting this, it is clear that any particular action is morally right when it is the best that any particular agent can perform at any given time.

It follows, therefore, that in order to know the best action possible for any particular agent with his particular gifts and opportunities it would be necessary to know all that the agent could achieve in and through his action down to its most distant effects, and to the minutest recesses of his soul and all that his soul has charge of; to know the values of all the possible alternatives that are, as we say, " open " to him, and to compare these with precision. Even if (as some philosophers say) we know ourselves better than anything else, we still do not know ourselves very well (as other philosophers have shown). We can only guess at our powers (at any rate, until it is too late for any considerable achievement), and at the best have only a short, dim, summary, schematic apprehension of what is likely to happen to ourselves and to our works if things continue to happen after their wont, and if unforeseen accidents do not occur. (Certain effects may indeed be foreseen—for instance, the effects of taking poison—but not the totality of effects upon others). In the same way, even if the facts were known, our knowledge and comparison of their values, to judge from a host of disputes concerning values, is highly, and perhaps radically, uncertain.

Let us consider these matters with more attention.

Our knowledge of the nature, possibility, and effects of any given action may be called practical sagacity. Sagacity in some degree is, of course, indispensable in moral matters, since anyone who does not have it does not know what he is about when he acts, and so is not a responsible agent. To hold, as some moralists hold, that ignorance and stupidity are not moral defects, although they may be highly mischievous, is to speak foolishly. If the stupidity in question is *born* and incorrigible stupidity, then certainly it cannot be helped ; and since no one can be commanded to do that which he cannot do, we may agree that moral imperatives apply only to those matters which an agent is not too stupid to appreciate. Unavoidable ignorance, again, and ignorance which, while not strictly unavoidable, is reasonable in those who are busied for the most part in other affairs (as a layman's ignorance of medicine or the law) is morally irrelevant for the same reason as before. Apart from this, sagacity *is* a moral requirement. It is a man's business to see what he is doing as carefully as he can—to trim his lights, as well as to act in accordance with them—and everyone knows that it is. A seaman who neglects to take seamanly precautions is *not* morally innocent, and the principle is universally applicable. In matters of common knowledge, ignorance is not an excuse, and the fault is moral.[1]

Accepting, then, the duty of practical sagacity, we have to consider the consequences of its inevitable limitations ; and so we should consider, in the first place, what these inevitable limitations are. The chief limitations are, I think, the following : Ignorance of our capacities, ignorance of our mode of acting in detail, ignorance of remote effects, and differences in the degree of ignorance reasonably to be expected in different agents. In each of these directions perplexities are concealed if they are not openly proclaimed, and all these perplexities have important consequences for moral theory. I shall endeavour to show, however, that these perplexities are less overwhelming than many suppose.

[1] From the recent trial of a medical man, as reported in *The Times* of October 30, 1924. *The judge :* " How does conscience, apart from telling a man to do his best for a patient, operate on your mind ? "

It is clear that we have often a very inadequate notion of what we might do if we tried. Our imaginations are starved and unready, and either refuse to tell us of expedients entirely possible, or tell us when it is already too late. Again, when we think of possible expedients, we may grievously mistake our capacity for them. It is a common complaint against the existing social order that young people, and older people too, have a way of drifting into the positions in which they find themselves ; and it is sometimes supposed that vocational experts might deliver us from this pass. So, very often, they might ; but the thing has deeper roots. The raw material of our capacities, and the faint outlines of a possible pursuit to the inexperienced, must often be the flimsiest guess-work. We may speak with some confidence of the premonitions of a talent, and with still greater confidence of the absence of some necessary requirement or peculiar aptitude. In the end, however, we remain marvels to ourselves and to others, sometimes meeting a dreaded emergency in a manner inspired (as if grace had been given us to meet our weakness), sometimes responding feebly and fumblingly as if we were novices or poor hirelings. There are times when nothing goes wrong, and times when nothing goes right, and although the occasions for these differences are sometimes outside ourselves, they are often within us and unknown.

This has to be said ; yet the question has another side. Whatever lines of promise are to be followed must at least be followed with regard to the existing situation, and the serious alternatives may therefore be comparatively few. Mistaken as we may easily be, it is past doubting that experience may tell us much of what we can make of our powers. We may never be too old to begin all over again (even when others suppose that we are), but at least we know something of the difficulties, and much that we may rightly expect if we proceed upon accustomed lines. For youth, in appearance, there is greater scope, yet although early promise may flicker and die, showing never a flame in the future, or conceal slow beginnings as by a screen, youth's is seldom a random adventure. In short, although there are risks and surprises wherever there is life, and although these risks and these surprises are as much in ourselves as in our fate, we may still guess shrewdly concerning ourselves, and instruct ourselves by the guesses of others.

Our ignorance of detail in the mode of our acting is in many respects very profound. Although we control our muscular movements, we do not know precisely how the thing is done; and when, by our thinking, we control further thinking, we again may not know how we do it. Moreover, the very signals by which we guide ourselves in the common affairs of life are for the most part gross ones and not minute. It has been the opinion of many philosophers, for example, that it is better for us that our senses are not refined. "Thus a dog," we are told, "in order to recognize water and to be able to satisfy its thirst by lapping it with the tongue, does not need to apprehend its molecular, atomic, and sub-atomic structure. That would be a harmful complication. The animal would be bewildered by the multitudinous dancing particles. . . . The animal preoccupied with the unnecessary would be unable to survive to take advantage of the knowledge thus obtained."[1] This is an odd way of trying to prove that it would be the worse for us if our senses were better; and we answer it, with some success, in practice

[1] N. K. Smith, *Prolegomena to an Idealist Theory of Knowledge*, p. 33.

whenever we bring a microscope to the assistance of unaided sense. The fact remains, however, that our senses, even when they are assisted, are at the best macroscopic not microscopic, and the same is true of our tastes and emotions, our attractions and our repugnances.

On the other hand, this detail is often irrelevant. The man who is steering his car through the traffic does not need to know how the mechanism works. All he needs to know is the gross, palpable fact of the car's response. Similarly, a better acquaintance with physiology need not have the smallest effect upon ordinary action. The Greeks, in our opinion, were hopelessly ignorant of this science. Aristotle, for example, regarded the heart as the sensorium for the common sensibles, but this in itself is no reason why his ethical theories should differ from other people's. If the effect is known, nothing else may matter. The ethics of a sword drawn in anger are not at all affected by a man's knowledge or ignorance of the nerves or the muscles which he uses in drawing it. And so we may agree that much of our ignorance of this kind is, morally speaking, irrelevant.

It is otherwise, however, with remote effects, for an action is undertaken in order to produce an effect, and plainly we have no right to pick and choose among these effects, acknowledging some of them and ignoring the others. Very often, indeed, the remote effects are more important than the immediate ones. Reforms, for the most part, do not come of a sudden. The voice of them at the outset is the voice of one crying in the wilderness, and they are effected only when opinion is ripe to receive them. Our objection, again, to mere " opportunism " (as we call it) is that, assuaging the moment, it wrecks or at least perturbs the future. There is no reason, indeed, to neglect any effect simply because it is remote, and it is always possible, although it may be very unlikely, that the remote effects of some very innocent-looking action may be very considerable indeed. This is why we hear of " a chance word spoken in jest," of " casting our bread upon the waters," and the like.

On the other hand, any effects which are the implicates of a given action must at least be its own proper effects, and remote effects are very seldom of this kind, since the action, from the nature of things, usually contributes to them in a very slight degree. An action which, so to speak, is preserved whole and entire (as the written word which remains, or the spoken word that is remembered) may, indeed, continue itself in its integrity, and grow and act again after a long interval of time. In these cases the remote effect must be ascribed to it, not indeed because it is the sole cause of that effect, but because it is the inciting and controlling occasion. Even the immediate effects of an action are not entirely due to it, since the action can but alter a situation or make use of an opportunity. The action, however, may be the dominating and initiating feature of the change either remotely or immediately. If so, the total effect is said to be due to the action, and rightly so. On the other hand, what we call an accident (that is to say, some occurrence uncontemplated in the action and beyond its purpose) is not, properly speaking, an implicate of the action (which therefore bears only a part of the responsibility), and an effect which is only influenced to some small degree by some given action cannot be said to be *due* to the action except in this small part. This is commonly true of remote effects. They are brought about by a multitude of concurring causes, of which the former action is only one, and it may be a feeble and insignificant one. A great many actions are such that things are all the same, not a hundred years, but a hundred seconds after them. It is true in these cases that some other action might have made a most critical difference (since we can always work mischief when we have a mind to it, and can usually do something that we or other people would regret for many thousands of seconds), but the action in question need not have made any particular difference, since its effects have a very short life, and so could not be distinguished from the results of most other short-lived actions. These are the deeds that rest in unvisited tombs.

Our practical sagacity, therefore, although sadly curtailed by these varieties of ignorance, may yet be effective and serviceable in all the cases (and they are many) in which we know what we can do, macroscopically if not microscopically, and may reasonably believe that effects too remote for serious contemplation are likely to be very little affected by our present performance. If this be granted, no one should allow himself to be puzzled by differences in the practical sagacity of different moral agents. We are accustomed, indeed, to speak of moral duties as if they were the same for all; and many of them may be, since a certain minimum of practical sagacity may be common to all the adult and responsible members of a given community at a given time, and since the best of such people may not be greatly superior to the worst in these particular affairs. Anyone may know that he should not murder or bear false witness, and anyone may know it as well as anyone else. It is impossible to suppose, however, that this democracy of moral knowledge extends to everyone in every matter (as if children or infants had the same practical sagacity as their elders, or as if the members of some profession did not differ from the laity in respect of their knowledge in their calling). This knowledge, quite plainly, does affect our action, and very often affects it morally. What is culpable negligence in a professional nurse need not be any sort of negligence in a mother.

Granting, however, that we may have a serviceable knowledge of our capacities and of our opportunities, it seems plain that this knowledge falls very far short of certainty. These uncertainties, as we have seen, are of two sorts, for they affect both our practical sagacity (or our estimates of what might be done) and our knowledge of the values of any action that might be done. We have to ask, therefore, what effect these uncertainties have upon rightness in conduct; and since problems should be considered one at a time, we may, for the time being, neglect the second type of difficulty (i.e. the difficulty concerning values) and consider the former only. Let us suppose, then, that we could tell whether an action would be good or bad if we could tell what it was and what would come of it, and so that we have to consider only the consequences of our ignorance concerning it and its implications, in the first instance.

What is commonly said in discussions upon this matter is that the knowledge which is morally relevant here is the knowledge, not of a certainty, but of a probability. It is always the duty of a moral agent to do what is *probably best*—that is to say, to choose the action which in itself and in its probable consequences seems better than any other action in itself and in its probable consequences.

This seems most reasonable. Whether the future is or is not uncertain in itself is a problem for metaphysical dispute, but there is no disputing that our knowledge of things to come, whether from our own action or otherwise, is and must always be uncertain; and it could not be anyone's duty to foresee events that could not possibly be foreseen. As Bishop Butler says : " We never, in the moral Way, applaud or blame either ourselves or others for what we enjoy or what we suffer, or for having Impressions made upon us which we consider as altogether out of our Power; but only for what we do, or would have done, had it been in our Power; or for what we leave undone which we might have done, or would have left undone though we could have done it." [1] In accordance with this principle, therefore, we must hold that no one can be commanded to guide his action by any species of knowledge better than the best available; and the best available knowledge cannot be more than a probability. Unless it is held, therefore, that foresight and careful scrutiny are not commanded at all, and that grace from above or the mere spirit and enthusiasm of virtue are sufficient of themselves, it is necessary, in principle, to assent to this view, and without reserve.

At the same time, certain explanations are necessary. An agent cannot be held to be morally accountable for the lack of any knowledge or foresight that is inevitable in the nature of things. Granting this, however, perplexities still remain. When we speak of the probable consequences of an act we are apt to speak loosely, since many things may be meant. It is essential therefore to be more explicit.

Probability is always relative to the evidence on which it is based. We have therefore to ask what the evidence is when we speak of guidance by probabilities; and different moralists, clearly, may answer this question

---

[1] *The Analogy of Religion*, Dissertation II. "Of the Nature of Virtue."

quite differently. Thus, according to some of them, the intention of the agent supplies *all* the relevant evidence, and even here there is a plain difficulty, since the expectations of the agent in regard to the effects of his intentions may not be the true probabilities according to the evidence of which his intentions take cognizance. Moreover, by these true probabilities, different things may be meant ; or, if we mean by them what the phrase naturally suggests (that is to say, the probability which an ideal intelligence would deduce from the given evidence), it may reasonably be asked where this ideal intelligence is to be found. For any practical purpose, therefore, we could not expect the " true probabilities " of any intended action to mean more than what the best opinion (relatively to the available knowledge at any given time) would take to be probable, and it would be foolish to suppose that there is any expressed opinion of this kind for the majority of the private intentions of John Doe or of Richard Roe ; that if there were one it would suit Doe's or Roe's particular case ; or, in general, that the best expert opinion on any probable matter (if there were one) could be accessible to ordinary people (for the most part) in the common affairs of life, or could conceivably determine their duty.

These perplexities may seem insurmountable. When we are dealing, however, with the voluntary or self-controlled actions of a responsible being it may not be impossibly difficult to determine in principle what his duty is. The principle here is that anyone ought to do what according to his knowledge and belief is probably best, provided he has done his utmost to inform himself of the probable consequences of his actions. More than this may not be commanded, since this is the utmost that could be asked from intentional action. Less than this should not be commanded. It is much to be honest, although ill-informed, but an honesty that is wilfully ignorant is very doubtfully sincere. The question is not what we expect, but what we ought to expect when we have tried to learn ; not what we happen to intend (forgetting what ought not to be forgotten, or neglecting what we ought not to neglect), but the best we might set about doing in so far as an estimate is possible for us.

The main distinctions in this affair are very neatly described by Mr. Russell when he distinguishes between the most fortunate, the wisest, and the right action.[1] (Mr. Russell says " subjectively " right, but the qualification, I think, is a mistake.) The most fortunate act, in this language, is that which together with its consequences achieves the best result. It is the act whose fate is the best. The wisest act is that which is based upon the best available information, and upon the most reasonable conjecture possible at any time concerning its probable fate. The right act for any agent is the wisest act which the agent with his measure of wisdom, and with his opportunities for reflexion, can attain.

The objections that may be raised against this view are not, I think, very formidable. The term " wisdom," indeed, may be misleading because we are accustomed to mean by it simply that practical sagacity of which I have formerly spoken. The "wisdom" here spoken of, however, is wisdom concerning the value as well as the nature and effects of the actions in question (for we are assuming this knowledge). Accepting this, there is no serious reason for objection. It is absurd to deny that consequences count (since, as we have seen, the intention of any action is to bring some consequence about). It is equally absurd to deny that the wisest action possible to man may still have unfortunate results,

[1] *Philosophical Essays*, pp. 22–6.

and therefore to deny that there is an important difference between the wisest and the most fortunate action. No one, again, should argue that it is not a man's duty to act as wisely as he can, or that it is possible for all of us to be equally wise in all affairs. If we assume, then, that the right action for any man is simply identical with his duty, the principle of these distinctions seems to be definitely accepted. It is clear, of course, that this injunction to act as wisely as we can does not and should not mean that we ought to deliberate to the top of our bent upon every matter. We may not have time for this, and we can prepare for such emergencies only by drilling and training ourselves to be ready to meet them. Many emergencies, again, cannot be provided for by education or earlier discipline ; and since we might deliberate (as madmen do) upon some small thing without end, or spend the greater part of our time upon some particular and perhaps trivial piece of training, it is plain that practical wisdom entails a sense of relative importance in life's concerns, and very likely a compromise. These facts, however, are not objections, but rather consequences. Finally, as we have seen, it is not an objection that what is right for one agent need not be right for another. Is it the less incumbent upon A to be a good man if he knows he can never be a good woman, or upon B to be a good citizen if he knows he can never be a good Cabinet Minister ? Was it an old man's duty or a child's to shoulder a musket in the war ? The principle here is that duty is *not* the same where there is a relevant difference, and that it *is* the same where there is no relevant difference.

Notwithstanding this, it may be contended, not unreasonably, that a great many of our moral duties, such as veracity or good faith, *are* precisely the same for all, and in general that our duty is by no means so variable as these arguments suggest to the first look. This opinion may be held consistently with the foregoing, and the effect of holding it would be to vindicate a very determinate casuistry over a wide range. The principal arguments here are the following : It may be held, firstly, that certain duties are in themselves completely determinate. Such are paying one's debts, keeping one's promises, telling the truth. Secondly, that certain duties are absolutely binding irrespective of any *other* consequences than those of obeying the duty. This may be argued on grounds of overwhelming probability instead of absolute certainty ; and in general it may be maintained that the well-established general rules of conduct are such that *probably* it is *always* our duty to follow them. This is the argument of Bishop Butler's *Analogy*. Probability, he thought, was the guide of life, but this probability was the probability of an orderly system of general moral rules, and therefore he bade us " instead of that idle and not very innocent Employment of forming imaginary Models of a World, and Schemes of governing it, turn our Thoughts to what we experience to be the Conduct of Nature with respect to intelligent Creatures ; which may be resolved into general Laws or Rules of Administration, in the same Way as many of the Laws of Nature respecting inanimate Matter may be collected from Experiments." [1]

I shall try to show that all these claims are something too absolute.

It may be true that a debt, for example, is a debt for so much, and is therefore completely determinate (although if the debt were merely to do someone " a good turn " this would not be the case). If so, the question still remains whether it is probably always our duty to pay this determinate sum ; and plainly we do not

[1] Introduction to the *Analogy*.

always suppose so. There is a Statute of Limitations against claims of very old standing. There are rules against usury. The debt must not be an overcharge; and it would generally be agreed that the International Debts which trouble us so much in these days may not be capable of settlement on any pellucid and indisputable principle. In some of these cases, at least, it is probably not our duty to pay the determinate sum which is called the debt.

More generally, a proviso of this sort seems to affect all the duties which are alleged to be duties of perfect (or completely determinate) obligation. Let us take veracity for instance. We are to tell the truth, the whole truth, and nothing but the truth. But are we? Are we bound to retail other people's secrets as a piece of mere gossip, to answer any question that is put to us even when we suspect that silence may mislead? Surely not; and if it be said that the truth should be told only when it is rightfully demanded, and when we are the proper persons to answer, it is plain that this question may be very difficult to determine. Even in the witness-box a priest holds the confessional secret; and although a doctor cannot claim this protection for professional secrecy in the courts, it is surely not to be argued that he should ignore the point altogether when he is a witness.

Since *suppressio veri* may be a lie, it is plain that mere reticence cannot always save us; and surely it is not always so very easy to know what is or what is not a lie. Is any falsehood that is uttered a lie? If so, the smallest inaccuracy uttered in perfect good faith would be one; and since inaccuracies can seldom be avoided, the only conclusion would be that no one (in all probability) should ever say anything at all. Shall we amend our definition, then, and say that any false statement made with intent to deceive is a lie? If so, we may still be perplexed. The kernel of the question now is the intention to deceive, and so it may be doubted whether a true statement made with this intention (as when a man, knowing that he is expected to lie, tells the truth in order to mislead) is not a lie. In any case, the difficulties are endless. It is the business of a teacher, or preacher, or lecturer to convey to his hearers the fairest impression of the matters with which he deals, and if anyone supposes that it is always easy to do this without evasion, suppression, or exaggeration I can only say that his experience is different from mine. A lecturer (as William James once delightfully reminded us) may even be justified in "cooking" his platform experiments. In a word, scrupulous veracity need not convey a fair impression. We depart from literal veracity at our peril, but it may sometimes be right to do so.

The second line of argument concerning consequences is also, I think, insufficient. As we have seen, to ignore consequences is simply to ignore the meaning of action, and so is not worth a debate. On the other hand, it may very well be contended that the results of disobeying any of the greater moral rules (even for what seems a sufficient moral reason) are, in general, so much more unfortunate than the immediate advantages gained by such a course that the "wisest" plan is always to obey them. The mere fact of disobedience, it may be urged, weakens the stability of these rules both in ourselves and in others ; and this general reliance upon them is precisely one of their greatest assets.

I cannot think that this reasoning is conclusive. What it proves directly is that if disobedience to the rule entails a weakening of it, and if it is good that the rule should not be weakened, then the mischief of this weakening is a positive evil which should only be overridden by some manifestly superior good. On the other hand, if the rule, apart from this circumstance, is plainly not the best adaptation in the given case, then the following of it, just because it is an accepted rule, is a positive evil.   The rule would be better if it could be modified so as not to be inequitable in the given case.   And if it cannot practically be modified, its occasional inequities, even if they are only occasional, sap the grounds of its authority.   In principle, all rules are justified by their value if they are justified at all ; and departures from them may themselves be justified on precisely the same principle.   If a rule provides for most cases, although not for all, it is better, surely, to discriminate carefully between the cases for which it provides and those for which it does not provide, than to follow it inflexibly in all cases because it is generally wholesome.   Misunderstanding apart, the rule is the better and the stronger on account of this discrimination ; and it is easy to fear misunderstanding too much.

Even if we admit, however, that the arguments on the two sides of this question are hopelessly entangled, it is still apparent that definitive practical guidance is not *always* to be expected in moral affairs.   In the case of " imperfect " obligations—those which, like the command to be generous, have to be entrusted to a man's discretion—this is abundantly plain ;   and we have already seen that, in certain cases at least, " perfect " obligations are subject to the same condition.   Even when the rule is determinate, it may not be plain precisely when and where it applies;   and if this, *per impossibile*, were always clear, even the best and the widest rules might still conflict.   As we all know, contradictory injunctions may apply to the same act.   Promise-keeping is a duty, and so is the avoidance of adultery.   What, then, if a man has promised to elope with his neighbour's wife ?   Veracity is a duty, but what if it enjoins the

betrayal of our friends? And treachery towards our
enemies (which cannot afford to be squeamish) is often
applauded. In the eyes of the Jews, Judith did right;
and in the valley of Sorek a woman of the Philistines
did as the lords of her country advised and was well-
pleasing to Dagon, their god.

These difficult cases bulk largely in the pages of
moralists because they compel our thought. It is hard
cases that make the best law. For the most part, to be
sure, easier instances prevail. The path of virtue is
usually plain. To be honest and candid, to avoid envy
and malice, to be hospitable, steadfast, sober, and
compassionate, are duties which in general are not at
all intricate or doubtful. It is past disputing, however,
that serious moral perplexities not only may occur, but
actually do occur to all of us at many times, and it may
be doubted whether any rule is such that it should
probably be followed on every occasion. It is well to
be temperate, but many are altogether too sober, and
it is better for some to be drunk with their zeal.

It may be contended, indeed, that all the more
specific commandments are subordinate to certain more
general commandments of the spirit and to certain
formal axioms. To be perfect, or to love one's neighbour as oneself, may be considered the great commandment of the spirit, and Mr. Sidgwick's Axioms of
Prudence, Benevolence, and Equity (of which the first is
that " a smaller present good is not to be preferred to a
greater future good, allowing for difference of certainty,"
and the last, that "similar cases ought to be treated
similarly,") [1] are the classical expressions of supreme
formal canons. Of the latter Mr. Sidgwick says that
he " regards the apprehension with more or less distinctness of these abstract truths, as the permanent basis

[1] *Methods of Ethics*, 7th ed., Book III, chap. xiii, p. 382.

of the common conviction that the fundamental principles
of morality are essentially reasonable " ; [1] and certainly
they are reasonable and most fundamental. Even the
most scrupulous attention to them, however, could not
be expected to settle the perplexities which have been
discussed in this chapter, or greatly to diminish the
latitude and the discretion which we have seen to be
implied in the application of our principles to practice.
As Mr. Sidgwick admits, these formal principles obviously do not give complete guidance. They are
necessary in all moral guidance, but insufficient for
much of it. Implied in every moral rule, they cannot
decide which rule (if any) is applicable, or with what
degree of precision. The same thing holds, with an
even livelier firmness, of the injunctions which I have
called " commandments of the spirit." The command
to be perfect is just the command to seek the best, and
this is the subject of our whole discourse. The command
to love our neighbour as ourselves does not discriminate
between the baser and the finer elements in our love
for ourselves, or in our love for our fellows.

Summing up, then, we would seem to have reached
the following conclusion. Morality is concerned with
what ought to be done, and everything that ought to
be done, or that can be done, is a particular action. It
is absurd to argue, therefore, that moral theory cannot
in principle be applied to individual cases, or, in other
words, that it cannot guide that which it is its business
to guide ; and although our ignorance of the future
compels us to choose probability for our guide, probability itself is neither irrational nor uninstructive.
Granting this, it follows (and, independently, it is
entirely plain) that our duty in many particular cases
is completely determinate, a thing not merely of the

[1] *Methods of Ethics*, Book III, chap. xiii, p. 383.

spirit but of the letter too; and in every particular case much at least is definitively forbidden. On the other hand, in many instances, we cannot expect moral guidance to have this exemplary degree of precision. The guidance in these instances permits, and indeed requires, discretion within a certain range. Moreover, in a few cases, duty may decree an entirely determinate action which is definitely opposed to what is usually a duty in other actions of the class; and there is an honourable and a wider discretion in certain exceptional cases less definite than these, but still on the whole exceptional. Such " exceptions " of course, are not arbitrary exceptions, but exceptions for a sufficient moral reason; and again, when we speak of " discretion," we do not mean a capricious or unprincipled discretion, but only a discretion which is not completely determinate in detail.

I shall conclude this chapter by endeavouring to defend the later portions of this summary by applying them to two distinct departments. These are the conditions of action and the nature of dominant goods.

Human action is part of the business of living. It is a doing and a becoming, a trust and a charge. Accordingly, any command to do as we ought should be regarded not from the standpoint of a dictator expecting servile obedience (if any dictators do), but from the standpoint of one who entrusts a commission to a free agent. Such a commission, to be sure, rightly implies the careful execution of much that is completely determinate. In a great part, however, it implies nothing of the sort, but is an injunction instead to deal with the situation to the best of the agent's ability. This is not arbitrary, but it is not a thing of rules. It requires tact, judgment, discretion, initiative, and what Pascal calls *l'esprit de finesse*. The commission, indeed, may

of the qualities of these principles as the righteous, the requisite, and the generous qualities respectively.

The first of these (or the righteous quality) may be illustrated by veracity, promise-keeping, and the like, and are indistinguishable from the moral rules (positive and negative) already considered. (If there is any distinction here between the conduct that is virtuous and the conduct that is right, the distinction at most is that these virtues consist in *habitual* obedience to their governing rules.)

Qualities like perseverance, steadfastness, and the like illustrate the second class—i.e. the class of qualities which are requisite but insufficient. These are necessary to a virtuous character, but may also be found in the vicious, and if they contribute to the excellence of the best they seem also to be a factor in the wickedness of the worst.

Virtues of the third, or generous, class, on the contrary, seem in part at least to redeem indefensible conduct, and greatly to dignify conduct which is conformable to moral rules. Thus, courageous emotion, as we saw when we considered Lord Camelford, has something splendid in it, morally and not merely æsthetically, even when it is shown in an unworthy enterprise. Again, loyalty to the worthless and compassion for the undeserving have always a strain of fineness in them ; and purity or chastity is by common consent indefinitely more excellent than the simple abstention from contaminating actions. In the same way the vices of this order detract immensely from actions which may nevertheless be right, and aggravate what is already an offence. Take envy or malice, for example. If a man has to choose between two candidates for a position, his action is right when he chooses the better of them, but if he feels a pang of envy at the rapid promotion

of the victor, or a malicious joy at the discomfiture of
the loser, his action is sadly tarnished ; and if he allows
his envy or his malice to determine his choice his fault
is proportionately the greater.

The examination of these three classes of virtue
cannot impugn, and may strongly confirm, our former
argument. Virtues of the righteous class do not
differ in any particular from the obligations already
discussed. They have therefore no independent bearing
upon problems of casuistry. Qualities of the second
class are plainly subordinate, and may either be good or
bad. Their guidance accordingly, if they give any,
must always be incomplete. Qualities of the generous
class, on the other hand, seem for the most part to come
very near to what we mean by intrinsic goods. In a
way, therefore, they would seem to be flawless mentors.
For the most part, however, this claim is the last that
should be made. The quality of courage, for example,
is never in itself even approximately a sufficient guide
to action. What is needed always is courage appropriate
to the situation, and courage grotesquely inappropriate
(as when a man bears bravely and cheerfully evils which
his dentist or his doctor could easily remove) can hardly
be said to mitigate folly at all. It is possible, indeed
(and it is frequently claimed), that qualities of this kind
quicken and sharpen the moral vision, and are even
accompanied by an intuitive insight into the good ;
yet these same qualities are often the retainers of rage
or obstinacy of prejudice, blunt things not sharp ones ;
and in general they are but features of a larger pattern
of conduct. If so, it is the whole pattern that is judged,
not simply the fineness of emotion and temper that is
woven into it.

The virtues, indeed, seen from this angle, are the
beauty and the bloom of certain patterns of living.

These patterns, in their turn, have the distinctness of perspectives rather than the individuality of agencies. They are not agents at all, or even departments of agency. They are seldom dominant goods, but often are the features which a dominant pattern reveals in some one of its perspectives, although in another some different virtue would stand forth. The greatest of them, indeed, love and compassion and courage, are to be seen, in some form and feature, in every moral pattern where the good is dominant, but these forms and features dissolve and commingle as the eye of the beholder turns. In their case, therefore, there is no caprice; and there *is* effectual guidance. This guidance, however, must often be impressionist; and different impressions need not always enjoin the same action.

CHAPTER V

THE KNOWLEDGE OF GOOD AND EVIL

Our discussion, up to the present, has assumed that there is such a thing as the knowledge of good and of evil, and has postponed consideration of difficulties that may be incident to this species of knowledge, supposing it to exist. These matters must now be dealt with.

The most serious difficulty is whether there is any such knowledge at all. It is granted, of course, that we all speak as if there were, using the same grammar and forms of speech when we say that pleasure is good as when we say that honey is sweet or poinsettia red. This grammatical identity, however, proves very little, and may mask a fundamental difference. It may very well be true that what we say, for short, is not what we mean in the long. And this is precisely what is commonly alleged. Our language, we are often told, testifies to the existence of a certain attitude of the soul ; and this attitude is not a knowledgeable one, or even cognitive, but something entirely different. This is the attitude of *approval*, and approval is really a state of feeling or of inclination, not knowledge or judgment at all.

I have to show, therefore, that the attitude here called approval does in fact have the characteristics which are proper to judgment and to knowledge of good and of evil.

It will be agreed, I think, that approval is at least potentially contemplative. We frequently say, indeed, that a man's actions are often the most convincing evidence of what he approves or disapproves. This is living, active approval. Clearly, however, we may do what we do not approve, as the Greek in the story feasted his eyes upon a loathsome spectacle, although condemning himself the while. Our actions, therefore, cannot be supposed to give indisputable evidence of what we approve, and since our approval or disapproval extends to the doings of other people in other ages (as when we condemn false Sextus or praise Joan the Maid) it is plain that the attitude may be, and frequently is, entirely contemplative.

Again, the attitude of approval may be analytical and comparative. When Cassius, in the play, resents Cæsar's dictatorship we may perhaps approve his republican spirit, but must certainly disapprove the meanness and petty jealousy which underlie his complaint that he himself has become an underling. We distinguish here and analyse. Comparison, similarly, is essential to this whole matter; for *better* and *worse* concern approval even more nearly than " good " and " bad " themselves.

The answer to these arguments, I suppose, is that, while they may show the presence of judgment and knowledge, they need not show that judgment and knowledge are directly concerned with good and evil. Thus the contemplative aspect of this question may be taken to mean that when we contemplate certain actions we feel that they are in harmony with our emotions and inclinations. The analysis, again, may be analysis into elements which severally are liked or disliked in a certain way; and *better* and *worse* may be taken to mean certain feelings of preference when comparison occurs. This view, however, becomes increasingly difficult to sustain when further and more considerable arguments are adduced.

It is plain, on any theory, that approval cannot be simple liking or inclination, even when it accompanies the contemplations of a disinterested spectator. It is not to be supposed, for example, that those who approve of the execution of a murderer have any liking for the hangman's deed, or any inclination towards it. Much that we approve is approved sorrowfully. Thus approval, if it is a feeling, is a feeling of a very peculiar sort, a sort of register of general consonance with the trend of our inclinations and desires, or perhaps an overflow spilt out of the plenitude of the consonance. Certainly there might be such a " feeling," or peculiar register of the current of one's wishes ; and perhaps there is one. This alleged feeling, however, claims to be true, and general, and submissive to the demand for logical consistency, and a " feeling " of *this* species seems altogether too peculiar.

The claim to truth, in short, is undoubtedly made ; and approval could never be what we take it to be if in fact it could never be true or false. When we condemn false Sextus we really do condemn him, and do not merely state that we feel in a certain way regarding his rape of Lucretia. Certainly, we do feel horror at his action ; but we also judge that this horror is appropriate and deserved. In other words, we ascribe to the action a quality of vileness which in our view really does characterize it. The action does not become vile when our horror arises, but is vile whether we are stirred by it or not ; and although the Tarquins may not have regarded this action as we do, we do not therefore conclude that because the Tarquins felt in a certain way and other people feel in a different way, this is all that is to be said on the matter. If the question were one of feeling this would be the whole of it. What we mean is that the action was truly vile whatever the Tarquins may have thought; and again, that if the Tarquins said it was not vile, what they said was false.

The generality of moral approval is similarly a necessary characteristic of it. Our approval of an action is not our private feeling. It claims validity for *any* act similar to the one approved, and for *any* judge who knows what he is doing when he approves. This is not the story of feelings or inclinations. The only generality that these can claim is the circumstance that they may be widely spread. Our constitution is such that most of us have them. Logical universality is not of this order. It does not depend upon counting heads, and it legislates for every rational creature. Approval, in this critical aspect, is therefore a logical thing.

It submits itself also, and of right, to the canons of logical consistency—not, indeed, because morality is an exercise in general logic, but because approval is self-stultifying if it does not pursue those logical implications which are part of its essence. The very profession of approval is a profession of fairness and equity, and if equity is not a logical thing it is impossible even to conjecture where logic can conceivably work. Its canon is the equal treatment of equals; its progress is the progress of discrimination in relevant equality. Have we the right to discriminate between Jews and Christians in respect of the franchise, or between men and women as holders of property, or to compel blacks as well as whites to serve in the army and yet to deny them the ordinary privileges of responsible citizens? Is it fair to call labour leaders mercenaries and hirelings, and to forget that soldiers and priests are also paid for their work? Is the scramble for oil essentially different

from piracy and buccaneering ?   In claiming to approve
an act we admit the relevance of such questions as
these, not as they happen to suit our inclinations or the
broadest outlines of our emotional constitution, but
because right reason is appropriate to them. It is false,
in fact, to suppose that inclinations ungoverned by these
superior canons could act as a substitute for them.
Our preference goes to our class and creed and kin.
It is equity and reflection that widens it.

Approval, then, must accept these claims, or else
cease to be approval. This is another way of saying
that it has the characteristics of truth and right judgment ;
or, in the alternative, if it is not itself a kind of judgment
and knowledge, there must be some other capacity of
the soul to which these same characteristics may pertain.
This latter was Brentano's belief. In his *Origin of the
Knowledge of Right and Wrong* he maintained that there
is " an inner superiority which distinguishes the moral
from the immoral will in the same way that it is an
inner superiority which distinguishes true and self-
evident judgments and conclusions from prejudices
and fallacies." [1]   " We call anything true when the
recognition related to it is right. We call something
good when the love related to it is right. That which
can be loved with a right love, that which is worthy of
love, is good in the widest sense of the term." [2]   The
better, again, is " something which, for its own sake, is
preferred with a right preference " ; [3] and from the
" better " the " best " may be learned.

Brentano's alternative, however, seems plainly in-
admissible. If the higher or the finer kind of loving
is, indeed, the standard of morals, we should at least be
able to distinguish it from coarser ways of loving, and

[1] English translation, p. 9.   [2] *Ibid.*, p. 16.
[3] *Ibid.*, p. 23.

to know that it is better than they.   Granting, therefore,
that love differs in quality, some knowledge and judgment concerning the goodness of loving seems quite
indispensable.   And if " that which is worthy of love "
means, as it seems to mean, not only that which may be
loved with the finer qualities of this emotion, but that
which deserves this nobler loving, then we must, in
addition, be able to recognize the goodness to which
a good love is appropriate.   It seems impossible,
therefore, to avoid the conclusion that ethics necessarily
presupposes a certain knowledge of good and evil.
If there could not be this knowledge, there could not
be ethics, but only the ape and pretence of it.[1]

Certainly, if it could be shown that all such knowledge
is impossible in principle, we should be forced to
accept this sceptical conclusion.   There is, however,
no way of showing this.   Judgments of good and evil
seem to be possible.   For we do make them ; and it is
not to the point to argue, as some do, (1) that at least
they are not descriptive judgments, or (2) that they only
pertain to " subjective " conditions or states of mind.

(1) " If you could enumerate *all* the intrinsic properties
a given thing possessed," Mr. Moore says, " you would
have given a *complete* description of it, and would not

---

[1] I am attempting in this chapter to deal succinctly with a
subject that may easily become enormously complicated, and
therefore have avoided much that, from many points of view, I
might reasonably have been expected to discuss.   If this is a short-
coming, it was committed deliberately, and the time for apologies
is past ; but for the benefit of readers not familiar with the vast
and increasing volume of literature upon this subject I may refer,
in English, to Mr. Urban's *Valuation : its Nature and Laws*, and,
for a shorter treatment, to the early chapters of Mr. Sorley's
Moral Values as well as to Mr. Mackenzie's *Ultimate Values*,
Book II.   On the Continent, the best-known discussions are
Mr. Meinong's *Psychologisch-ethische Untersuchungen* and Mr. von
Ehrenfels's *System der Wert-theorie*.

need to mention any predicates of values it possessed ; whereas no description of a given thing could be *complete* which omitted any intrinsic property." [1]   This statement (taken, on its own showing, as applicable to " intrinsic " goods) seems to be either false or incomplete.   The goodness intrinsic to a thing *is* a property of that thing ; and if we say, as we may, that it is a property of a higher order than any of the characteristics which (as we are accustomed to say) *describe* a thing's *nature* (being as it were the attestation of the goodness of *all* these properties), no important theoretical consequence would appear to be involved.   To goods not simply " intrinsic " the statement does not apply.

(2) So of " subjectivism " in the sense here stated. There is none of it, if the argument be only that nothing is good or bad except states of the soul.   For these are not unknowable, and there is nothing in principle to prevent the true discernment of their value or the true discrimination of their goodness from their badness.

The only other argument which seems to bear directly upon the possibility, in principle, of this knowledge of good and evil is an indirect psychological argument.   The good, it is said, must be something capable of attracting, moving, and governing.   Knowledge and judgment, being cold and neutral, can never perform this necessary task.   I shall consider this argument when I come to treat of moral psychology at greater length.   Apart from it, we have now seen reason for concluding that the knowledge of good or of evil is not impossible in principle.[2]

---

[1] *Philosophical Studies*, p. 274.

[2] According to the doctrine of Mr. Moore's *Principia Ethica* (unless I have mistaken it sadly) this result might have been obtained directly from inspection of the *meaning* of "good."   For " good," as he maintains, is entirely simple and indefinable, and is seen at once to be something that we *judge* of the entities we

Agreeing, then, that there may be such knowledge, we have to ask of what kind it is, with what things it deals, and what confidence we may place in our beliefs concerning it. In discussing these matters we have to remember that our investigation deals with better and worse, as well as with good and bad simply ; and also that value or disvalue is a wider thing than moral worth

believe to be good. Personally, I cannot but agree with him here, and I have even a certain sympathy with those who say that agreement with Mr. Moore in this particular is almost indefinitely wider than he himself seems to suppose. I have preferred, however, to argue the question more indirectly, and am content if it be granted me that " good " is a character that really does characterize, a quality that really does qualify. This, I may repeat in passing, is the only proper sense of its " objectivity." The puzzles in which certain authors allow themselves to be involved at this point seem to be entirely verbal, and to depend upon nothing more important than the irrelevance of the sense of " objectivity " in which it is implied that " objective " is equivalent to " pertaining to an object that is never a subject."

I should like to explain, however, that the *definability* of the *concept* " good " seems to me to be seldom a problem of major importance, and usually to be definitely of very minor moment. In Mr. Moore's language "indefinable" seems to mean "unanalysable," and most of us would be ready to grant that " good" *is* simplex as here it is declared to be. If so, it is *not* unintelligible. On the contrary, these " simple natures " (to use a seventeenth-century phrase) are, if they are grasped at all, precisely what is most readily, most completely, and, indeed, finally intelligible. On the other hand, mistakes are very easy here, and if " good " proved, in the end, to contain a lurking complexity, I cannot think that the discovery need involve more than a further refinement of ethical doctrine. The essential point is the irreducibility of values to non-values. Again, "definable" may, logically and with full appropriateness, be conceived in many ways, and need not be taken to be the same as "analysable" at all. Many writers, indeed, appear to mean that to be " definable " is simply to-be-equivalent-to, and although, in this sense, it may be argued that the concept " good " is-equivalent-to no other concept besides itself, it seems also possible to maintain that *any* standard of value, or *any* account of what value is-equivalent-to is *therefore* a definition. If, so every moral theory would " define " good.

or moral evil.   In the present chapter, however, I shall
restrict the discussion to questions of moral value so
far as possible, and shall consider comparative questions
only where they appear to need distinctive mention.

Theories which deal with the *kind* or species of our
knowledge of moral values may be distinguished,
broadly speaking, into those which assert that this moral
knowledge is akin to perception or to the æsthetic
judgment on the one hand, and those which maintain,
on the other hand, that it is fundamentally reflective.
I shall try to show that there is no insurmountable inconsistency between these opinions, and that each of them
may be correct in what it asserts.

A perceptual judgment deals expressly with particular
fact.   An intellectual or reflective one deals expressly
with general fact.   Clearly, therefore, many of our moral
judgments are akin to perception.   They claim to give
direct intuitive insight into the particular value of some
particular act.   Indeed, writers of the " moral sense "
school who (like Shaftesbury) speak of a " taste and
relish " for virtue akin to *sensation*, are in a measure
describing a relevant possibility.   The earliest steps in
moral education, again, are commonly concerned with
the rightness of this action or of that, intuitively evident
in the particular case.   This is not quite accurate, it
is true, since abstractions, viciously inflexible, are almost
as primitive as they are stubborn.   On the whole,
however, the general trend of our proceeding in moral
education is the passage from relatively particular
intuitions to a more general survey.   Judgments of
better and worse may similarly be perceptual in this
sense—that is to say, they may be (and often are) direct
visible comparisons, analogous to the simple perception
that one's hand, say, is longer than one's finger.

The æsthetic attitude must certainly be distinguished

from the moral one, even when both apply to the same thing. Although there is beauty in holiness, this beauty is not its moral worth ; and duty may enjoin much that is not at all pretty. Courage, again, may be spectacular and splendid (like the noblest courage in Aristotle's analysis), but this need not be the right courage ; and a lumbering pedestrian fortitude may sometimes be better still. On the other hand, certain types of moral judgment seem to be æsthetic in a moral way. When we speak of certain sins as foul and repulsive, we are saying, in truth, that they are *morally ugly*, as well as æsthetically so. When we extol purity we extol a kind of moral beauty. In these latter cases, therefore, there is literally a moral sort of æsthetic judgment, and in other cases there may easily be a wider analogy.

Nevertheless, our intuitive or perceptual acquaintance with values impels and requires further reflection upon them. The good (and the better) which are seen to be so when encountered as particulars, have also a general significance, and are valid for all cases that are similar in relevant respects. This has already been shown ; and although the inductive elaboration of moral standards, having to deal with special problems, may require a method and a technique which in certain respects are peculiar to itself, it has the general characteristics of all inductive enquiry. The aim of induction is to see the general essence and catholic significance of the particular case, to distinguish crucial from trivial elements, to follow connections wherever they lead, to avoid hasty judgments and extravagant conjectures. In arguments of this type, particular experience sets the problem and supplies the basis ; and the conclusion, while it sustains and enlarges this basis, is in principle conformable to it. Every joint in the structure, however, must be able to withstand the assaults of logical criticism, and this may entail the revision and correction of portions of the initial evidence. I do not say that moral standards are evolved by calculation and measurement after the fashion of experimental physics, but a parallel, nevertheless, may be usefully drawn. The data for the experimental sciences, with or without the aid of instruments, are ultimately the observations and comparisons of our senses. Such a planet is observed to cross the meridian of the telescope, the meniscus of the mercury is observed to touch some line on the tube, lengths are observed to be equal or greater or less, stars to be brighter or not so bright, our sun to be one of the " yellow dwarfs." At the same time precautions have to be taken in all such matters, the personal equation allowed for, the meniscus observed from a fixed point, and the like. It is a controlled and self-critical (not a chance) observation that is needed, and much that seems to be evidence does not declare what it appears to declare. So in morality.

It is sometimes argued, indeed, that even if reflection has a place in moral matters, it should at least be forgotten and overcome in action of the finest kind. The best of the virtues are easy, graceful, and inevitable, as the best art is inevitable ; and the man who is always thinking of his virtue is simply and finally a prig. This criticism is in part itself forgetful and in part perverse. Certainly, we should not always think of our own goodness—perhaps the less the better—and, if it is possible, it is best that our action should be easy and, as we say, spontaneous. The question for moral theory, however, is not whether a man is asking himself about his virtue, but whether his acts are virtuous. If he sees what is good and does it he need not ask questions, and he may have something better to do. Moral theory, on the other hand, has to ask precisely these questions and to reflect upon them. Our objector, therefore, has forgotten much, and he may even become perverse. The right course is not always plain and inevitable even after the hardest thinking, and it is idle to suppose that we can fulfil our obligations either to ourselves or to others without strenuous analysis, comparison, and inference. Self-consciousness, it is true, in many of its senses may be always a sickness or a useless vanity of the soul. We mean by it sometimes a withdrawal from the business of doing in favour of a lazy and complacent posturing of the dear self before its own partial mirror, or, again, an unhealthy and, in its root, a selfish preoccupation with our interesting infirmities. " I was both a burthen and a terror to myself," Bunyan wrote in his *Grace Abounding*. " Nor did I ever so know, as now, what it was to be weary of my life, and yet afraid to die. How gladly would I have been anything but myself ! Anything but a man ! and in any condition but my own." Such reflections may well be temptations of the devil. It is quite another thing, however, for us to know and admit that *we* have a duty before us that needs the best of our intellect for its unravelling, that principles may have to be tested and understood, that perplexities may need a patient head as well as an honest heart. Such matters as these pertain to reflection, and they are commanded morally.

When we turn to the things that we count good or bad, better or worse, we are commonly told that nothing can be good or evil (save in some derivative and wholly unimportant sense) unless it is a state of the mind and alight with consciousness. The truth of this is sometimes supposed to be intuitively evident. If not, it is supposed to be amply confirmed by an empirical survey of the things we admit to be good or to be bad.

Take the inventory of goods and of evils set forth on an earlier page—happiness, beauty, truth, and moral values. Happiness is something that is felt and consciously liked. If not it would seem to be meaningless, like an ache that never hurts. Moral values pertain to conscious moral experience, truth to the knowledge and understanding of fact, beauty to a loveliness that touches and stimulates the soul. It is held, accordingly, that *without* conscious experience there could be no values at all; and that *in* conscious experience, value or disvalue is a quality of the experience. It is conscious happiness, conscious well-doing, and the like, that are valuable at all.

This confident opinion, I believe, is not very firmly founded. Both in the case of moral values and in the case of natural beauty, it would seem at least possible that there might be values in the absence of conscious experience. Unconscious consciousness, indeed—the Unconscious of so many psychologists—is not, in my view, a legitimate conception. On the other hand, unconscious behaviour is, and I cannot suppose it impossible (or even very generally denied) that some of our unconscious behaviour might be good or bad in a moral sense. Of this more later. Again, it would seem to me possible that the beauties of Nature might exist (and be good because beautiful) apart from a hearing ear or a beholding eye. It is often maintained, indeed, that colours and sounds are not properties of natural things, but a garment with which Nature is clothed upon by our senses. If so, the wind does not moan in the forest when no one is there to hear it, nor sunsets glow with a riot of unapproachable colour when no one sees them. This view, however, cannot be said to be certain; and if the wind really does moan in wide uninhabited forests, or sunsets irradiate antarctic wastes, it is hard to deny that beauty, too, may be there. Again, even if Nature herself is not as our senses reveal her, but an imperceptible rhythm of electrons instead, it is not quite evident that this hidden dance and musical motion might not itself have beauty.

Even if there could be no value apart from mind, however, it would not follow that good or evil pertain solely to mind. When the mind, for example, becomes a partner with other things, the values which may accrue might pertain to the whole of the partnership. This is commonly believed in the case of a good like health. Where there is a sense of well-being without its substance, as in *spes phthisica*, pity seems more appropriate than true value; and although this illusory cheerfulness (as we call it) is better than any misery founded on fancied or perhaps even on solid causes, it is still a pathetic thing. The same seems to be true of other goods. If knowledge, regarded simply as a mental occurrence, contained all that is valuable in the pursuit of truth, it would seem that our assurance of insight and shining certainty must ultimately determine this species of worth. Yet in a dream we may have this assurance, and be suffused with a sense of ineffable understanding; and such baseless insight is worth at the best a whimsical smile and a reluctant sigh. These shadows and images of truth are not the worth of truth; for truth is negligible unless it grasps and understands what it sets out to investigate. The mere sense and thrill of beauty is similarly qualified. We speak of barbarous art, or of perverted æstheticism; and not without a meaning. So, too, in moral affairs. A life, like Hamlet's, devoted to revenge " with wings as swift as meditation or the thoughts of love " is not, without qualification, a worthy thing, even if this revenge seems to the agent an ineluctable and a pious duty. The mind's scope and power and reach and accuracy are as essential to the worth of it as any private quality or introspective flavour.

When these facts are forgotten, the mistake, I believe, is due to a confusion between dominant and intrinsic goods. If ultimate value were simply intrinsic, and if nothing could be good apart from conscious experience, the mind, by a very simple inference, would necessarily be the sole repository of value. A dominant good, on the other hand, may include everything that experience touches, or informs, or controls, even if it be granted that without conscious experience there is no such thing as value.

In the third place, we have to ask what confidence we may place in our judgments of good and of evil. Have we any rational certainty in this thing, or are we, like the schoolmen of Paris, overwhelmed by *præsumptio sensuum et dissensio sententiarum et desperatio inveniendi verum*?

One very usual opinion is that no genuine confidence can be placed in any such judgment. One man's meat is another man's poison. Head-hunting, cannibalism, and incest, at stated times and of a determinate sort, are part of a sacred ritual among certain tribes. Men have died from conscientious shame because their alien conquerors have forbidden a ceremonial murder or a suicidal pilgrimage. As has been said somewhere, "Nothing is more precious than honour, and nothing more wayward." The same seems to be true of other values. Beauty and the sources of happiness seem to vary from clime to clime and from age to age. A true or general judgment seems therefore impossible. Who would trust his judgments of sense if the Andaman islanders clearly perceived that to be brown which we see to be green, and if other tribes were confident of its inky blackness? Yet differences of this magnitude are not uncommon in judgments of good and evil; and the thing is so notorious that the reader may be spared any superfluity of examples.

It would appear, however, that the issue in all these cases is immensely over-simplified. In moral questions, for example, it has to be remembered that anything held to be good is commonly a function of exceedingly complicated factors. Who can say what obscure motives are fulfilled, or used to be fulfilled, in the sacred customs of Central Australia, or in any religious festival? The whole environment to which such duties conform is enormously complicated, and it should not be supposed that the simplest judgments of sense are at all a fair analogue. A fairer one, let us say, would be the signs of glacial action on the rocks, or the knocking of the engine of a motor-car. These to trained observers are spontaneously and unreflectively perceptible, and the mere fact that they convey nothing to an untutored folk, or to an unmechanical passenger, is not at all to the purpose. It is only the simplest judgments of good and evil that could be expected to be common to anyone not afflicted with a moral amaurosis—judgments like " This is blue," and not judgments like " This is a volcano in eruption about thirty miles away."

It is not to be denied that there are such simple judgments of value. The values of love and happiness and warmth and sunshine may surely be taken to be universal, or very nearly so. The appreciation of these needs no special training, and is seldom overthrown by any. The subtler values which depend upon training and habit are manifestly less universal; but our confidence in them need not be shaken upon this account. Let us consider once again the analogy of trained perception. The volcano to some may be the outpouring of terror

and sorcery, and to geologists quite another kind of
thing. This does not prove that the geologist is
wrong, and if he is right his rightness is none the
less due to wary and tested inferences from simple,
indisputable perceptions. Is it wholly impossible that
moral or æsthetic training might proceed in the
same way ?

An appropriate and considerable variation, again,
is rationally to be expected in these matters. When it
is claimed, for example, that the joys of health, exercise,
good food, and the like are approximately universal
values it must not be supposed that the sources of
these joys are the same everywhere and always. What
is good food in the arctic zone need not be good in
the tropics. The exercise that an old man finds enjoy-
able need not suit Mr. Dempsey. A very large proportion of the difficulties mustered under this head are
manufactured on these flimsy grounds. It is supposed
that the effects of like causes on unlike persons must
necessarily be the same—or else that there is Bedlam
and pure unreason. This is not true, and the differences
that spring, more indirectly, from habit and association,
are often of the same order as differences due to climate
or constitution. No Western audience, I suppose,
could abide the music in a Chinese theatre, or regard
the action of Chinese plays as other than tedious.
What these Westerners hear and see, however, is really
not the same as what the Oriental audience hears and
sees, although the physical stimuli are the same. With
a certain education, the Occidentals themselves would
receive different impressions, and they might come to
perceive beauty where, at the first, dissonance and tedium
prevailed.

In short, these disagreements are often only superficially about the same things ; and when there is

genuine disagreement there need not be hopeless disparity in our judgments of value. When an ascetic
condemns all pleasures, he may do so, not because he
takes them to be vile, but because he regards them as
dangerous or enervating, or at least as never so good
as other things which, as he thinks, should be chosen
in place of them. This is not really to contradict his
opponent, but to offer a further consideration also
defended by a judgment of value.

We may claim, then, I think, a very reasonable
confidence in our judgments concerning the simpler
constituents of human welfare, and may hope for rational
improvement in more complicated valuations. In our
own case, and in the case of those we know very intimately, there is, of course, most to be expected from
this knowledge. Nevertheless, we have reason to make
fairly confident judgments of a wider sort. We know the
grosser forms of cruelty, for we know certain at least
of the things that will make anyone suffer. We know
that without food, and shelter, and clothing no one can
lead a contented or a dignified life ; that avoidable
solitude and social ostracism are almost always terrible
things. These are simple judgments concerning
happiness and misery, and are relatively easily adapted
to the standards of living which prevail in any given
community at any given stage. The same is true of
other dominant goods. We know a great deal about
the needs of the intellect at particular levels of education.
The canons of beauty, in their simpler applications, are
tolerably plain, and perhaps very firm. The moral claims
of equity, fidelity, and the like are not seriously in
dispute. In the face of this it is unreasonable to maintain
that our knowledge of goodness and our standards of
comparison are thoroughly untrustworthy or radically
inapplicable to our tasks and conditions. The most that

should be said is that they are still extremely imperfect, and that in many ways they are likely to remain so.

Our argument has been that ethical standards must ultimately be based upon particular judgments of good and evil, and upon particular comparisons of better and worse, and that in the end they are generalizations from this basis, mainly of an inductive sort. Since all achievable goods are relevant to this enquiry (for the problem ultimately is the best use we can make of our lives), it is plain that, somehow, we must be able to estimate values and disvalues upon a single basis. This is implied whenever we speak of " weighing " advantages and disadvantages, or of " greater " and " lesser " goods. Indeed, the appropriate language seems to be the language of calculation and measurement; and if we renounce this aim, with a fine gesture, we should indicate, in some fashion, what we mean to put in its place. I shall ask, accordingly, whether a *calculus* of values is at all possible ; and if not, whether any rational substitute may be found for it.

As we know, certain philosophers have dreamed of establishing morals upon a mathematical basis. Thus, Locke " doubted not, but from self-evident propositions, by necessary consequences, as incontestible as those in mathematics, the measures of right and wrong might be made out, to anyone that will apply himself with the same indifferency and attention to the one as he does to the other of these sciences " ; [1] and others thought with him. This was partly, no doubt, because they supposed that mathematics had a monopoly of impartial reasoned certainty (such certainty, in their view, being undoubtedly appropriate to morals), partly because they believed that the due amounts of retribution and reward, and generally of justice, *were* mathe-

[1] *Essay*, Book IV, chap. iii, § 18.

matical things.   A moral ledger, again, is not entirely unknown.   " I made a little book," Benjamin Franklin tells us in his *Autobiography*,[1] " in which I allotted a page for each of the virtues.   I rul'd each page with red ink, so as to have seven columns, one for each day of the week, marking each column with a letter for the day.   I cross'd these columns with thirteen red lines, marking the beginning of each line with the first letter of one of the virtues, on which line, and in its proper column, I might mark, by a little black spot, every fault I found upon examination to have been committed respecting that virtue upon that day."   This quaint ledger, he tells us, was not at all futile, at any rate until he was " employ'd in voyages and business abroad, with a multiplicity of affairs that interfered " ; and perhaps it was not.   It is not very hard, however, to see the reasons why moral mathematics and moral book-keeping are much less dependable than the usual exercise of these pursuits.   I shall try to show this by pointing out some of the difficulties admittedly present in the calculation of one of the great varieties of value, that of happiness and misery, and considering thereafter what appear to be the greater difficulties of a wider calculus.   The advantage of this course is that serious and persistent attempts have been made to defend and elaborate the hedonic calculus of pleasures and pains.

In any such scheme it seems essential to treat pleasures as *plus* quantities and pains as *minus* ones, and there must be some way of judging that so much pleasure is precisely equal to so much pain.   It needs a good deal of effrontery, I think, to pretend that anyone has this capacity, or that there is any intelligible sense in which so much toothache, say, is precisely equal and opposite to so much good music or to so much

[1] Everyman edition, p. 101.

pleasing oratory. The best that could plausibly be said, I think, is that when we are just prepared to endure a certain amount of pain for the sake of a certain amount of pleasure, this particular quantity of pain might reasonably be judged to be a *minus* quantity just smaller than the *plus* quantity that is sought. This, however, need not be true. For most of us (let us hope, if we can) it is pleasant to be alive, but it is absurd to say that a margin of anticipated happiness determines what we are just prepared to put up with. We *are* alive, and we put up with life because we have to.

The usual hedonistic argument is that duration and intensity are the crucial circumstances which determine whether pleasures are greater or less. Of these, duration is a measurable quantity ; and all would agree that the longer a pleasure lasts the better, provided that the pleasure is unchanged and unabated, and that nothing but its pleasantness is in question. It is not at all certain, however, that two minutes, say, of a given pleasure are precisely twice as good as one minute of it, or that, if this is not the correct numerical ratio, any other is. The most we can say is that, other things equal, the more enduring the pleasure the better.

Intensity is even more perplexing, since it is very difficult to measure. My toothache, I may know, is becoming worse ; but how do I know when it becomes twice as severe as before ? A physiologist, I dare say, might determine the point at which I groan twice as loudly as I did, but it does not follow that this is the point at which my toothache becomes twice as sore. Let us suppose, however, that by a miracle I know precisely how intense my sufferings are. Is it, then, to be assumed that the toothache which has become twice as intense is therefore worse by a definite assignable fraction ? And what are we to say of intensity and duration taken together? By what arithmetic could it be said significantly that the short, sharp pain of a blow on the cheek has the same numerical disvalue as the slower but more prolonged discomfort of a tedious sermon?

If there is such an arithmetic it is clear that we do not know it, and I do not see why there should be one. A non-arithmetical standard, however, while logically possible, would not yield a calculus of any ordinary kind; and the inherent difficulties of this idea may be illustrated by a further puzzle concerning the greatest happiness of the greatest number. Is it really certain that ten million reasonably contented people are collectively at all more valuable than ten thousand who are equally contented? And, if they are, is it likely that they are a thousandfold better? The writers of our Utopias clearly do not think so, for they prefer a small number to teeming hordes.

In England, to be sure, the utilitarian formula of the greatest happiness of the greatest number was taken to embody a practical programme of social and political reform; and the Marchese Beccaria, in Italy, spoke of a " cool examiner of human nature, who knew how to collect in one point the actions of a multitude, and had this only end in view, the greatest happiness of the greatest number." [1]   In their estimates of happiness and of misery, however, the utilitarians relied, not on any psychological analysis, but upon what they took to be the experience of the race concerning the welfare and security of the members of societies. Neither the race nor any individual has ever made this elaborate argument, and the utilitarian procedure was rather to assume that goodness and happiness are identical, and then to argue that what men call good ought to be the same as the race's experience of pleasure. This flagrant

[1] *An Essay on Crimes and Punishments*, Introduction.

begging of their own question makes it impossible for us to suppose that the practical achievements of utilitarianism yield the smallest confirmation of the soundness of their theories in this matter.

We have assumed, in this argument, that pleasures and pains do not differ in quality, so that the only question for this calculation is how many and how great they are. As is well known, however, J. S. Mill, in the second chapter of his *Utilitarianism*, maintained that " neither pains nor pleasures were homogeneous," and that the greatest distinctions among them are distinctions in their quality. " Few human creatures," he says, " would consent to be changed into any of the lower animals for a promise of the fullest allowance of a beast's pleasures ; no intelligent human being would consent to be a fool, no instructed person would be an ignoramus, no person of feeling and conscience would be selfish and base, even though they should be persuaded that the fool, the dunce, or the rascal is better satisfied with his lot than they are with theirs. . . . It is better to be a human being dissatisfied than a pig satisfied ; better to be Socrates dissatisfied than a fool satisfied." We must, therefore, consider this form of the argument.

It is sometimes supposed that this doctrine is one of J. S. Mill's acute and honourable inconsistencies—one of the instances in which, setting out to support the doctrines of his father and his father's friends, he elaborates in their place something richer but passing strange ; and, history apart, the doctrine has been declared to be either downright impossible, or at least inconsistent with hedonism.

If pleasure or pain were nothing but general names for an entirely simple experience of liking or disliking, there would certainly be no room for differences in their quality; and some appear to suppose that when we speak of qualitatively different pleasures (as the satisfactions of Circe's swine on the one hand, or of a Socratic intellect on the other), we do not mean that the *pleasures* differ in quality, but that certain other aspects of these experiences do. This opinion does not seem to be true. These pleasures really seem to differ in quality, although all are pleasures. They seem to differ just as much as colours do; and although red, green, and the rest are certainly colours, they are just as certainly different. It is not merely possible, then, but plainly the truth that pleasures differ in their qualities, and this truth is *not* inconsistent with hedonism. There is nothing illogical in maintaining that pleasure is the only good, but that some varieties of pleasure are preferable to others, any more than there is an inconsistency in arguing that nothing is worth drinking except champagne, but that some brands of this fluid are better than others. And if hedonists maintain, as Mill did, that nothing but pleasure can be sought, they may also consistently argue that certain pleasures are better worth seeking than others. On any theory, indeed, there must be a general category of " the seekable," and there may be distinctions of quality within it.

Mill's general line of argument, therefore, seems consistent enough, although his applications of it were pretty certainly inconsistent in detail. If the *pain* (or dissatisfaction) of Socrates is better than a fool's pleasures, it is hard to see how pleasure is the only good; and Mill, in fact, substituted nobility or dignity for pleasure in this part of his doctrine, and was prepared to renounce and override all pleasures for its sake, although he also insisted that these renunciations must always be useful. It would be possible, however, to avoid this inconsistency and still to retain the substance of Mill's doctrine.

Manifestly, any such theory would make a striking difference to any hedonic calculus ; for quality as well as quantity would have to be counted, and a small amount of a finer pleasure might easily be better than a large amount of a coarser or a tamer one. A few crowded moments of high fruition might be worth many lifetimes of dull contentment. These complications, indeed, may seem to dispose altogether of the calculus ; and Mill made no attempt to save it. Like Plato long ago, he was content to say that the judgment of those who have tried both kinds of pleasure must be allowed to determine which of two pleasures is the better in quality. This is hard on the sot and on the fool who cannot experience what Socrates experiences ; yet the sot and the fool may actually find pleasure where Socrates finds none, and if Socrates prefers his own soul to the soul of any animal, it is hard to see how he does so on the basis of personal experience, since he never was a fish or an eagle or a deer. The standard, in short, limps badly. It is probable, even, that the Socratic estimate of feminine pleasures might often be mistaken.

We may legitimately contend, however, that the recognition of qualitative differences in pleasures does *not* overthrow the theoretical possibility of a hedonic calculus, and even that it might simplify this calculus in important respects. (For it might be true that pleasures of a certain quality were so enormously superior to pleasures of some other quality that the smallest amount of the former would always be greater than the largest amount of the latter.) This type of argument, indeed, is quite commonly maintained by those who are not hedonists. Thus it is held by certain enthusiasts that a world in the extremity of the greatest agony would be better than a world which was sullied by a single lie, or that the comforts of a pusillanimous peace can never compensate for its dishonour. The qualitative differences in the values of pleasures, therefore, might possibly be of this order, and if these preponderating differences of qualities could be arranged on a definite scale the task of the calculus would be simplified. The reckoning would only have to apply to pleasures like in kind, and would there be entirely necessary. An overwhelming difference in the value of *unlike* pleasures, *ex hypothesi*, would dispense with it.

Even in this case, however, a precise *numerical* calculus would seem to be wholly impossible; and certainly we could not hope to achieve one.[1] This result is important for our general problem. It is manifest, I think, that pleasure is not the only good; for there are other goods, as truth or virtue or beauty; and, as Mill said (inconsistently, yet truly), the discontent of Socrates, which is *not* a pleasure, may nevertheless be divine. It is easy to conceive of a universe of contented slaves, or of graceful, healthy animals; and yet to prefer our own discontented one. On the other hand, while virtue and the rest are not happiness, they are commonly allied with it, and there is usually a certain ease and appropriate pleasure accompanying and enhancing the greater excellences. As Aristotle maintained, pleasure is normally an ingredient in the superior activities. Therefore, *because* pleasure is a good, the calculus of pleasures (if there is one) would have to be a part of a larger calculus of values (if there were such a thing), and the difficulties of the more special problem, accordingly, are pertinent, quite directly, to the more general question. Our discussion, indeed, has been wider than it professed to be. There *are* qualitative differences in pleasures, but the superior pleasures are important, not so much on account of

[1] See Note at end of chapter.

their superior pleasantness, but because of the superior worth and dignity of the pursuits to which they are appropriate ; and the logic of their qualitative comparison is also the logic of a more general conspectus of dignified and lovely and excellent things.

From this larger standpoint, then, we may agree (without special enquiry) that a numerical calculus is impossible, and we are bound to conclude that any non-numerical reckoning, in terms of a definite scale of preponderating excellence, is full of difficulties. These are partly highly general and partly quite specific. In the general case, if we had simply to deal with so many intrinsic values, each of them isolable and complete in itself, our task, although formidable, might not be impossible.   What we have to deal with, however, are values of interlacing patterns—as subtle a web as life itself.   Here values in their intermixture may yield a disvalue, disvalues combine into values, and a value emerge from neutral things (just as a man's body may be valuable, although the constituents of this body, taken separately, may never be worth more than five shillings).   In the face of these facts, *à priori* appeals to " unity in variety," to " harmony encompassing a wide expanse," or to the " right mean " which " right reason " is said to prescribe, are little better than harmless puerilities.   The more special questions, again, are not less difficult.   If we say, for instance, that " mental " values are superior to animal ones, and avoid extravagant nonsense concerning the necessary evils of the flesh, do we seriously mean that even bespectacled highbrows should make health and sunshine wholly subordinate to intellectual pursuits, or that the state should compel all uninterested dullards to study geometry and fine art ?   In short, as Mr. Lowes Dickinson says,[1] " if

[1] *The Meaning of Good*, p. 67.

all conduct turned on such simple choices as that between thick soup and clear " these matters might be easy; but when the choice is between " leisure and liberty now, or £1,000 a year twenty years hence; art and fame at the cost of health, or sound nerves and obscurity: and so on and so on through all the possible cases," it is not at all easy either in principle or in practice.

And yet—it is precisely these choices that we have to make; and we make them rightly when we give heed to their value, and then only. Certain values, indeed, are dominating, others plainly subordinate; yet none, perhaps, is entirely incommensurable with the rest. Religion itself, which claims the whole of a man for an ineffable purpose, has always permitted what seems at least to be a working compromise in its practice, and enjoins ploughing and reaping and sheep-shearing as well as prayer and meditation. We laugh at Shelley's hearty supper coming close on the heels of his scornful outburst upon the vanities of food, or at De l'Hôpital asking half-seriously whether Newton ate, drank, and slept. Twist it as we will, however, a certain commensurability of values is implied in all these things; and if a calculus is impossible, something not utterly dissimilar is indispensable. " Solid joys and lasting treasures " are better than fleeting ones of the same kind; subsequent health is worth the pain and dis-comfort of an operation, and subsequent debility is not. If we sacrifice ourselves or others we ought to do so only for a greater good. These are not problems to be stifled, and they do require some species of reckoning.

If the arguments of this chapter have been sound, however, we would seem to have rational grounds for a discriminating confidence in our moral beliefs. In the simpler cases at least our beliefs concerning values are not untrustworthy. Inference, analysis, and reasonable comparison are as possible and as appropriate as they are necessary. Our own experience, winnowed and tested by reflection, is fitted to tell us much concerning the values we ourselves may hope to achieve. The examined life of a Socrates did tell him much concerning right living, and tells all of us not a little. Our knowledge of the tendencies of action, with the experience of the race to guide it, gives instruction both concerning the personal and the contingent fruits of our deeds. Even when our estimates are impressionist, or directed to wavering patterns, they are not, therefore, misleading or unreasonable. Tact and *l'esprit de finesse*, although they may not calculate, need not be unthinking, or impervious to reflection and incapable of being improved by it. These varying sources of our evidence do not in principle conflict, and the more general dubieties I have mentioned are subject to a wholesome correction. A thing that is good may certainly have neutral constituents, or constituents which in some other connection might be (or work) what is evil. This prevents us from legislating *à priori* concerning combinations which have hitherto been without example. It does not, however, prevent us from assessing the instances that have occurred, or the types and patterns of living that are congruent with a very wide experience. Such merely general perplexities, therefore, are for the most part entirely irrelevant.

NOTE TO P. 113.

Despite his modest admissions concerning the limitations of his results, the most serious effort hitherto made to examine these hedonic ratios with " quantitative " precision appears to have been made quite recently by Mr. J. C. Flügel in an article published in the *British Journal of Psychology* for April 1925. Believing that modern experimental psychology, with the greater accuracy of its methods, is able to achieve results on this question (at any rate for short periods and in ordinary circumstances) far more precise than any hitherto obtained, he has undertaken an enquiry which had for its principal objects : " (1) a quantitative evaluation of the duration and amount of pleasure and unpleasure experienced ; (2) a rough description of the chief mental states that appeared to be intimately connected with the occurrence of the various pleasures and unpleasures —a description such as might eventually also lend itself to quantitative treatment " (p. 320).   And he obtained such results as (a) that the total duration of the more intense pleasures and unpleasures is much smaller than that of the less intense feelings ; (b) that pleasure occupies a very considerably larger proportion of human life than does unpleasure ; (c) that there is some general tendency for those who frequently experience high degrees of pleasure to experience frequently high degrees of unpleasure ; also (d) that there is an inverse ratio between the tendency to experience intense feelings and the tendency to be generally happy ; (e) that the six most important (ordinary) states of pleasure are, in order, Interest, Joy, Contentment, Pleasant Sensations, " Positive Functional Feeling," Food, while the corresponding order for states of unpleasure is Unpleasant Sensations, Anxiety and Worry, Anger (and Irritation), Fatigue, Boredom and Depression.

These experiments are only a beginning, since the subjects of them were but nine London students familiar with the work of Mr. McDougall.   It is questionable, therefore, whether such a result as (b) could safely be generalized to older persons, or to those of a different social status, and pretty certain that the pleasures of Food, say, would not come sixth in a child's list.   (By

the way, is not Food itself a "Pleasant Sensation"?)
Even making the fullest allowance, however, for revision
consequent upon less slender *data* it is difficult to see
how Mr. Flügel's methods could answer any of the
difficulties I have mentioned in the text.   I say nothing
of the restriction to "ordinary" cases, although the
things that commonly sour a man's life or irradiate it,
are *not* ordinary, and yet may be vastly more important
than the sum of what is "ordinary."   Let us keep to
the major difficulties.   With regard to one of these,
the question whether a doubled intensity can, with any
significance, be said to be the equal of a doubled duration,
Mr. Flügel expressly admits that "it is difficult to find
any certain ground for deciding questions of this kind"
(p. 332), and he can only assure us that he has adopted
two different systems of weighting (!).   And on the
still more general point of quantity it is obvious, upon
examination, that Mr. Flügel's method is only apparently quantitative.   In his attempt at a "quantitative
evaluation" what he really does is to distinguish seven
grades of pleasure-unpleasure, reckoning $+ 3$ for "the
most intense pleasure you have ever experienced,"
o for a neutral state (either indifferent or on balance);
and correspondingly in the pain series.   There is no
reason here for supposing, say, that $3 - 3 = 0$, or that
$1 + 1 + 1 = 3$ (although there is excellent reason for
supposing that within a month, this being the period
of the experiments, neither $+ 3$ nor $- 3$ is likely, in
strictness, ever to occur).   The argument, in fact, is
just about as quantitative as an estimate of ability based
upon the assumption that a person who is awarded a
first class in the Moral Sciences Tripos ought to be
supposed to have precisely three times as much ability
as one who is allowed a third class in the Classical
Tripos.

CHAPTER VI

THE PSYCHOLOGY OF MORAL ACTION

At this stage of our study, I mean to make a definite break in the course of the argument, and to pass from the analysis of moral conceptions to the psychology of moral agency. In the present chapter, then, an attempt will be made to discuss this topic generally; and its two successors will deal with more special problems, also, in the main, psychological. Since these chapters are part of a study and not of a treatise, much, of course, is omitted in them that is both relevant and of high importance. Even in a study, however, it is a reproach, I think, to be desultory, and I hope that the course I am minded to pursue will be vindicated (in so far as such things may) by the peculiar significance of the subjects selected for treatment, and by their preponderant relevance to the points in moral theory which (if there is any soundness in the foregoing pages) are, in reality, the critical ones.

As we have seen, moral theory has to do with justifying not with explanatory reasons. Even necessity does not justify. It follows, therefore, that ethics can never be based upon psychology, since psychology, if it succeeded, could be only an explanatory science. On the other hand, moral obligation, while it cannot be deduced from psychology, is a mere idea if it does not apply within a certain psychological field. There is no obligation to pursue a good unless we can see this good (at least when it is pointed out to us), and unless the pursuit is psychologically possible, at any rate to the best of our belief. Conscience, again, is a psychological thing with a moral direction. It is the name, not only for judgments of good and evil, but also for all the emotions, feelings, and sentiments which have to do with moral action, and for that in us which commands and controls in the service of what we believe to be good. For some (as for Mill) it is primarily a sentiment and first cousin to an oracle ; for others a judge and an " umpire " (as Milton says) ; for others, again, an executor of the law bidding (and even compelling) us to do or forbear.

All our problems, then, have a psychological aspect, and this, perforce, has appeared in our attempt to discover the anatomy of moral action. We have insisted, indeed, that morals need not be simply a human affair, " planetary and telluric," and that even if moral notions do not strictly apply to sub-rational creatures (although many would believe that a dog's fidelity to his master is virtuous and morally good) they would apply in principle to all rational creatures, and to any conscious superhuman agents. This view, in its turn, however, is not without its own psychological aspect. These other beings are assumed to have the knowledge of good and of evil, and therefore to be capable of accepting moral obligations. The inference to their case (if they exist) depends upon the analysis of the meaning of what we find in ourselves ; and for the most part we have to deal with the moral direction of our own psychological selves. It is psychological control, to be sure, not secluded introspection, that concerns us for the most part.[1]   But the dominant facts are psychological.

I propose, in this chapter, to follow out some of the psychological implications of our analysis, with the object, more particularly, of testing the psychological possibility of our opinions.   Here the first difficulty that is urged is also one of the most considerable.   It is necessary, on our view, that, seeing the good, we should be able to respond to its direction ; and that, often at least, reflection upon it should be capable of improving us.   If so, knowledge taken generally, and reflection more especially, must have a certain power and efficacy.   The good has authority ;   and although authority is not mere power, an impotent authority is a thing to mock at.   It is a common psychological opinion, however, that " reason " is *never* a motive to the will ; and even that knowledge of any sort is cold and neutral and powerless.   The opposite view, of course, is also held.   There are some who believe ideas to be the strongest things in the world, and many who are afraid of them as the most dangerous.   These contrasted psychological opinions provoke and require discussion.

It is easy to show, I think, that certain ideas actually do move us, and certain psychologists have even maintained that *all* psychological behaviour is at bottom ideo-motor.   According to this analysis, action occurs whenever the idea of action obtains an exclusive (even if only a temporary) possession of the mind.   Such ideas, it is claimed, are always the *immediate* antecedents of conscious behaviour, and the work of the will (as we call it) is the work of permitting or encouraging

---

[1] Cf. H. Head, *Proceedings : Seventh International Congress of Psychology*, p. 182.   " With an expert shot, the gun is an active member of his body, and the pace with which it swings is an exactly regulated somatic function."

these moving ideas to hold the field and develop themselves (as their nature is) into movement and action. Thus in general, when we are lying in bed the mere thought of getting up (when there are no competing ideas) is already the beginning of this action; and when there is conflict, when the idea of lying still *also* attracts us, we wait until the idea of getting up catches hold of us exclusively, and then, before we know it, we are getting out of bed.

This analysis, in many instances, seems insufficient. In my own case, at any rate, I do not seem to find this exclusive dominance of an idea of movement just before I intentionally move. The rejected ideas seem still to be present, and very often to continue when a movement opposed to them is already in train. During deliberation, again, I seem often to hesitate, although only one idea is consciously before me. A man may easily delay without any explicit idea of delaying. Furthermore, ideas of movement are not the only ideas of action. One's control over one's own thoughts, when one has it, is just as truly action and efficacy as one's control over one's muscles. When it is said, then, that an effort of attention is the fundamental attribute of the will, it seems to be forgotten that this effort of attention is itself active, so that somewhere choice and resolution (or the *fiat* of the will) is certain to enter. There seems no good reason, therefore, why it should not enter at the inception of a movement (as seems to be the case when we make up our minds, reluctantly, to get out of bed). On the other hand, it is plain that any conscious and intentional movement must be preceded by an idea of that movement. This idea, therefore, is a part at least of the total antecedent which we call the cause of the movement; and in many cases ideo-motor action seems an entirely sufficient explanation of the movements that occur. To choose Mr. Stout's instance, a man notices a speck of dust, for example, and at the mere sight of it flicks the dust away. Again, in the " willing " game the experimenter, by merely thinking of the direction in which he wants the subject to go, makes slight muscular movements which, in fact, guide the subject. And so of a host of other examples. We have to conclude, then, that ideas —mere ideas—may move us, and often do so.

The truth of this conclusion, it should be noted, is often obscured by a plausible irrelevance. The function of ideas, it is often said, is the ascertaining of fact and of truth ; and this function is not action. The obvious and sufficient reply to this contention is that ideas *are* psychological facts which, like all facts, have their effects. They are parts of the life process, and they influence further living. When we speak, then, of their function in truth-getting we legitimately ignore their other functions, but we have no right to deny the existence of these other functions.

To admit, however, that mere ideas may move us (as they do in ideo-motor action) is to take a comparatively short step, for it may readily be contended that ideo-motor action, in its pure form, occurs rather seldom ; and that it presupposes, when it does occur, either a formed habit or a ripe impulse. In the general case, we may be told, it is desire, appetition, or inclination that moves us, not bare ideas, and although desire, properly speaking, is an ideal thing (being a species of unrest induced by the idea of something lacking), appetite and inclination may be un-idead. If this be denied, on the ground that blind striving never occurs —*ignoti nulla cupido*—it may at least be maintained that any ideas that may enter are dim and subordinate things, hurriedly generated by the inclination itself.

I have no intention of disputing these arguments, for they are irrelevant, in substance, to the contentions of these pages. As a matter of psychological fact it does not seem to be true that ideas or any form of cognition occur quite alone ; and although, as we have seen, certain active consequences seem sometimes to be due to nothing but ideas, it is comparatively unimportant to consider what ideas might conceivably do " by themselves." Even if it were true, as is often alleged, that the apparent good is always determined by wishes and inclination, the moral question proper is about the *control* of action in accordance with our knowledge of good and evil. A controlling force acts upon other forces, not in a vacuum, and if our knowledge of good and evil were able to modify and direct our appetites and desires, the most ardent rationalist would have every reason to be content. The psychological possibility of this control is therefore our proper subject, and as reflective control is the most important and the most disputable variety of it, I shall proceed at once to discuss this question.

The most formidable opponents we have to encounter are Aristotle among the ancients and Hume among the moderns. It is also necessary to consider certain opinions widely expressed at the present time. I shall deal, therefore, with these matters in this order.

According to Aristotle, " thought by itself moves nothing," [1] and as Mr. Burnet explains, " thought simply universalizes and formulates the material furnished by appetition in the same way as it universalizes and formulates the material furnished by sense-perception." [2] Examining these assertions further, we extract the

---

[1] *Nicomachean Ethics*, Book VI, chap. ii.
[2] *The Ethics of Aristotle*, p. 256 (cf. Appendix A, referring to *De Anima*, 433*a*).

following opinion.   Practical thought is concerned only with variable and alterable things which may be within our power.   The end of theoretical science is that which cannot be otherwise—the eternal verities—or else that which has its source of motion within itself. Here, then, is one cardinal distinction between the theoretical and the practical reason, and the analysis of the occasions for deliberation completes the story. We deliberate not about ends but about means.   The end is set by wish and we deliberate about the best means towards attainable wishes.[1]   Hence the practical reason is ultimately concerned with the furtherance of wishes and appetitions, although the best of these are held to be in accordance with right reason, and reasonable wishes are even regarded as belonging to the rational faculty.

In its intention, to be sure, Aristotle's moral psychology is highly rationalistic, but much that he says might readily be construed in support of a very different theory, and he may be thought to have made very damaging admissions.   It is important, therefore, to ask whether his reasons are sound ;   and many of them seem plainly unconvincing.   There is *no* reason, we may say, why science should be concerned with unalterable, not with alterable things ;   and, again, if reason is capable in principle of being self-moving, or a first cause, it *is* capable of moving, and does not merely move " as desire moves."   On the other hand, moral deliberation has certainly to do with alterable events believed to be within our power.   In this sphere, however, it is utterly false to allege that we deliberate in fact only about means and not about ends.   The more important aspects of moral reflection, on the contrary, are just about ends.   We are concerned fundamentally with the

[1] *Nicomachean Ethics*, Book III, chaps. i–v.

justification of dominant goods. Such ends, even granting that they have inclination behind them (or, for that matter, a Freudian wish) are the proper objects of moral scrutiny; and reflection is a subordinate and unavailing thing if it cannot direct control and modify our evaluations of them. It is important to notice, therefore, that Aristotle's position is, in the end, dogmatic; and that such general reasons as he gives for it do not compel assent.

Hume's argument may be summarized as follows.[1] Reason alone can never be a motive to the will; and, properly speaking, can never influence it. For morals excite passions, and produce or prevent actions, whereas reason itself is utterly impotent in this particular, since it consists of the calm and indolent judgments of the understanding. Being perfectly inert, it is and ought only to be, the slave of the passions, and can never pretend to any other office than to serve and obey them. Again, reason is the discovery of truth or falsehood, and this is the discovery of an agreement with real relations of ideas or to real existence. Our passions, volitions, and actions are not susceptible of any such agreement, being original facts and realities "compleat in themselves." In a strict and philosophical sense reason can have an influence on our conduct only after two ways : Either when it excites a passion by informing us of the existence of something which is a proper object of it; or when it discovers the connection of causes and effects, so as to afford us means of exerting any passion. More generally the province of reason concerns either the abstract relations of ideas, or inductions concerning matters of fact. There is no room for moral distinctions within this province, and the cause

[1] *A Treatise of Human Nature*, Book II, Part iii, section 3, and Book III, Part i, section 1.

or original of these distinctions must therefore be found elsewhere. The belief in the functions of reason in this matter is due to a careless confusion between the indolent understanding and the " calm " passions which cause no disorder in the soul.

The objections to these arguments are, I believe, overwhelming. As we have seen, reason by itself, reflection which reflects upon nothing, is nobody's concern. The question at issue is the effect upon action of reflection about action. Here Hume does admit a certain influence. Reflection, according to him, may excite a passion by causing us to think of some desirable thing which we should not have thought of without it ; and, as he elsewhere admits, it may show us the hollowness of objects of desire which, before reflection, excited a lively passion. (These are not the functions of a slave, and they are not trivial.) Our discussion of ends and means, in an earlier chapter, again, has shown that if reason were concerned only with means and not with ends, the relation between these is far too intimate for Hume's airy dismissals. It is more important to notice, however, that Hume's fundamental contention simply begs the question. The thesis which he has to dispute is that the knowledge of good and evil permits of reflective analysis, comparison, and consistent argument, and that such reflections may influence conduct. In reply to this he states that reason is not concerned with these reflections, but only with mathematical ones, or with inductions not concerned with value. This is no answer at all. Instead of asking whether reason can perform these functions, Hume simply states that he proposes to define it in such a way as to make these functions out of accord with his definition. It is quite true that inclinations are neither true nor false, but the statement is irrelevant unless moral distinctions are a matter of mere inclination. Indeed, it is irrelevant unless our inclinations, *per impossibile, are* the knowledge of good and evil. (If we speak of a reasonable inclination we mean one which is inclined to something which is reasonable.) In effect, then, the whole of Hume's pretended argument either shirks the issue by an arbitrary definition, or relies upon the dogma (later modified and in principle denied) that reason can never have any effects whatsoever. It is entirely plain, however, that the psychological process of reflecting does have psychological effects. Men have died on account of it. Moreover, it need not be "calm"; for often it is fierce and disturbing and desperately exhausting. In short, the whole position is grotesquely misrepresented in Hume's pages.

The modern varieties of irrationalism, although they owe little to the study of Hume, seem to present very similar arguments. There is a great deal of tiresome irrelevance to the effect that political propagandists, doctors, journalists, mothers and nurses employ methods of suasion which do not correspond to the canons of school logic. This shows that the irrationalists do not know where to look for the signs of reflection and intelligence, but it shows nothing else. For the rest we are presented with a quasi-science of "instinct" and "impulse." It is usual to say that these, by definition, are irrational things, and to dismiss the palpable evidence that mankind, in many obvious ways, is a thinking species, by speaking vaguely of sublimation and education. Along with this goes, rather amusingly, a touching faith in the usefulness of psychological science (presumably reflective) for the improvement of human life; and sometimes we are shown a really admirable comedy which attempts to correct the irrationality of the instincts by admitting the existence and operation of an *irrational*

instinctive tendency towards *rationality*. Another form
of the comedy is to use the word " rationalization " to
mean the giving of *bad* reasons, on the ground that
although " reason " is frigid and useless, the finding of
false reasons is an effective and, indeed, a necessary
part of the human constitution. The unreason of this
comedy is certainly a proof that human reflection is
often imperfect ; but this, so far as I know, has never
been denied. And since certain psychologists have
a way of supposing that outside their own science lies
utter darkness, I shall quote some wise words from
a writer whose psychological competence cannot be
disputed.

" Impulse," Mr. Dewey writes, " is needed to arouse
thought, incite reflection, and enliven belief. But only
thought notes obstructions, invents tools, directs
technique, and thus converts impulse into an art which
lives in objects. Thought is born as the twin of
impulse in every moment of impeded habit. But unless
it is nurtured, it speedily dies, and habit and instinct
continue their civil warfare. There is instinctive wisdom
in the tendency of the young to ignore the limitations
of the environment. Only thus can they discover their
own power, and learn the differences in different kinds
of environing limitations. But this discovery when
once made marks the birth of intelligence ; and with
its birth comes the responsibility of the mature to
observe, to recall, to forecast. Every moral life has its
radicalism ; but this radical factor does not find its full
expression in direct action, but in the courage of intelligence to go deeper than either tradition or immediate
impulse goes." [1]

Stating the issue otherwise, we may say that human
action is often guided by ideas ; and that we have ideas

[1] *Human Nature and Conduct*, pp. 170–1.

of good and evil.   These play their part in our guidance
and direction.   Therefore, when these ideas reach the
reflective level (as manifestly they may) there is no sound
reason for denying that they play their part in regulating
our conduct.   Reflection, to be sure, is a distinctive
stage of intelligent process.   It may never occur in
many intelligent species, but it does occur in the human
species.   *Our* minds have a trick of reflecting themselves
back upon the principles they are pursuing, and this
trick of self-reflection, psychologically incontestable, is
just what the irrationalists vainly attempt to deny.   In
important matters, nothing can be more fundamental
than this capacity ;   in trivial ones the capacity should
not, perhaps, be called upon (although often it is).
Psychologically speaking, however, all human ideas
tend towards the reflective level, seeking it, as it were,
of their own accord.   Naturalism itself admits this,
and has done a service in admitting it.   We are inevit-
ably and incurably a reflective species, looking before
and after, and pondering invisible principles.   Certainly
we are not always employed in this way, or in all things,
and most of us often reflect very badly.   But that is
another thing.

Reflection upon good and evil, therefore, is capable
of effective influence upon the regulation of conduct.
It is not, however, the sole agent in this affair ;   and
unreflecting ideas are not the sole agent either.   The
emphasis which so many moralists place exclusively
upon the emotional or appetitive aspects of conscience
is an exaggeration and not a fable.   Ethically speaking,
quia multum amavit is not at all an amiable subterfuge.
We must turn accordingly to these other aspects of our
psychological problem.

Conscience has to do with the guidance, control, and
regulation of conduct in accordance with the appeal

of the best. From the emotional standpoint, therefore, we have to consider the part which our feelings, and our whole affective diathesis, play in this conscientious regulation; and even a cursory glance at the language we employ in describing these matters is sufficient to show that this emotional aspect is highly important. Love and loyalty and dignity; shame and self-abasement; reverence and respect; sympathy, compassion, and honour—all these are either emotions or patterns prevailingly emotional, and we have already seen how important the emotional qualities in courage, or chastity, or pity are for many of the virtues. It is not enough to think rightly or to act rightly. We should also feel rightly. The truth of this is entirely indisputable, and it has many witnesses.

We may begin by enquiring whether any single emotion is peculiarly or exclusively moral. The answer to this question, I think, is doubtful. A great many of the emotions which have to do with morality, such as pity, or shame, or tender emotion, quite plainly are not. Many are ashamed, for example, of a club foot, or a rounded back, or a ridiculously diminutive stature, and there is nothing moral or conscientious in this distress. Animals, again, may show the signs of shame, but need not therefore be moral creatures. Similarly, if there are righteous kinds of anger, or proper sorts of fear, it is plain that neither fear nor anger need be of a moral kind. On the other hand, such distinctive emotions as envy or malice seem to be always bad, and never to be *un*moral. It is not unlikely, therefore, that certain single emotions are peculiarly and exclusively *im*moral.

Whatever the truth of this may be, it seems clear that our primary concern is with moral sentiments and not with single moral emotions. The distinction, here, is that a sentiment is an organization of emotions, not a single one, and that it evokes, or is manifested in, a great variety of exceedingly *different* emotions according to the situation of the object of the sentiment. This is clearly true of loyalty, honour, love, reverence, dignity, and the like. The sentiment of loyalty evokes anger when the object of our loyalty is attacked, pride and joy when the object of our loyalty is accorded the status we think it ought to have, shame when we are convinced it has shown itself unworthy. A man's loyalty to his country calls upon all these emotions and upon many more. The emotional side of conscience, then, is plainly of this order, as Mr. A. F. Shand, who has done so much to explain what " sentiments " are, and to trace them to their roots in the foundations of human character, himself explains. " That there is a calm joy in fulfilling the dictates of conscience," he says, " and a peculiar sorrow in our failure to fulfil them, is familiar to everyone. When we rebel against it, and persist in our evil courses, this sorrow becomes remorse. Its fear is that apprehension of punishment which follows the violation of its laws ; and its anger is known as " righteous indignation.' " [1]

According to this statement, there *is* a distinctive moral sentiment or emotional organization, and this is conscience in one of its aspects. It must be conceded, however, that this moral sentiment is so closely allied with other sentiments, such as reverence, honour, loyalty, or self-respect, that its distinction from them may seem nebulous and confusing. " My countrymen," a Spanish gentleman once told me, " are for the most part quite unmoral, but they have a very strong sense of honour." He meant, I suppose, that they were not Puritans, but what he said was quaint. A certain

[1] *The Foundations of Character*, p. 57.

blending and fugitive union of the patterns of different sentiments seem, however, to be natural to these organizations, as is often remarked concerning hatred and love ; and the fact, if fact it were, that moralizable sentiments, such as love and loyalty, need not be moral would not prove that there is no such thing as a peculiarly moral organization of the emotions, or that this emotional pattern need not strongly resemble a pattern (say, of dignity, or of reverence) which is not distinctively moral. On the other hand, *all* the sentiments have to do with the regulation of conduct, and therefore are good or bad in a moral sense. An undisciplined, fanatical loyalty, a sightless ambition, a reverence hardly to be distinguished from lick-spittle abasement before a monster, the pathetic devotion of women to worthless mates, are not, I suppose, conscientious devotion to the best, but they certainly seem to be moral sentiments. I think it is very doubtful, therefore, whether there is *any* sentiment which, in its own way, may not be a moral sentiment, or whether conscience, regarded purely as a sentiment, is an entirely distinctive emotional organization.

Indeed, we should rather suppose that conscientious loyalty and reverence differ from the unconscientious varieties of these sentiments not because of a specifically different emotional pattern, but because of the dependence of the conscientious pattern upon the knowledge of right and wrong. Morality, as we have so often observed, has to do with the regulation of our conduct in terms of what is seriously believed to be the best. These beliefs lay claim to authority, and are appropriately accompanied and sustained by the emotional dispositions which befit a being that is submissive to an authority which he imposes upon himself because he accepts its worth and uprightness. It is this appropriateness to our beliefs, I think, that makes our sentiments a part of the conscience. Here we have self-respect which is humble because of its littleness and proud of its high calling; self-reverence, too, and a devout seriousness. These sentiments are austere but not harsh, kindly but not complacent. We have also the tortures of remorse and the bitter cry of the man who feels himself smirched with sin. This anguish, we may hope, should never reach the depth of self-loathing and of self-abasement which is so frequently felt, yet a rational being who is neither infallible nor a saint ought to be susceptible to shame and horror and deep regret. In all these cases, whether of self-respect or of " conviction of sin," these sentiments are matters of conscience when, and only when, they are the children of our beliefs concerning right and wrong.

Certainly these children are also helpers; and it is past disputing that there may be a relatively considerable independence and a very marked divergence between reflection and sentiment in moral action. The " head " may be employed with little of the " heart " to succour it, and the heart in its turn may reck little of the head. Who does not know of warm, impulsive natures, caring very little for inconsistencies, or even for demonstrable unwisdom, contradicting themselves far oftener than " once a day," yet good and lovable ? To deny moral value to natures of this kind would be as unjust as the opposite error of denying all merit to scrupulous considered actions which strike us as frigid, dry and strigose. There is, in fact, no such thing as moral action which is all head and no heart, or all heart and no head; but there may be a pronounced leaning towards either extreme. What I am suggesting is only that no emotional disposition is properly a matter of conscience unless it is subordinate to the discrimination of good from evil. It is this that has authority, and sentiments which are devoid of this authority are not our concern. When the authority is granted, different natures may respond to it in different ways, and although the "head" and the "heart" need not pull different ways, they may indicate distinctively different types of psychological organization.[1]

It may be interesting to compare this view with the two main lines of opinion among those moralists who agree that "reason" or reflection has an indispensable function in these affairs. One of these views is most concisely set forth in Mr. Burnet's statement concerning Aristotle already quoted. The office of moral reflection is simply to universalize and to formulate the material supplied by appetition. The other view is Kant's, in his doctrine of what he calls "respect for the law." This latter needs discussion.

" The essential point in every determination of the will by the moral law," Kant says, " is that, being a free will it is determined simply by the moral law, not only without the co-operation of sensible impulses, but even to the rejection of all such, and to the checking of all inclinations so far as they might be opposed to that law." So regarded, the moral reason has a certain effect upon feeling. It strikes down self-conceit, but this negative feeling (which Kant even calls humiliation) is not the only effect. There is also a positive feeling of esteem. This esteem " is of such a peculiar kind that it seems to be at the disposal of reason only," and

---

[1] Cf. Vauvenargues, *Introduction à la connaissance de l'esprit humain*, xii: "Il faut avoir de l'âme pour avoir du goût : il faut avoir aussi de la pénétration, parce que c'est l'intelligence qui remue le sentiment. Ce que l'esprit ne pénètre qu'avec peine, ne va pas souvent jusqu'au cœur, ou n'y fait qu'une impression faible ; c'est là ce qui fait que les choses qu'on ne peut saisir d'un coup d'œil, ne sont point du ressort du goût."

it is "morality itself subjectively considered as a motive." In illustration Kant says : " Respect applies to persons only, not to things. The latter may arouse inclination . . . but never respect. Something that comes nearer to this feeling is *admiration*. . . . But all this is not respect. . . . Fontenelle says, 'I bow before a great man, but my mind does not bow.' I would add, before an humble plain man, in whom I perceive up-rightness of character in a higher degree than I am conscious of in myself, *my mind bows* whether I choose it or not, and though I bear my head never so high that he may not forget my superior rank. Why is this? Because his example exhibits to me a law which humbles my self-conceit when I compare it with my conduct ; a law the practicability of obedience to which I see proved by fact before my eyes. Now, I may even be conscious of a like degree of uprightness, and yet the respect remains. For since in man all good is defective, the law made visible by an example still humbles my pride, my standard being furnished by a man whose imperfections, whatever they may be, are not known to me as my own are, and who therefore appears to me in a more favourable light. Respect is a *tribute* which we cannot refuse to merit, whether we will or not ; we may, indeed, outwardly withhold it, but we cannot help feeling it inwardly." (*Practical Reason*, chap. iii.)

Kant's psychological valuations to the effect that no sentiments or emotions (other than this feeling of *respect*) are lower or higher, that all such emotions are utterly selfish, that they do not co-operate with " reason," and that our esteem for the moral law is due to the coercion and restraint of " reason," cannot be defended. He does, however, emphasize the authority of conscience, together with the submission of con-scientious emotions to this authority ; and it is true, as he says, that when the best coerces us in spite of our inclinations, we have a peculiarly striking instance of its authority. Our moral sentiments may be joyous and free, but they are also obligatory, and our acceptance of these obligations may entail a very onerous but inescapable self-compulsion. This essential and true feature in the Kantian analysis seems to be neglected in Aristotle's ; and Aristotle's, accordingly, should be corrected by it.

To conclude : The moral sentiments may have themselves a very high value, and they participate effectively in the pursuit of the good. Moreover, since they are regulative organizations of emotions, they are psychologically similar to other regulative features of our constitution, and this analogy may very fairly be pressed. For the same reason, they may readily simulate a conscientious regulation. They should therefore be accorded a high position and function in moral theory, but they should not be assigned a commanding one. They are not our counsellors, although our counsellors should take account of them. Even if the " tigers of wrath " are " wiser " (sometimes) than the " horses of instruction " they are unable to justify their wisdom or to reflect upon it. It is the head that judges, not the heart, and the authority of the head is therefore in principle supreme. An uninstructed sentiment, not discerning good and evil, is not what we mean by conscience.

Up to the present, our discussion in this chapter has dealt with moral counsel and with moral sentiment. These counsels are counsels of action, and these sentiments enliven and sustain action, either fromwards or towards. It is therefore very natural to suppose that moral action is simply the utterance of these counsels and sentiments working together, or, in other words, that the union of these regulative forces is precisely what we mean by the will.

This analysis seems insufficient. To take thought or counsel about action, to admit that the counsel is proper counsel and the thought true thinking, is one thing; to accept the counsel as an obligation and to resolve to follow it is quite another thing. Counsel does not govern unless it enacts; and similarly the sentiments, being only certain systems of inclinations and solicitations, do not govern. When we follow or reject them with our might, and in the teeth of adversity, because of our belief that we *ought* to do so, we have a plain example of this truth; and the force of these arguments does not seem to be diminished when counsel and sentiment are considered in their union. In " will," therefore, we appear to have a further factor of choice or resolve, a unique moment of acceptance or acquiescence—in a word the will's *fiat*, or let it be done. This is the psychology of enactment.

Choice or resolution, indeed, giving heed to the counsels of value, and influenced by the sentiments and regulating impulses and the other forces of behaviour, is the supreme fact in moral psychology. It is the executive authority which as a whole is conscience, and its province would seem to define the domain of moral psychology when its influence upon habits, dispositions and character is taken into account.

Accepting this, our immediate task is the description and examination of this fact of choice in the more important of its moral aspects. This discussion will occupy the remainder of this chapter.

Choice may occur either with or without deliberation. In the former we consider and weigh alternatives; and deliberate choice is the better in proportion as the review of possible alternatives is as complete and accurate as may be, both as regards fact and value. The phrase, however, denotes all degrees of deliberation. Very often our decisions, in the end, appear to be an acquiescence of a rude and truculent kind in which alternatives are brushed aside rather than duly pondered, and the result is only a solution dimly divined, or even the product of weariness. There is, however, a measure of deliberation even here; for there is a pause during which we collect ourselves and consider.

It may be said that since choice involves alternatives, it implies at least a minimum of deliberation. This, however, is a verbal point which seems to overlook a variety of free resolve, and in general it is plain that we may accept or resolve upon some particular mode of action without perpending other possibilities (although we *might* act otherwise), and may be said to be acquainted with the fact (although we do not consciously consider it). In rapid decisions this very often occurs, and there may be semi-deliberative action in which we delay in order to give ourselves the chance of changing our minds in altered circumstances, although there is no weighing of serious alternatives.

Another important distinction is between momentary and settled choice. Choices, in general, are not isolated events, but the expression and continuance of habits and of character. They may illustrate the law of secondary automatism, and dispense, after practice, with the attention that was necessary before the habit became fixed and formed. Even in important and crucial decisions, moreover, which involve much thought and are consummated in a single decisive action (as, for example, the acceptance of a life-work in a foreign country), the ultimate decision, for or against, seems rather to be a process of settling down in the mind than anything else. This is not always so, and the urgency of immediate action may make certain momentary decisions enormously important. In general, however, our settled choices are the weightier. It is also very usual for a momentary choice to be governed by a previous decision. We have given our word, let us say, and it only remains for us to choose the time and the manner in which we implement it. Aristotle's account of deliberation as the study of means for an end *already fixed* refers entirely to decisions of this order.

In our settled determinations the stages of the process are very often hard to mark, just as the highest point in a watershed is very frequently insensible to the eye and has to be determined indirectly by watching the course of the streams. It need not even be true, as the more moderate believers in the necessity for a sudden " conversion " maintain, that there is any moment at which a new, strange rush of emotion indicates that a process of reorganization has actually taken place. None the less, there is such reorganization. What was formerly only a strong inclination is now an adopted activity of the soul, a trend of action which we acknowledge and acquiesce in. Competing inclinations, although they still incline us and may sometimes be very forcible, assume, in the main, an aspect of memory, imagination and unreality. It is argued, therefore, that the essence of will is adoption by the self or self-determination.

To me this statement is a problem rather than a solution, and I should like to give my reasons for this opinion. When we speak of this self-determination we can scarcely mean determination by the idea of the self, or by the ideal of what the self may become. For the ideal of the self is an obscure matter which cannot be explicit in most ordinary willing, and although we may speak very truly of our ideals as being that which *we* hope to achieve or become, we can hardly suppose that any explicit idea of the self can be the governor in these determinations. Accordingly, if these statements are true, it must be the *fact* rather than the *idea* of the self that is operative, although, to be sure, we may be consistently supposed to have an obscure or "virtual" acquaintance with this fact.

This fact of selfhood is certainly fundamental, since all our psychological processes are members and phases of it. On the other hand, even the language we use about it shows that many perplexities are concealed. According to Professor James, for example, we speak of overcoming or conquering our impulses and temptations, " but the sluggard, the drunkard, the coward never talk of their conduct in that way, or say they resist their energy, overcome their sobriety, conquer their courage, and so forth." [1] If this language were conclusive, it would appear to show that *we* are identical with a certain *part* of ourselves, the part, namely, which is good and authoritative. This seems a flat contradiction, and the contradiction does not seem to be avoided (but only declared impenitently) by those theories which allege that " our " good and authoritative self is our only *real* self, the rest being illusory. On such a view courage and sobriety would be real, cowardice and drunkenness unreal, and since we also speak of succumbing to unworthy fears, or of being overcome by them, it would seem, on the theory, that we are overcome by nothing. This would be odd. The truth is, however, that language of James's kind, the language of ethical partiality, is not at all conclusive, if for no other reason than because the same language is used, in other instances, of evil as well as of good.

[1] *The Principles of Psychology*, vol. ii. p. 548.

Nothing is commoner than to speak of " stifling one's conscience," and this critical example is precisely opposed to James's.

Again, when we speak of a " divided self," or of a " war within ourselves," we seem to be using language at least equally appropriate. The distinction, indeed, between a good self and an evil one (or, again, let us say, between a carnal and a spiritual) need not be taken to mean that there are *two* selves in these cases, which are also a single one. Apart from strange and wholly pathological instances, what we describe in these cases is a tension within the same personality in which there is either an obstacle to a settled determination, or, more seriously, a tension of opposing organizations, each (in a sense) competing for general mastery and control.

Perhaps, however, this latter conception gives a clue to the difficulty. Although every thought, every feeling, every impulse, and every desire is included in the self, we may properly draw a distinction between the controlling organization of selfhood and its subordinate, incidental portions. If so, something very like a fission between competing controls might occur not infrequently, and lesser tensions of this kind might be very common. I think this is what we do mean, and I think it is true. The conception is appropriate to dominant goods and to besetting sins, and more generally to the opinion that moral value pertains to the regulation of the whole of a man's being in pursuit of excellence, moral disvalue to the wrong use of ourselves. This opinion, as we have seen, seems to be true.

CHAPTER VII

CONSCIOUS AND UNCONSCIOUS REGULATION

EVEN if the reader, in his charity, is inclined to accept the principal outlines of the psychological analysis in the preceding chapter, he must still, I am sure, be sensible of a host of psychological difficulties springing up to trouble him. I cannot even conjecture, I am afraid, what the chief of these troublers are, but I suspect, from recent literature and from more general observation, that certain difficulties may be felt with regard to the precise fashion in which the sovereignty of the best should be held to be a conscious regulation; and it is undoubted, I suppose, that the sense in which the freedom of the will must be presumed to hold in a world of moral persons needs the closest scrutiny. In a small way, then, I propose to employ the next two chapters in discussing these two problems, and in this order. An examination of both of them is clearly required for elucidation of the standpoint I have tried to set forth.

As everyone knows, the conception of the " unconscious," while not entirely novel, is supposed to have effected a revolution in " modern " psychology. In consequence, it is often stated that the psychology of all previous moralists, together with the opinion of responsibility held by lawyers and by the man in the street, must be radically revised. It seems important, therefore, to consider this question in so far as it affects our argument.

This new-fangled revolution is very heedless of its logic, as the term "unconscious" shows. Since wishes and ideas, for example, are conscious phenomena, it is nonsense to speak of "unconscious" varieties of them. What appears to be intelligibly meant, rather, is wishes and ideas either not explicitly attended to by "introspection," or incapable of such attention by ordinary means. The former undoubtedly exist, the latter may possibly do so. For the rest, we need not attend to controversies of this type. The conception of different systems of conscious ideas, impervious to one another, but belonging to the same personality (i.e. *co*consciousness), while not inconsistent, need not be supposed to apply to anything. To speak of elusive memories, as surviving, unknown to us, in the "unconscious" may be a natural expression, but supplies no evidence that anything is remembered when it is not recalled. And to say that there is *something* in us which, while not conscious, acts as if it were, is not to assert any positive theory whatsoever.

On the other hand, as we have seen already, the unconscious regulation of our behaviour is obviously an entirely consistent notion ; and plainly it does occur. I quote an account of the process of breathing. "Under ordinary conditions the constancy in the pressure of carbon dioxide in the lung alveoli provides for the supply of oxygen to the lungs and blood ; but quite evidently the breathing is, under abnormal conditions, regulated also in direct relation to the oxygen supply ; and the action of the lung epithelium, the concentration of hæmoglobin in the blood, and the mode in which oxyhæmoglobin is dissociated in the blood, play an important part in helping this regulation."[1]

[1] J. S. Haldane, *Mechanism, Life and Personality*, pp. 87-8.

While there is a certain conscious regulation of breathing, the primary regulation, as the above extract shows, is unconscious. Similarly, if we were to follow modern researches into the functions of the ductless glands, or into the " protopathic " as opposed to the " epicritic " system, or into distinctions within the reflexes, we should find abundant evidence of unconscious regulation. Digestion, for the most part, has always been regarded in this light by common sense.

Accepting this, let us begin by considering the orthodox view of responsible control, and proceed to examine the need for revision.

In the orthodox view, it is assumed that a man is responsible for what he does with intent, that action may be intentionally controlled, and the intentions made reasonably adequate to the facts with which they have to deal.

The conception, then, is one of conscious government, a ruling executive capable of acting with wisdom ; and since it is entirely proper for a ruling executive to make use of other forces and organizations, it is quite irrelevant to argue that conscious intention is not the sole operative agency in these matters. Of course it is not. The regulation of movement, for example, presupposes a certain bodily strength and co-ordination, yet it may be thoroughly intentional. The argument, therefore, that consciousness is not the sole or the strongest " driving force " in our constitution is not to the point. It is like saying that the commander-in-chief does not control his army because the force of the army is the force of the rank and file. The relevant question here is whether the " new " psychologists have shown that intentional control has an enormously smaller field than is commonly supposed.

Again, as we have already seen in another connection, it may not be necessary for us to know how we control the forces which we do, in fact, control. A man may know how to set his watch without knowing how the wheels go round. Accordingly, if the new psychology really has enlarged our knowledge of this question we need not infer that the principle of the orthodox opinion, having been examined, has been found utterly wanting.

Our laws, institutions and social behaviour are based upon the orthodox opinion, and our ideas of our own selves are very largely a reflection of this circumstance. It is likely enough that this fabric is sustained, quite appreciably, by prejudice and misleading assumptions, but it is not at all likely that the opinion is baseless. If conscious control is powerless it must at least indicate something powerful; if its range is smaller than we usually suppose, we should still believe that the range is large. Otherwise the bubble would have been pricked long ago, and we should have forgotten the vestiges of it.

On the whole, I think, the claims of the orthodox opinion are really rather moderate. To determine this, let us consider the plain man's view of the two principal species of his conscious intention, the control of movement and the control of thought.

In the first of these we seldom seem to claim more than we can reasonably establish. We do not claim that we can jump thirty feet or lift a ton. In short, experience teaches us our powers in these matters with very fair accuracy. It teaches the baby that he can suck his toe, and the man that he cannot; that feats of endurance are possible after special training that would not be possible without it; and the like. Odd and exceptional facts may come to our knowledge here, as when we learn that hysterical patients may have to lie immovably in bed until some faith-healer persuades them to get up. This may enlarge our current conceptions; but on the whole these very ordinary ideas are very accurate indeed.

In the ordinary way, again, we are pretty modest in our claims concerning the *immediate* control of our thought (in the wide sense of conscious experience) by express intention. In sense perception we can relax and concentrate our attention, and direct different senses to different parts of the environment. The limits of this variation, however, are very narrowly restricted. In memory there is much we can recall at our bidding, much that we cannot. In imagination there is a certain voluntary loosening of the mind and a greater emancipation; but there are shackles, too. Our intellect certainly is freer. Up to a point we can analyse, compare and infer wherever we choose. We may create interests as well as follow them. This choice, however, is itself restricted. Our ideas, commonly, have a straitened orbit, and even if we are free in the choice of them we are not free in the lessons they teach us. Our beliefs are *ours*; but the facts, as we understand them, decree the beliefs. Even faith exists *quærens intellectum*.

It is often maintained, again, that we have *no* immediate control over our emotions and affections, although we may directly control the expression of them. This, I think, is false. We *have* a certain immediate control —at least very often. It is plain, therefore, that the common opinion is exceedingly (I think unduly) modest in this particular.

Certainly we claim, and with reason, a more remote and indirect control over our mental processes. Intellectual discipline, training of the memory or senses, and most that is called " education " pertain to this; and although education is not the panacea that some have supposed, and the doctrine that (since each man is the best judge of his own interests) society must rapidly improve when all are " educated " has not been supported by the somewhat indifferent attempts at education which experience has shown us, it is not to be doubted that our thoughts may be disciplined, and that a measure of control may gradually emerge from this training.   The same is true of the remoter control of beliefs, faith and creeds.   When Tolstoy and others tell us that a man's beliefs cannot be forced, although his utterance may be compelled, they are thinking of immediate, not of remoter results.   A great deal of our thinking is manifestly *ex parte*, and it is a very short step from making a case or from defending a brief to believing in the conclusions of our one-sided pre-occupation.   When penalties are attached to the expression of certain opinions, most people judge it prudent not to think (even) about these things very much.   And so forth.   Suspense of judgment can be cultivated and so can the inhibition (and the lazy rejection) of ideas not likely to be profitable.   In short, while we cannot seriously deny what we see to be true, we can easily contrive to forget it ; and we may gradually cheat ourselves into believing the opposite.

An indirect and comparatively remote control by conscious intention over the emotions is, again, entirely possible.   In part this is due to control over their expression.   We form a " crust " or a " hedge " round ourselves, and for the most part do not reveal our feelings when we do not want to do so.   Everyone guards himself thus, not merely the lawyer or the doctor, or the unfortunate being who is tried for a criminal offence ; and there can be little doubt that this control over the expression of the emotions does on the whole diminish them, although sometimes, to be sure, it aggravates them by penning them in. More important, perhaps, is the indirect control which results partly from inhibition, partly from attending to something else. A forced cheerfulness, to be sure, is comparatively empty and unsatisfying, but, except in the more extreme forms of misery, it is certainly possible to check the thoughts which aggravate our wounds, and to turn our attention to something brighter. A cynical temper can be avoided as well as cultivated, and habitual sourness may sometimes be prevented. Indirectly, at least, we can do much to prevent these evils by taking thought and by recollection of the dangers of brooding upon our woes. It may be better still if we wait for the grace and healing of time, but these gifts are not given us without our co-operation, and a certain effort and intention and wary endeavour is also required of most of us.

On the whole, then, it may fairly be claimed that the orthodox opinion, as I have called it, makes rather moderate assertions. And yet these assertions are quite sufficient to justify its beliefs. If we really have this degree of responsible control, the ordinary view affords an appropriate and an adequate reason for the facts with which it has to do. A revolutionary psychology, therefore, has to show either that an alternative explanation fits the facts better than the usual one, or else that there is illusion, not fact, at the roots of the orthodox doctrine.

To judge from the burden of opinions on this general subject with which the printing-press still groans, anything approaching an adequate discussion of it would need a treatise to itself. A slighter treatment, however, strenuously circumscribed to the effect of these modish opinions upon the meaning of moral responsibility, may have some value. This is what I propose to attempt.

The first and the most general line of argument
employed by the " new " criticism has the object of
casting a general doubt upon all the knowledge we
obtain by conscious self-examination with the further
purpose of indicating that the ultimate regulation in
these matters is due to something unexaminable in the
ordinary way.   A portion of this argument has already
been considered, and does not seem very formidable.
When " rationalization " is used as a piece of semi-
scientific jargon, and taken to mean the finding of bad
reasons for what we believe upon instinct, we may
counter it, in Mr. Mackenzie's fashion, by pointing out
that these reasons need not be always *bad* or always
for.[1]   Similarly, when the stress of the argument is only
to show that preachers, teachers, propagandists and
politicians commonly employ irrational methods of
suasion, we may admit the point with some necessary
reservations, but may reply with some confidence that
human beings are also capable of employing intelligence and good sense in the control of their affairs.
There is no call, so far, for a revolution of psychological
principle.

Indeed, many of the arguments used to support the
new opinions do not even pretend to run counter to
older ones.   " It is the people with secret attractions
to various temptations," Dr. Ernest Jones tells us, " who
busy themselves most with removing these temptations
from other people ; really they are defending themselves
under the pretext of defending others because at heart
they fear their own weakness." [2]   This has been known
for a very long time, and it has been expressed quite
sufficiently.   Thus, take King Lear : " Look with thine
ears : see how yond justice rails upon yond simple thief.

[1] *Manual of Ethics*, Preface, p. xi, footnote.
[2] *Papers on Psycho-analysis*, p. 95.

Hark in thine ear : change places ; and, handy-dandy, which is the justice, which is the thief ? . . ."

> Thou rascal beadle, hold thy bloody hand !
> Why dost thou lash that whore ?   Strip thine own back ;
> Thou hotly lust'st to use her in that kind
> For which thou whipp'st her. . . .
> Get thee glass eyes :
> And, like a scurvy politician, seem
> To see the things thou dost not.

Or, again, La Rochefoucauld :

" Si nous n'avions point de défauts, nous ne prendrions pas tant de plaisir à en remarquer dans les autres." " Il semble que la nature, qui a si sagement disposé les organes de notre corps pour nous rendre heureux, nous ait aussi donné l'orgueil pour nous épargner la douleur de connôitre nos imperfections." [1]

As is plain from these quotations, three things may be meant by arguments of this species : first, that, like the hangman, we know the fact well enough ; second, that, although we know it, we do not acknowledge it to ourselves ; third, that, although it is true, we do not know it and could not acknowledge it.

The first of these is conscious hypocrisy, and needs no special mention. When Mr. Thomas Trumbull in *Redgauntlet* remarked that it was " not his custom to become a chamberer or carouser thus late on Saturday at e'en," but " sanctified his liquor " by a peculiarly long grace, or when he presented Alan Fairford with *Merry Thoughts for Merry Men : or Mother Midnight's Miscellany for the Small Hours*, bound as a hymn-book for the Sabbath that was passing so cannily off, we recognize his breed and know quite enough.

[1] *Maximes Morales*, xxxi and xxxvi.

Instances of the second variety, in their extreme forms, may very well be hypocrisy, and perhaps a commoner form of it. For the most part, however, what is meant is a degree of self-deception that is "indifferent honest" and normally to be expected. Our idea of our own moral character, either from lack of self-examination or from carelessness in the examining, may not correspond at all accurately with the truth about our character. For the most part it seems probable that our judgments of this sort are biased in our own favour, and so that we are somewhat hypocritical. Quite frequently, however, the mistake is in the other direction, since we take ourselves to be worse than we are ; and in the best of cases, as La Rochefoucauld also says, "Nous n'avons pas assez de force pour suivre toute notre raison." [1]

Certainly, when it is said that we *know* our frailties yet refuse to acknowledge them to ourselves or to others, there is a verbal difficulty in the language that we use. What we know, that we also acknowledge. What is meant, however, is really pretty plain. We are acquainted with facts of our nature which are evidence of a different character from that which, when we think of it, we take ourselves to have. Mistakes of this order are naturally very frequent, since rigid self-examination is a very hard exercise and sometimes a profitless one. Its results, moreover, are often exceedingly hard to interpret. On the whole, then, arguments of this type do not seem to imply very startling conclusions, although they undoubtedly have weight.

The third of these arguments seems much more revolutionary, for it maintains that these secret inclinations are necessarily and incorrigibly concealed from the

[1] *Maximes Morales*, xlii.

agent himself. His unconscious hypocrisy, or his un-grounded humility, is revealed only to others.[1]

To be sure, a great, if not the larger, part of the evidence adduced in favour of this third contention seems actually to support the second only. An ado-lescent, for example, is said to be disturbed without any (*sic*) awareness of the cause of his callow malady, to be in love without knowing that he is in love, to seek a short dark maiden, if he himself is tall and blond, without knowing Nature's secrets concerning the attractions of opposite types. This should not and does not mean that there is no emotional disturbance, no conscious experience of love and attraction in the stripling. A studious youth, again, may be morose and disconsolate without knowing why, but this need not indicate any " unconscious " springs of sadness. He does not know the natural consequences of immuring himself with books, and that is all. Similarly, in the former case, what is unknown is the usual interpretation of the symptoms that plainly are experienced.

On the other hand, there may sometimes be plausible evidence of a source of disturbance necessarily hidden from any ordinary process of self-examination, and impervious to any ordinary interpretation of the sig-nificance of conscious experience.

We may take the case of claustrophobia cited by the late Dr. Rivers [2] as a sufficiently apt illustration. In this case, the patient, as a child, was frightened out of his wits by a growling spaniel in a dark passage. Later he forgot all about the incident, but was troubled by an irrational, haunting dread of enclosed spaces. There

---

[1] The name *Bovarysme* (after Flaubert's heroine) is sometimes used (rather unnecessarily) as a technical term to describe this attitude.

[2] *Lancet*, August 18, 1917. Appendix II to *Instinct and the Unconscious*.

were stammerings and other neurotic symptoms ; then a war neurosis due to life in a dug-out. After probing and much questioning by the psycho-analyst, the forgotten incident of the spaniel returned in a dream, and when this memory was restored and firmly grasped the claustrophobia disappeared.

According to the psycho-analytic explanation the " manifest " or overt neurosis was due to the " latent " persistence and regulation of this incident in a buried past. Such heroic interpretations, however, do not seem to be required. In place of them we may reasonably suppose that the boy became afraid of all enclosed spaces after his fright, never knowing what might lurk in them ; that when he forgot about the spaniel, this dread became a mysterious horror marking him off from his fellows and making him a frightened, abnormal thing. Psycho-analytic treatment and suggestions have, *inter alia*, the effect of inducing an abnormally persistent effort to recall childish experiences ; and in a dream this recollection came. Conceive, now, the effect on the patient. A sufficient cause has been assigned for his peculiar distresses, and a cause which might have had this effect upon anyone. He is no longer a thing apart, and, in a fortunate hour, might readily be persuaded, with enduring results, that his troubles were entirely due to this early mishap.

It is probable that many of the other cases are less simply to be explained than this one, but it is hard to see how the cathartic cure which is the culmination of psycho-analytic treatment, and consists in the restoration of " buried " memories to the conscious waking personality could have any actual efficacy unless this conscious waking personality were the genuine governor of our actions. Again, if this is not so, it is quite unintelligible why we are not all neurotics, not merely in the occasional misspellings, mispronunciations, accidental breakages and forgetfulness which Freud brings forward as evidence of the psycho-pathology of everyday life, but radically and generally. If, in fact, we are all compounded of a repressed, infantile, irrational, unconscious, pleasure-seeking system, and an adult, rational, conscious, responsible reality-seeking one, there ought to be not, as we find, an alternation of relaxations and tensions with occasional neurotic disturbance, but a permanent incorrigible tension in which smothered complexes are permanently at war with intention and design. In other words, our " manifest " consciousness could not, on this hypothesis, work as it does, and could not be cured by catharsis. This is the main point, and it seems clearly to show that official psycho-analysis, despite its protestations, is in the end a curiously willing convert to the very ideas it so often derides.

On the whole, then, we should conclude that the principal ethical lesson of this much-debated evidence is the extreme difficulty and the need for caution in the process of self-examination. If the psycho-analysts are right, the history of our emotional diathesis, and particularly the impressions of early childhood, are much more important than most grown people suppose. These, to be sure, are beyond the reach of our memories, but a certain instruction may be obtained (if only from others), and perhaps a useful point of view. It may be possible, also, to care for children more wisely. Some theory of pre-disposing history, again, basing itself upon heredity and "instinctive" repugnances like the horror of snakes, while enormously speculative, should perhaps always be kept in mind ; and on these matters we have to learn from other sources than our own private self-examination.

This historical ignorance, however, is not the only

perplexity which besets us in our endeavour to estimate the " significance " of much of our conscious experience. The greater part of the difficulty, as moralists have constantly averred, is fundamentally that our knowledge of the trend and tendency of the strivings and purposes of an aspiring creature is necessarily very obscure. Even when life repeats itself, it does so, for the most part, with a difference ; and even if we remembered (as generally we do not remember) precisely how our past fruitions felt, we can still only guess at the future condition that would gratify us. The thing is always a species of divination, and often it is hasty and imperfect.[1] Urged by wants and solicited by desires, with only a guess at the states they portend, it is only to be expected that much which seemed fair in its promise should be Dead Sea fruit in the eating, and generally that we should often pursue what we do not " really " want. Indeed, we may " really " want one thing and believe that we want another. A commoner case, however, is that in which we do not " really " want anything specific, but are a tangled mass of inconsistent impulses, inclinations and aspirations. The event cannot fulfil all of these, and therefore, whatever happens, we are restless, perturbed and foiled.

The young may not know the experience of old age, the youth how he will feel when he is head of a family, the old man wearily getting rid of his harness

[1] Cf. Wilfrid Ward, *Last Lectures*, p. 197: " In one sense autobiography brings us closer than anything else to its subject, for the writer's testimony about himself is the testimony of the most intimate witness, yet, in fact, nothing needs more careful scrutiny in determining its true historical value. Some see themselves very truly, others very falsely. Some write frankly, others fail completely in frankness. Some do their best to get at their own thoughts and motives, others write for effect. Some remember the past accurately, others see it deeply coloured by the glasses of their present feelings."

whether the ease which he has earned may not, after all, be a tiresome inactivity. They think, perhaps wrongly, that it is better to have these experiences, whatever betides, than not to have them at all. The man who craves distinction may not be content when he achieves it. The prospects which seem so fair may have a dull inevitableness when finally they are reached. Youth is underpaid because it lives on hope, age too much remunerated (among the wealthier) because it needs a consolation. These commonplaces have never been forgotten by anyone who is sane, and they certainly show the limitations of the wisest self-regulation. What they do not and cannot show is the futility of this wisdom.

Another line of argument sometimes adopted by the " new " psychologists, and rather loosely connected with the question of what is or is not " conscious," may be illustrated by Mr. Russell's opinions concerning the evils of what he calls " desire," and by what exponents of M. Coué's ideas call the " law of reversed effort."

The main points in Mr. Russell's contention are given in the following sentences: " All human activity springs from two sources: impulse and desire." [1] " Will as a directing force consists mainly in following desires for more or less distant objects, in spite of the painfulness of the acts involved and the solicitations of incompatible but more immediate desires and impulses. . . . But desire governs no more than a part of human activity, and that not the most important, but only the more conscious, explicit and civilized part." [2] " Impulse is at the basis of our activity, much more than desire " ; [3] yet " Desire, as opposed to impulse, has a large and increasing share in the regulation of men's

[1] *Principles of Social Reconstruction*, p. 12.
[2] *Ibid.*, p. 13. [3] *Ibid.*, p. 16.

lives." [1] "Almost all paid work is done from desire, not from impulse; the work itself is more or less irksome, but the payment for it is desired." [2] "The complete control of impulse by will, which is sometimes preached by moralists and often enforced by economic necessity, is not really desirable. A life governed by purposes and desires, to the exclusion of impulse, is a tiring life; it exhausts vitality, and leaves a man, in the end, indifferent to the very purposes which he has been trying to achieve." [3]

In its plain meaning, the contrast here set forth pertains to the subject-matter of our last chapter, not of the present one; and since Mr. Russell, in this volume, sets himself to show that "creative" impulses and desires should be preferred to "possessive" ones,[4] it is clear that he does admit the value and the efficacy of certain desires and our capacity, by taking thought, to curb, and indeed to annul, a certain class of impulses, namely the acquisitive ones. The problem in this case is one of value and of possibility. Possession, in the sense of an admitted claim to private use, is a necessity of secure existence; its limits and its value are a question of general ethics. So far, therefore, the principle of conscious regulation is not affected, and other criticisms which Mr. Russell's arguments seem to court (as that work or desire implies the readiness to persist in the face of obstacles rather than a perpetual warfare with them, or that the rational control of impulse, while it may require coercion for sufficient cause, need not in general meddle or restrain overmuch) are not our present concern.

[1] *Principles of Social Reconstruction*, p. 16.
[2] *Ibid.*, p. 17. [3] *Ibid.*, p. 18.
[4] In the hands of certain authors this cult of "creativeness" seems to become an adoration of "the life force" and not to be readily distinguishable from phallic worship.

On the other hand, it is possible (and not illegitimate) to interpret theories of this type in a way that is thoroughly relevant to our present subject. While impulses are *not* unconscious, for the most part, they *are* unforeseeing, and action in accordance with them is therefore not the regulation of conduct with conscious prevision. Again, it may plausibly be held that impulsive action arises from unknown springs, so that, while it reports itself to our consciousness, it has, properly speaking, no conscious intention. In the greater instincts, at least, it is the unconscious regulation of an unconscious pattern of adaptation, something primeval and hidden which touches the mind without instructing it, and some of the more ancient and stubborn of these primitive vital patterns may never report themselves directly at all. This seems part of the lesson of Dr. Rivers's *Instinct and the Unconscious*. Again, these impulses may report themselves spuriously. To quote Mr. Russell once more: " Impulses bring with them a whole train of subservient fictitious desires ; they make men feel that they desire the results which will follow from indulging the impulses, and that they are acting for the sake of those results, when, in fact, their action has no motive outside itself. A man may write a book or paint a picture under the belief that he desires the praise which it will bring him ; but as soon as it is finished, if his creative impulse is not exhausted, what he has done grows uninteresting to him, and he begins a new piece of work." (This is alleged to be the cause of false " rationalization." *Ibid.*, p. 16.)

None of these arguments seems properly to impugn the authority of conscious regulation in the full sense. Certainly they may show that the great part of our conscious control holds sway over unknown forces whose effects alone are within our ken. This, however, would not show that the control does not exist, or that the effects cannot be ascertained. The best we can make of them is still something we can intentionally make. We are still responsible in the ordinary sense for exhausting ourselves on the one hand, and for losing self-command upon the other. And the concluding argument, if examples are to be trusted, is quite singularly weak. The number of authors and artists with strong creative impulses, who work, in their own eyes, for fame alone, is probably rather small; and if they do grow tired of their work at the end (which is intelligible enough for very ordinary reasons) it does not follow that they ever grow tired of the fame it brings them. So far as I can ascertain it is very unusual for anyone to be tired of his renown, although many are tired of the effort to live up to it.

The "law of reversed effort" of the New Nancy School may seem, indeed, to supply a strong argument for the co-ordinate or superior importance of unconscious regulation as opposed to conscious. What this law enjoins is the cessation of conscious effort, when this effort is useless in any case. Instead of *trying* to become better every day, the patient is enjoined to relinquish the struggle, and simply to believe that he will grow better without any effort on his part. If, as we are invited to do, we have to interpret this event as auto-suggestion operating upon the unconscious, and effecting the cure through *its* agency, a serious revision of our main contentions would seem to be implied.

This argument, however, is only superficially formidable. We all know very well, as a matter of very ordinary experience, that sometimes we could not and should not force ourselves, that we cannot always work when we are tired or *invita Minerva*, and we also know that if we never force ourselves we never accomplish anything. Other things being equal, we should make every task as easy as we may, and avoid effort (or, rather, avoid *strain*) wherever possible. These facts need no special explanation, and their application to persons who have tired themselves out, and are for the time being incapable of *any* effort, needs no special explanation either. It is impossible for anyone to make an effort if he is convinced that the effort is bound to fail, and M. Coué's patients are precisely in this position. They are convinced of their impotence, and their confidence must somehow be restored.

The answer, I suppose, is that the confidence is restored by an appeal to an *unconscious* regulation. If this were really so, it would appear that a certain initial voluntary effort and intentional regulation is still presupposed. Voluntarily and intentionally the patient ceases to struggle—" quits struggling " as a certain dialect puts it—and the marvels begin to happen. This is like sleeping upon a resolution or upon a problem, hoping that the delay (and the unknown occurrences during it) will be helpful on the whole. In the main, however, there is no occasion to suppose that the " unconscious " is peculiarly concerned. An effortless suggestion, if it can be induced either by M. Coué's methods or by a psycho-galvanic battery, is not necessarily or distinctively " unconscious," any more than faith, or confidence, or arrogance, coming unsought and without express resolve, is necessarily or usually unconscious. All that follows is that the regulation in these cases is not a matter of *trying*.

CHAPTER VIII

FREEDOM

THE problems of freedom, crucial for all moral theory, are also of outstanding difficulty, as an age-long discussion has shown. We need not hope to resolve them, but we may diminish the difficulty by removing some of the commoner misunderstandings, and perhaps describe, in general, something of the degree of freedom which moral theory seems to require. In attempting this I shall begin with a psychological discussion and pass to an ethical one.

In any ordinary sense of the words, an action is said to be free in so far as it is not restrained. When it is restrained to the point of entire compulsion there is no freedom. Short of this there is a measure of freedom. It is in this sense that a physicist speaks of a particle as having so many degrees of freedom.

Proceeding, then, with this antithesis of freedom-compulsion, we may ask how we are to judge whether an action is or is not compelled. Here we have at least one important witness—the *sense* of compulsion. Often we feel ourselves constrained or borne along, and then we have no sense of freedom. Such compulsion may be either physical or psychological. It is physical, say, when fetters prevent our moving, or a gag keeps us silent, or when we are dragged behind the wheels of a chariot. It is psychological when we are compelled by someone's threats or penalties.

The sense of compulsion and the sense of freedom do actually exist and are of great importance. Everyone knows, for example, that freedom has been a political ideal for a longer space of time than our records extend to, and that rebellion against tyranny or slavery has been among the commonest of human practices. This ideal and this vast unrest have been neither the idolatry that is prostrate before an abstraction nor the product of acute reasoning, although reasoning and abstraction have played their part in it. For the most part it has been an attempt to get rid of restrictions *felt* to be irksome, and to achieve the *sense* of emancipation. The spur comes from our own experience and not from a catchword. The irksomeness of constraint and the positive joy of experienced liberty are undeniable constituents of the human mind. The liberated captive, always supposing that he has not become so habituated to his cell as to be bewildered and uninterested out of it, tastes one of the sweetest delights of our human existence. He is rid of an incubus. This sense of liberty, moreover, is not simply a reaction from the burden of a restraint removed, but normally present in our action. As such, it is habitually felt and greatly to be prized.

Despite the importance of these feelings, however, it is entirely legitimate to argue that they are very often illusory, and that the fundamental question is not whether we *feel* free or constrained, but whether we *are* free or constrained. Let us address ourselves, therefore, to this problem, and begin by attempting to examine it more precisely.

In the first place it is necessary to consider what is or is not to be accounted compulsion. This is not easy.

When an agent is said to be compelled it is naturally

to be supposed that he is compelled by some other agent, by some force outside himself. Accepting this interpretation, then, we may regard human agency as the agency of a mind-body partnership without for the moment attempting to consider the nature of this partnership more closely. So defined, a clear and not unimportant sense of compulsion is physical compulsion on the part of some agency outside the body, although it is probable that what doctors call a " foreign " body or other recalcitrant matter within our skins should be reckoned as " outside " for the purposes of this discussion. The more important problem, however, is what outside *compulsion* means. The body maintains itself by adapting itself to its physical environment and by utilizing the same. External influences and conditions cannot therefore be what is meant by compulsion ; and compulsions felt as such are for the most part the result of external conditions which in some way thwart the body's action. A physical definition of thwarting, however, is not at all easy, and may indeed be impossible. When unfavourable conditions, for example, lead to stunted growth, we may speak, metaphorically, of thwarting, but the truth seems to be that the body grows as well as it can whatever its environment may be. It may be doubted, therefore, whether restraint in the sense of compulsory thwarting has any proper meaning except a psychological one. We are compelled only when we are forced to do what we might try not to do, or, if this is not the *only* sense of compulsion, it is vastly the most important.

Psychologically, then, a man is thwarted when forces outside him frustrate his intentions. Even here, however, there is a plentiful crop of dubieties. A child's intentions, for example, or the unreasonable arrogance of elderly children may be frustrated by forces which to a balanced, serious will are not compulsions at all, but simply the conditions of our living. In general the will is the will to make use of opportunities, and we usually speak of compulsion when opportunities reasonably supposed to be such are forbidden in special circumstances, or where a regulation that is normally possible is forcibly overridden. In such cases there are all degrees of compulsion, as is shown by Aristotle's illustration of the sea-captain who may have to throw the cargo overboard to prevent his vessel from foundering. It is his business in general to bring the cargo to port, but in the special emergency he may have to choose between losing both ship and cargo and losing the cargo only. Here his general intention is thwarted by circumstances, while his special intention is not.

These instances might be multiplied indefinitely. So-and-so is said to be compelled by a threat of blackmail. Yet he might choose ruin. What is the truth about his freedom? Perhaps all the threats and all the blandishments of our fellows leave us a certain liberty.

In the main, however, and in any reasonable sense, our fellow-men can certainly compel us by threats and other psychological means, and they certainly limit our freedom. Our social environment, indeed, which is as much a condition of our existence as any physical one, may restrain and intimidate us purposely and capriciously. Nature does not; and on the whole we have more to fear from the meddling and the obstinacy of our fellows than from drought or floods or a niggardly soil.

By contrast, our fellow-men may compel us for our own good, while Nature does so by metaphor only. It is claimed (and with reason) that children, citizens, and the members of associations have their freedom, on the whole, immensely enlarged, even by being forced to learn, and by social conditions which involve compulsory tax-paying, sanitation, industrial insurance and the like. We may sometimes, indeed, be forced to be free and forced to rely on our own judgment and initiative.

While these matters are intricate, they do not seem to involve any insuperable theoretical difficulty. Actions which are forced upon us *are* forced, whether they are or are not for our good. We may be glad of the compulsion afterwards, as some in later life may be glad of the compulsions which they resented when they were children. We may be glad, upon the whole, of a compulsion which, unpleasant in itself, is judged to be part of a system necessary for our advantage. This might cover the effects of an unpopular Budget. We may be glad, even, to have a decision taken out of our hands if we regard it as too intricate for us, as some preferred military conscription to voluntary enlistment.

The last example certainly illustrates the truth that compulsion is a wider notion than negative restraining compulsion, or thwarting. A part of us, indeed, might rejoice at the thwarting of some other part, but our entire consent and acquiescence in a course that is forced upon us is another thing. Its analysis, also, presents perplexities. The difference between a willing and an unwilling conscript, I suppose, after both have avoided voluntary enlistment, is principally that the former accepts an accomplished fact in a way in which the latter does not accept it. The former loyally accepts the implications of his enforced station; the latter has constantly to be goaded into doing what is required of him. In short, after the fact, there is still a possibility of a certain effective control with a limited choice in the way a man conducts himself; and compulsion without this minimum of elective choice would seem wholly opposed to freedom in any intelligible sense. The attitude of invincible fatalism, in which our fortunes and our very soul are taken to be completely fixed without the smallest regard for anything we may try to do, is definitely opposed to a freeman's. On this view, what has to happen has to happen irrespective of anything we do. When there is no control and no electiveness there cannot be freedom. On the other hand, there may be a very important and a very effective degree of freedom within a narrow range, and subject to an acquiescence which, speaking generally, is quite unavoidable.

To these obvious compulsions from the outside, unseen and supersensible ones must be added according to the testimony of many witnesses. The voice of God and of immaterial forces greater than ourselves or the visible society within which we live (whether they are manifested in visions or some other way) may seem foreign to the worshipper and yet be part of his spiritual environment. He is even as an oblate child.

All of these compulsions, as we suppose, are external, and there are also internal compulsions and restraints. In this respect, however, the problem of freedom seems to change its aspect. When we restrain or compel *ourselves* we are obviously acting freely. The truth is that we are pitting a part of ourselves against the rest, even when there is the greatest resistance and the hardest of obstacles within ourselves. On the whole, therefore, we are free agents in such cases, however taxing and wearisome the struggle may be, and the same is true in principle when we voluntarily relax control and succumb to what we consider an unworthy temptation. In a sense, however, we may abdicate from our free estate, and enslave ourselves by permitting a gradual loss of self-restraint and of self-control. This weakening of the moral fibre is properly to be considered a loss of personal liberty.

Such a process takes time, although frequently it is swifter than we think ; and time is precisely the factor which is commonly supposed to complicate the problem of freedom within the self most seriously. Is it not possible for a man freely to make himself unfree, to surrender his right of private judgment to the authority of an institution, to sell himself into literal slavery for the rest of his life, or to sell his soul to the devil for all eternity ? And is it not quite usual for our past lives to dominate us even more than our past contracts, and so to narrow our choice and restrict our freedom ? What middle-aged man could allege the contrary ?

Nothing else, indeed, could be expected. The self is a continuing entity owning, at any time, what has gone before, and determining in a great measure what it will become. Its decisions may be as unalterable as they are irrevocable ; and any decision, besides influencing our future, affords a circumstance of which, in the future, account should be taken. Here again, however, it is the intricacy, not the difficulty, of the problem that bewilders us. The self is a continuing and a changing thing having a narrow but effective power over its own future. There must therefore be a difference between its state and decisions at any given time, and our estimate of it as a whole. A free decision taken at any time belongs to the self as a whole, but it may fetter the whole of the subsequent actions of the self. This is not a contradiction, but an inherent complication in the fact of continuing selfhood, and as such it must simply be accepted. It is true, of course, that momentary decisions may liberate as well as restrain ; that unalterable ones should be very carefully pondered ; that the loss of freedom involved, say, in the choice of a profession may be more than compensated by the opportunities for free endeavour which the profession brings; and so forth. These truisms, however, do not mitigate the original problem—which is quite inescapable, but not a contradiction.

Proceeding upon these lines, then, and making use of reflection upon our experience of action instead of the mere sense of freedom or compulsion, we appear to arrive at the conclusion that there is freedom wherever there is self-determination, provided that this self-determination includes, in some degree, the power of effective choice.

To this it may be objected that freedom and self-determination cannot possibly be the same, since everything which has any effect is in a measure self-determining, and since no particular thing determines itself alone, but, on the contrary, co-operates with other things. A doctrine which implies that a material particle is partly free, and that none of our actions upon other things is ever entirely free, cannot (we are told) express what we mean by freedom.

These objections, I think, are not convincing, although the arguments used to destroy them are sometimes unconvincing also. What these counter-arguments set about to prove is (commonly) that the self-determination of a mind-body system is very different indeed from the self-determination of any other known system or thing. The suggested inference is that the former is free and the latter not; but this further inference is much more dubious.

A wider and very usual variety of the argument is the following: It is declared that all inorganic things and systems are "mechanical" in their action. All living things, on the other hand, are essentially non-mechanical. To be sure, there may be *certain* mechanical effects upon living things. A falling dog and a falling log are subject, as we say, to the self-same laws of gravity, and bones may be broken " mechanically." Life, and growth, and assimilation, however, belong to a different order of events—the biological order, not the mechanical.

As everyone knows, the discussions on this subject are interminable, and we may therefore be excused if we consider those, and those only, which are relevant to this problem of self-determination. We shall not enquire, therefore, whether the phrase " mechanical " is well chosen—or, in other words, whether mechanics is co-extensive with physics and chemistry—and we shall not debate the general problem of " mechanism " and " vitalism."

On the main issue that confronts us the answer is not doubtful. " Mechanical " systems may determine themselves very well, and they are thoroughly democratic in their constitution. Every portion of a mechanical system plays its mechanical part strictly in proportion to its mechanical ability.

What may consistently be maintained are two contentions, each of which is quite legitimate. In the first place, there may be a range and kind and degree of self-determination possible in a " non-mechanical " system which could not be matched in a " mechanical " one. Thus it is held that organisms utilize their forces for continued life according to a certain pattern, for dominating their immediate surroundings, for selecting appropriate nourishment and rejecting inappropriate, and all for the end of self-maintenance. If this be truly " non-mechanical," then, since organisms do these things (until they die) they must have a special kind and degree of self-determination. If it is " mechanical," then " mechanics " has rather peculiar potencies in this direction ; and when we come to a self-regulating mind (in so far as the mind really does control itself and that over which it has charge) we may have reached a still more important and effective kind and degree of self-determination. In other words, the range, degree and manner of self-determination possible to any system are matters for enquiry. Living bodies have potencies of this sort which dead ones do not have; minds have potencies which mindless organisms (although living) are without. Being different, they determine themselves differently ; and plainly the self-determination of certain systems relatively to their environment may *count* for more in some cases than in others.

A second possible contention is equally legitimate. If a "minding," a living and a dead system do, in fact, determine themselves differently, then a system normally and appropriately determining itself at any one of these levels may be said to be unfree if, for any cause, it determines itself at some other level, at any rate if what we consider a " higher " level gives place to a " lower " one. The same contrast may appear within the mind when a rational or spiritual organization gives place to a bestial one through the influence, say, of a drug. More generally, if we take the control of ourselves to be non-mechanical, and if it were proved that our actions, in fact, are mechanical, we should rightly infer that we have been shown not to have the kind of freedom and potency which we had supposed ourselves to have. Certainly we have some control on any theory, and therefore if we are mechanical systems, " mechanism " would be proved to have enormously higher capacities than are usually assigned it; but if our definitions of " mechanics " had been correct we should have shown, in proving ourselves mechanical, that the kind of self-determination we formerly supposed ourselves to have is a kind that, in reality, we never had.

Accordingly, if freedom and self-determination are the same, we should conclude that everything is free or self-determining in a measure, but that this self-determination is important in proportion as the thing's self-regulation does or does not dominate the events that happen to it. In the case of organic self-determination this distinction takes the crucial form of using or of being used, and plainly a user determines itself in a more important way than a thing that is used. In the psychical self-determination of sane and responsible human beings there is the further possibility and appropriateness of determining conduct by ideas and ideals. What has to be vindicated here is the truth that we do, in fact, determine ourselves in a way appropriate to a creature who may regulate himself reflectively in accordance with his ideals of value.

Plainly, this comes very near to what many of us mean by our freedom. We think of it as self-determination of a special kind. The man who makes use of his opportunities, and commands his own actions for an adopted purpose, is properly to be regarded as playing a freeman's part.

On the other hand, many believe that a " freedom " of this sort need not be freedom at all. The opposite of freedom, we are told, is neither the sense of compulsion nor other-determination as opposed to self-determination. It is necessity; and if our actions are necessary actions they cannot be free.

An action is said to be *necessary* when it must occur —when its absence or any other action is entirely impossible. Accordingly, if we say that any action is not necessary (i.e. that it is *contingent*) we must mean that something else could have occurred under the same conditions, for if we deny this we assert by implication that conditions do always necessitate, and if we distinguish between necessitating and non-necessitating conditions we imply that some conditions are only contingent —influences that incline without necessitating.

An action is *known* to be necessary when we know with complete certainty that it must occur. The case most usually contemplated here is that in which the occurrence of the action may be inferred from necessary laws which govern the phenomena in question.

The theory that every event (including every action) is necessary (or *must* occur precisely as it does occur) I shall call *determinism*, meaning thereby complete and ineluctable determinism down to the minutest details. The opposite theory I shall call *tychism*, such tychism being either general or restricted.

Our knowledge of all events (including our own actions) is plainly very short. Of past events we may know that they have occurred, not that they must have occurred; of present ones that they occur, not that they must occur; of future ones, at the best, that they are likely to occur, not that they are bound to occur. All our inferences which deal with the inter-connections of events are inductive inferences; and induction, at its best, cannot yield more than a high probability. This ignorance on our part, however, does not settle the general problem. We never know in detail all the conditions of any event, or, completely and quite certainly, the laws of these conditions; but it is often maintained that induction itself presupposes determinism, that is to say, that in all inductive inference it is taken for granted that every event has conditions from which its character necessarily flows. Our ignorance, therefore, only concerns what in detail these conditions and consequences are. In this we have to speak with the accents of mere probability, and if conditions apparently the same yield different effects, we have to suppose the concealed presence of some other condition. Our governing principle, however, is always that there are conditions which always necessitate.

These assertions are over-confident. The principle of them is not self-evident, and if they describe the *policy* of the inductive sciences they cannot determine more—in fact, this policy needs further assumptions which no one should assume light-heartedly. In looking for general principles of this species we also suppose that they are relatively simple (so that we can grasp them if we take pains), not incalculable (so that, given the patience we may apply them with precision), congruent with one another (so that with the aid of imagination we may proceed by analogy from one sphere to another) ; and so forth. It may be reasonable to follow this policy, since it is the one that pays best, if it pays at all ; but theoretically the procedure is full of hazard. In short, tychism in some form is not inconceivable, and it need not dispute the measure of success which the inductive sciences, pursuing for the most part an opposite policy, have actually achieved.

In point of fact, our general beliefs in this matter fluctuate considerably, and perhaps with reason. In the case of inorganic things we put our trust in the sciences, and believe that all their actions are uniquely determined by their own nature taken in conjunction with the nature of their surroundings. There is faith here, to be sure, and as much authority as sight, but it is part of the modern outlook, and we should treat any hint of caprice or contingency in these things as a relic of demon worship or of primitive animism. Probably also, as Mr. Jennings says, " experimental determinism " is part of our outlook in purely biological matters.

While the self-preservation and self-regulation of organic things count for more (relatively to their environment) than the self-maintenance of inorganic ones (despite the stubbornness of the everlasting hills) we commonly suppose that they also are uniquely determined, if we only knew how. Relatively to our knowledge there are genuine alternatives of growth, but not, we suppose, to omniscience. In the case of the higher animals, however, and in the case of ourselves and of our fellow-men, we do not, on the whole, suppose this. Here we think there really are alternatives and the possibility of genuine choice. Their behaviour, we consider, is influenced, not completely determined, by their nature and circumstances.

This combination of a limited tychism with a limited (although more general) determinism is not in itself inconsistent, and might be sustained if there were sufficient grounds for distinguishing between these different classes of actions. It may reasonably be demanded, however, whether there are any adequate reasons for this discrimination, and it seems probable that the reasons which appeal to us most are not, argumentatively, entirely convincing. If challenged we should probably appeal to our own experience and urge the facts of spontaneity and initiative, of fresh beginnings that surprise us and inceptions unheralded by the past, of an " authorship " not determined by former events, but freely adventuring into the future. These phrases undoubtedly describe our experience as we know it; but then we know so little, and because of our ignorance it is open to anyone to argue that these crises and inceptions have, in fact, sufficient causes in ourselves and in the influences we encounter, and are probably uniquely determined. It is our ignorance of these extremely complicated matters, we may be told, which suggests

a difference in their principle when in reality there is
none. Our " authorship " seems capricious because we
do not know in advance what ideas will suggest themselves ; but looking back upon the process we can see,
in general, how the links forged themselves, and we need
not doubt that, if we knew all, we could supply all the
links in detail.   Even choice itself would probably tell
the same story.   To be sure, these *post-mortem* revelations
are themselves suspect in a certain way.   Although we
can trace a certain influence and connection, we have no
business to assume an inevitable consequence.   In this
M. Bergson is absolutely right.   On the other hand, the
argument for contingency is sensibly weakened by these
considerations.

Let us ask, then, whether more general arguments
may be adduced, and let us examine their sufficiency.
Of these the more important, I think, are the following :
Human action, it is said, is unpredictable, and therefore differs in principle from determined action.   It is
individual, and in a certain sense unique, and therefore,
again, is essentially different.   Thirdly, it is teleological.
And lastly, it is the flower and extreme instance of
" emergent " evolution.

Strictly speaking, any action is predictable if it can,
in any sense, be foreknown.   It is clear, however, that
the mere fact of knowledge cannot affect the freedom or
unfreedom of an action.   Our present actions may be
free, although we know what they are, and our past
actions may have been free, although we may know
what they were.   Certainly they occurred, but perhaps
they need not have occurred.   The same thing is true
of the future.   Whatever occurs at any time (past,
present, or future) must be entirely determinate.   Whatever will be, will be precisely—what it will be.   It will
never have an indeterminate, alternative, half-and-half

being. Yet it is quite consistent to maintain that the
future *need not* be what it will be; and this might
still be true if we had (as, in fact, we do not have) a
prophetic prevision of it.

Less strictly, but more usually, we mean by prediction an inferential forecast of the future from data in
the present and in the past; and it is plain that the
power of the sciences depends entirely upon their capacity
for these inferences towards the future, since the past
and the present are unalterable by the sciences or by
anything else. Accordingly, this application of scientific principles to the future attracts our attention very
forcibly, although these same principles have necessarily
a wider application. The very principles which enable
us to predict the return of Halley's comet also require
us to infer that the sun did not stand still during Joshua's
campaign. They have no peculiar affinity for the future,
although the practical importance of inferential forecast
directs our thoughts rather specially towards prediction.

Admitting this, we have to say that a great many
human actions may be predicted with the utmost confidence, others with less confidence, and others with
none at all. We have the greatest confidence in our
predictions concerning the professional actions of
postmen and engine-drivers, less concerning politicians,
and none at all, perhaps, concerning the people we call
eccentric. To be sure, the postman *may* suffer a
" brain-storm " and scatter all his letters to the winds,
but the delivery of the mails is less likely to be affected
by this cause than by the weather. Considering,
indeed, what complex creatures postmen are, our
calculations concerning their work are quite singularly
simple. Accordingly, if the problem of freedom is
simply the question of predictability or its opposite, we
should have to maintain that some of our actions are free

and some not; that as our data increase, actions that used to be free may cease to be so, although the agents may not alter in any relevant respect; and so forth. In other words, we should have to believe what is absurd.

The possibility of prediction, in a word, is not the same thing as necessity or its absence. Given certain creatures who generally or always act in a certain way, we may infer, without any further hypothesis, that they will probably continue to do so. This could be inferred, and predicted, on the most extreme forms of tychism. What we may not infer, without a further hypothesis, is that, probably, these creatures *must* continue to act in this way; and this additional hypothesis is precisely the question in dispute. If we could argue, indeed, that without a necessary connection the regularities which we find in human behaviour would be entirely inexplicable, we should have supplied a strong reason for determinism. But human action, as we know it, does not seem to demand this hypothesis.

The alleged uniqueness of human individuality in each several moral subject seems irrelevant to the problem of freedom or its opposite. If we were free we might not be unique, and we might be unique if our actions were determined. Even on mechanical principles, any given system might necessarily differ from any other, and be determined in an individual fashion. Indeed, when initial collocations are different, this, according to the principles of determinism, must necessarily occur. Different things must behave differently unless they are undetermined, and therefore capable of behaving in the same way although they are different.

Teleology, again, while of the greatest importance, is not inconsistent with necessity. Unquestionably we act with intention and purpose, seeking an end. It is entirely possible, however, that we are so constituted that we *must* seek precisely these ends and form precisely these intentions. This appears, indeed, very clearly from a rather desperate device that certain teleologists employ. Teleological action, they say, is literally *a fronte*. The future itself enters as a determining factor. All other action is completely *a tergo*. It is necessitated without remainder by the pressure of the past. Certainly it is very hard to see that there is any reason for this opinion. When we act with an eye towards the future, it is our present intentions that direct us, the thoughts which we now have concerning what may be achieved in the time to come; and no further explanation seems to be needed. Let us suppose, however, that the future does enter into these matters as an operative incitement to present action, that what is about to be draws us towards it *now*. If so, we have admitted another determining factor, and this additional factor may also act with necessity. Indeed, unless the future itself is indeterminate, there is every reason to suppose that it does.

Finally, the concept of " emergent " development is not inconsistent with necessity. When matter passes into life, or life into mind, or mind into spirit and thought, we are told, according to this doctrine of " emergence," that a new order of being has come into existence. There is not merely growth, but a sudden, subtle, profound reorganization. Descriptively, this doctrine appears to be correct. It has long been admitted by the majority of competent enquirers that growth does not imply preformation. Gametes are not little men, or eggs little chickens. Development, in other words, is a genuine process of becoming (or epigenesis), not the mere unfolding of an unalterable pattern. The doctrine of " emergent " evolution carries these conceptions a stage further forward.   Just as growth does not involve preformation, so it need not be gradual.   There are crises in it, and the sudden, relatively discontinuous arising of a new thing.   The mutations of species or of men come about *per saltum*, at critical epochs.

If we suppose all this to be true (and, personally, I do not doubt it) important conclusions follow. Instead of *pre*arrangement, or of mere *re*arrangement, we have the emergence of genuine novelties and of fresh patterns characteristically different from an earlier order of things.   Venerable and cherished doctrines go by the board.   It is no longer possible to argue, for instance, that the later stages of a developing process must really *be* the same as the earlier, although thinly disguised on the surface ; or, conversely, that the end must be present, although concealed, in the beginning. The theory of inference and prediction, again, is profoundly affected.   Certainly, when we *know* the laws of an emergent series we can draw inferences concerning it in the ordinary way.   The grub, we know, will become a fly, the tadpole a frog, the pilidium a nemertine.   It does not follow, however, that before we have this knowledge of emergent process it would ever be possible to infer what the new stages would be or how they would act.   The new patterns and potencies, although they are begotten of the old, are different patterns, and there is no sufficient reason why the old, of themselves, should supply data theoretically sufficient for determining the new.   Those who are afraid of Laplace's " calculating demon " (who was supposed to be able to infer the event at *any* time from the events during any short stretch of time) may therefore take comfort.   There is no sufficient reason for supposing that the demon would ever be able to calculate in this fashion, and to predict either a man's own development or the development of any species. On the other hand, even if the development is discontinuous at its crises, if it is " emergent," and incapable of yielding necessary inference, there is no reason, on this account, for maintaining also that it is capricious or devoid of necessity. Quite possibly the tadpole *must* become a frog, and certain portions of protoplasm, given a certain history, *must* become a Brutus or a Cæsar. There is nothing in the theory to prevent this view or strongly to support the opposite.

Neither these general arguments, then, nor the more special ones derived from our own experience, are able to prove that our self-determinations are not necessarily what they are ; and it has to be admitted that if there is complete determinism throughout the whole of Nature except in a few privileged cases, it is not unlikely that human conceit is responsible for the claim of privilege. Certainly we are apt to lay too great stress on analogies, and it is undoubtedly true that responsible self-determination, with foresight and intelligence, is something *sui generis*. It is also quite manifest that a " little dose of contingency " might permit all the difference in the world in our actions, and yet be too minute to be detected by such methods of measurement (they are not very accurate) as we are able to apply. We determine ourselves in a true and important sense, but we did not make ourselves ; and if determinism, in the end, were true of our origins, it does not seem very likely that the later products could be other than deterministic. The emergence of new patterns is one thing, their *uncaused* emergence quite another, and if there are no uncaused emergences the self would certainly seem to be determined by its origins, however distinctive its pattern and however illimitable the potencies of its new and higher destiny. If we do not believe this, what are we to believe ? That minds arise from some other source than their biological antecedents and for no reason associate themselves freely with organic bodies? That everything has a mental side which is free, although its bodily side is not, and yet that this mental freedom influences behaviour only in the case of a very few mind-body systems? These are possible suppositions, I concede, but they are not very plausible.

Indeed, if there is true and final contingency in human action, the most probable philosophy for this circumstance is a species of universal tychism. It is easy, indeed, to state this hypothesis in a form which is quite unconvincing, but it is also quite possible to improve it. Out of chaos, we are sometimes told, settled habits begin to appear. These habits tended to become extremely settled in material things, and therefore we came to expect regularities, and our expectations were confirmed by the way in which physics and certain other sciences pursued, with success, their investigations into the habits of the most settled things. This fails to convince us because tychism, in itself, is properly the denial of any causes in the ordinary sense of necessary antecedents; and if there are no causes, there is no reason why habits once begun should tend to continue, or why the habits of any part of Nature (whether they are manifest to common sense, like the seasons, or only to men of science, like electro-magnetic equations) should *cause* any expectations whatsoever in the human mind. If we suppose, however, that everything which we call a cause influences without necessitating, and merely *tends* to have a certain effect without *requiring* it, the pith of this criticism would be absorbed. Chaos, in this case, might tend to become less chaotic, and our late-born era might be as we see it to be. Our self-determination, accordingly, *may* be unnecessitated.

The existence of freedom or of its opposite is clearly a question of fact which must therefore be examined in the manner attempted in this chapter. The problem concerns psychology and the regulation of a mind-body system. It also raises those wider questions which we call philosophical; and although these wide and varied terms of reference authorize a much fuller discussion than we have been able to supply, what we have said, let us hope, is at least to the point. The moral aspects of the question, however, have their own peculiar claims, which must now be considered. A sufficient indication of their scope and character, I think, will be given if we consider, first, the objections that may be raised to determinism on moral grounds, and secondly, the moral objections to tychism.

A.—Moral Objections to Determinism.

(a) Determinism makes us the captives of the past and forbids hope for the future. It is the " dull rattling off of a chain whose links were forged many ages ago." It therefore stifles moral achievement and aspiration.

This is false. There is no conflict between determinism and improvement; the law, indeed, might quite consistently be a law of progress, and it need have no limits. In any case determinism and emergence are not opposed, and so the conclusion does not follow. It is another question, no doubt, whether there is progress or whether there is emergence, but these problems are independent of the truth or falsity of determinism.

(b) Determinism denies spontaneity and initiative; and these are of the essence of moral endeavour. It transforms us into mere puppets.

This again is false. Puppets only simulate human behaviour, and they act when strings are pulled by other beings. Self-determination is another thing, and is not at all inconsistent with determinism. Certainly determinism forbids an *uncaused* spontaneity, or an initiative which springs out of nothing, instead of evolving from the situation in which it arises. A swift and profound mutation, however, readjustments on a new pattern, or an orientation profoundly new are not at all forbidden by it, and there is no sufficient reason for supposing either that we have any experience inadequately described in this way or that morality, exerting itself to the uttermost, could properly lay claim to any other potency. The claims of a " creative " ethics, indeed, are sometimes urged, but this creation is not creation *ex nihilo*, and it does not seem to imply any further spontaneity or initiative than is permissible to a sane determinism.

(*c*) Determinism and fatalism are the same, and fatalism extinguishes the moral life.

It is not at all evident that fatalism in many of its forms does extinguish the moral life. The fatalism of soldiers at the front or of the civil population during air-raids does not seem to have done so ; and those who believe that the larger issues of their destiny are in God's keeping do not seem to be the worse on this account. It may be conceded, however, that even the best-grounded varieties of fatalism, prescribing, as they do, a lack of concern in the major issues they take to be beyond our control, have the seeds of a dangerous quietism in them. They tend to accept what might perhaps be averted ; and the extremer forms of fatalism, which assert that all our endeavours are unavailing, obviously do assert the uselessness of moral (as of all other) endeavour. This is pernicious ; but it is not a logical consequence of determinism. On the contrary, if the language of fatalism is to be employed, we may be fated very well to do great things by our own effort and to undertake responsibilities which, being what we are, we may not renounce. There is such a thing as *believing* in one's destiny. Neither the lazy acquiescence in things as we find them, nor the bitter reflection that although we are born to be busy, all our busy-ness is a vain thing, like scribbling with glass upon a diamond, is in any sense a proper consequence of the determinist theory.

The belief in one's destiny may, indeed, have all gradations, from the superstitious reverence for one's luck, or mascot, or horoscope, to the mystical yet not unreasonable sense (conveyed by so many of the greatest writers) of the immense impact of brooding, Titanic forces upon our little lives. Even the majesty of these cosmic impressions, however, seem sometimes to imply a concern of Destiny with particular human beings that belongs to the order of ideas which in an earlier age was expounded, with a different purpose, in the doctrine of a " particular Providence." Literature apart, this sense of our littleness is or is not an incubus or oppressive according to the state of our feelings ; but essentially the problem is one of perspective, proportion and flint-like truth, and in the main it is independent of disputable theories concerning psychological laws. Whatever our conclusions, however, quietism is not a logical consequence, and neither good sense nor an appreciation of the realities of our existence need be offended.

(*d*) Determinism is opposed to responsibility.

If this objection were true, it would be conclusive, but it is possible for determinists to accept responsibility in a sense which seems to meet the fundamental requirements of ethics. As we have already seen, a being is accountable in so far as he is the cause of his own actions. Anyone, for example, who in the quaint phrase of our lawyers is "guilty, but insane," is accountable for the act performed. Such accountability is plainly the same thing as self-determination. Responsibility seems to connote, in addition, a certain level and species of self-determination, in which actions are performed with some foreknowledge and intention, with a knowledge of their good and evil and a recognition of their accountability and desert. None of these things is inconsistent with determinism, for all may exist and operate, although they have necessary causes.

It is possible, indeed, and very usual for determinists to carry the war, at this point, into their opponents' camp, and to maintain roundly that without determinism there could be no responsibility. Responsibility is in part a matter of individual actions, but it affects more importantly the whole body of their effects, and especially their effects upon character and future conduct. Why should we beware of the beginnings of vice if our freedom were the paramount truth and a totally fresh beginning occurred at every moment? If tychism were true we should be no more likely to continue in vice than to take the first steps. Why should it be so great an offence to poison the mind of another if contingency were the rule and the effects of the poison could be shaken off at any moment, leaving never a trace behind? It is *because* there are causes in these matters that our responsibility is what it is.

These arguments have manifestly a certain force, and they would be conclusive if the only alternatives were complete determinism on the one hand and immitigable contingency upon the other. They fall, however, if the contention is only that we have to do with influencing factors which do not necessitate. In this case it would be harder to break bad habits than to prevent the formation of them, but it would never be impossible. If the determinists believe this to be true, they would have to add that the thing is impossible without a sufficient cause. Their opponents, on the other hand, do not need to accept the addition.

(*e*) According to determinism, our future actions could be foreknown and predicted. This we resent.

As we have already seen, these statements need not be true ; and, if they were true, they need not be peculiar to determinism. Prediction with certainty would require, not merely necessary laws, but data sufficient for the inference. Prediction with probability only would be possible according to the hypothesis of freedom ; and beings which, unlike ourselves, had direct vision of the future might have this foreknowledge in a chaotic universe. It is the moral aspects of the question, however, that interest us now.

It is plain that we do not always resent predictions of this kind. " You know me well enough to trust me " is surely a common remark, and one that implies that others may predict with confidence concerning us. Certainly we resent predictions of evil conduct or of weakness on our own part ; but this is not because they are predictions, but because they are imputations upon our moral character. This resentment of prediction, therefore, if it exists, is a curious thing ; and I would suggest that it is part of a wider phenomenon which has nothing to do with the future in particular. The fact seems to be that despite occasional impulses towards confession, we do resent any other person having an intimate knowledge of the secret places of our hearts. Many, in fact, resent the claim to this knowledge, even when the claim is Deity's.[1] A cynical interpretation of

---

[1] As an entertaining example of a " howler " on this topic I quote the following from a printed pamphlet in my possession : " The fact of the foreknowledge of God necessarily implies that such foreknowledge is not revealed to man until the events foreknown have been fulfilled. . . . Otherwise the certainty of predictive knowledge would, paradoxically, cause man to alter the sequence of events predicted."

this circumstance leaps to the eye ; but perhaps it is unjust.   There is something, at least, to be said for the pride which refuses to bring everything to the notice of our fellows, something indecent in allowing even perfectly harmless confidences to become public property. Apart from this, I doubt whether any of us do resent the intimate insight into our character which a doctor, a priest, or a wife might have. If we do, it is because we would fain be better than we are.   And I cannot think that the future has any peculiar relevance.   If it has, the reason is that we truly believe in our freedom, and are convinced, although others doubt it, that it is always possible for us to become new and better creatures if only we have another chance.   This is not a special argument in favour of freedom, but an assertion of our general belief in it.

In any case, the moral question is what we ought to resent, not what we do resent ; and there is little in the above discussion which concerns justifiable resentment.

(*f*) Determinism is opposed to self-mastery.

Not at all.   It is opposed to contingent self-mastery.

(*g*) According to determinism, the past determines the future.   Self-determination is therefore an illusion, for the self is the product of events which happened before it was born, and is therefore a dependent thing.

This is strictly inaccurate.   According to determinism, every phase in the totality of being is necessarily connected with every other.   The earlier, therefore, requires the later as much as the later requires the earlier.   More particularly, determinism implies that everything which comes into existence (for whatever reason), and remains existent, actually and necessarily does maintain itself during the term of its existence. It is no matter if our selves arise from something not ourselves, or from something not a self at all.   What ever they control and regulate during their existence they necessarily regulate and control. It is difficult to see what more could be asked. On any theory, we were born, although we did not bring about our own birth, and it would be possible for us to determine ourselves either if we were born to be free or born to develop our capacities in accordance with our opportunities.

B.—Moral Objections to Tychism.

(a) Tychism is ultimately the principle of chaos— the theory of a disorderly self in a disorderly world. Instead of trying to remove irrationalities and perplexities, it glories in them. This makes morality chaotic, too.

This is a fair objection to simple, unmodified tychism, but would not appear to hold of the modified tychism which maintains that causes incline without necessitating; and since this modified tychism is not gainsaid by the facts as we know them, it is not unfair to reply that modified tychism is really the more rational theory since it does not, like determinism, force us to accept a creed which the facts do not prove. To this, however, the determinists invariably reply that any modifications of tychism are on its own principles themselves contingent; so that the last word is always caprice and mere randomness. This, I think, is begging the question. These philosophers *assume* determinism to be the only rational theory. On the other hand, their opponents often speak in this way, and are fond of asserting that the last word at least is with indeterminism. I quote from a statement of Dr. Schiller's (with ironical meiosis, he says it " may be true ") : " It is true that nothing ever arises out of absolutely nothing. There is always something out of which it grows. But that does not explain it wholly. It does not account for the *new* in it. It is only in so far as it is still the old, or the old over again, that it is accounted for by what it grows out of. In so far as it is new, it remains unaccountable, unpredictable, uncontrolled, undetermined, free. *That* factor in it, therefore, *has* arisen out of nothing, and Novelty as such *means* Creation out of nothing ! " [1]

(*b*) Tychism denies all control, and therefore denies self-control. Self-control, however, is fundamental in moral matters.

This is false. What is denied is necessitated control of action either by the self or by something else.

(*c*) Tychism, in forbidding prediction of human behaviour, destroys the basis of the good life, or even of a tolerable existence, in all human societies.

It is well that modified tychism, at least, does permit of probable prediction, for if it did not this objection would be very serious indeed. I need not labour the point, but am content to quote a sentence from Mr. Hobhouse concerning a requirement of security : " Men can neither shape their own lives nor co-operate with one another unless they know what to expect and what is expected of them under given conditions—unless, that is, they have recognized rights and duties." [2]

(*d*) Tychism destroys the basis of all moral advance, since it denies all security and all retention of what has been gained.

Again, it is well that modified tychism does not involve this consequence and that life does not present us with the alternatives of immovable conservatism or radical contingency. On any theory we know that we cannot afford to stand still. Perpetual adaptation is our lot. On the other hand, many of our achievements have the seeds of permanence in them, and the things we have done do not simply disappear. If " contin-

[1] *Proceedings of the Aristotelean Society*, 1921–2, p. 19.
[2] *The Elements of Social Justice*, p. 16.

gency is ineluctable," as Mr. Schiller says (perhaps nodding for the moment), *our* nature has consequences, and no one denies the fact.

On the whole it must be confessed that the determinists are usually wiser than their opponents in this matter. It is one of life's illusions to hope for what we do not seriously expect, and the advocates of freedom are accustomed to point to a roseate dawn which never comes. The principle of contingency has in itself *no* tendency towards optimism. It is simply that anything in the world *may* possibly happen, and without a reason. In this there is no encouragement of any kind.

(*e*) Tychism denies moral responsibility, and puts caprice in its place. In so far as we are responsible, we are responsible for consequences. Tychism denies that there are any consequences.

This has already been discussed when we allowed the determinists to defend their position by attacking upon this issue. The usual opinion upon this matter is a modified tychism, and this seems to be consistent. We believe, on the one hand, that our intentions presuppose a knowledge of justifiable consequences, and conform to the necessary conditions of continued existence. On the other hand, we suppose that (whatever may have gone before) it is possible for us to encounter any given problem strictly *de novo*, to make a fresh start, and to choose, no doubt for a reason, but in a way that is *not* uniquely determined.

(*f*) Tychism is the nursing mother of a great illusion. From conceit and from ignorance, man regards himself, not as a part of Nature, but as superior to it, and preens himself upon his aloofness and his solitary dominion. Even death and the vicissitudes of this miserable planet do not teach him his proper station. Tychism is just the flaunting of this indurated superstition in the face

of reason and of knowledge.   True morality is based,
not on empty conceit or on the mere chance that what
is unknown may not be merciless, but upon a recognition
of the facts of Nature and a sane understanding of the
place of human nature.   Nature may be merciful to us,
and even friendly.   In any case we are parts of her, and
a moral attitude which ignores this circumstance is
simply boastful and ignorant.   What we have to do,
in Mr. Santayana's words, is : " Starting with the
immediate flux, in which all objects and impulses are
given, to describe the Life of Reason ; that is, to note
what facts and purposes seem to be primary, to show
how the conception of Nature and life gathers around
them, and to point to the ideals of thought and action
which are approached by this gradual mastering of
experience by reason." [1]

When tychism is regarded simply as a human attribute
and opposed to everything else in Nature, this criticism
is undoubtedly very weighty ; for we are earthbound,
even if our duty is not merely planetary.   As we have
seen, however, a more general tychism may be defended
and is not impossible.   Nevertheless, it may be conceded
that apart from the supposed freedom of our own
experience we should probably make no great fight for
contingency in the rest of Nature.   While modern
physics lays stress upon discontinuity in the Quantum
Theory and is prepared to accept the transmutation of
chemical elements, while modern biology is not always
the advocate of " mechanism," there are no sufficient
grounds for believing that any of the natural sciences
at the present time is prepared to relinquish its " experimental determinism," although most of them may have
renounced certain earlier conceptions of fixity.   Nevertheless, just because we are a part of Nature, and know

[1] *The Life of Reason*, vol. i, p. 32.

this part pretty well, it is legitimate, and indeed essential, for us to treat the knowledge as a piece of independent evidence. Consequently, if freedom seems an integral part of it, either for psychological or for moral reasons, this appearance would supply evidence, without any conceit on our part, for a more general variety of tychism. On the whole, therefore, this objection also is inconclusive.

Summing up, then, we conclude that both determinism and tychism have to meet formidable moral objections, and that both of them are capable of answering these objections, at least up to a point—tychism by asserting that influences may incline without necessitating, determinism by asserting, as it may consistently do, that the operative causes in moral determination may be rational and include foresight, self-regulation and admission of the authority of the good. This conclusion is what we should expect. As we have seen so very often, morality has to do with *justifying*, not with *explanatory* reasons; and the debate between tychists and determinists is directly concerned with the causal explanation of our actions. Moral arguments, therefore, move in a different region from the chosen purlieus of this debate.

In the vast majority of instances the plain man's reaction to deterministic theory is palpably absurd. He speaks as if the theory could *argue* him into a condition of servitude in which he never was placed before. If so, the theory itself would plainly be false, for it purports to give an account of what everyone always is, and a man's new-found discovery of its truth (if this were a discovery) would be no more and no less of a cause than his previous happy disbelief. Again (to proceed with these summary repetitions), the moral repugnance that is often felt towards it is quite egregiously unjust in most of its commoner aspects. If determinism, we may say, implied that *we*, once we come into being, are completely determined by something *not* ourselves, or that we have always to act puppet-wise, this repugnance might have a solid basis. As we have seen, however, there is no such implication. To be sure, *we* have causes ; for our fathers begat us, and our environment affects us. Yet on any sane determinism, as on any other theory, we are what we are, and act as a man may act, soul and spirit and mind and body. Our self-determination, therefore, may, with the fullest consistency with determinism, be held to be potentially rational and righteous. If the determination is psychical, and our spiritual constitution is such that we can distinguish good from evil and admit the authority of the good, we have within ourselves a proper cause for moral action, over which reasoning and exhortation may have control. Determinists, not unreasonably, therefore are inclined to ask what *more* a man could want.

Caused or uncaused, it is plain that certain actions, and again certain agents, are better or worse than others. Similarly, a decision, even if it has determining causes, may nevertheless be a decision to pursue what is right and good. Moreover, it may be an effective decision. In a sense, then, choice and decision are entirely consistent with determinism, for they have causes, and are operative besides. And this is the fundamental moral phenomenon.

If we maintain, however, that all our choices are themselves uniquely determined, it follows that the language by which a moral decision is usually described contains something of inexactitude ; and it is possible, at least, that this circumstance is neither accidental nor superficial. In a certain sense, indeed, it would be true that there are genuine alternatives in a man's action, even in terms of deterministic theory. This is the sense in which we should say of a physical body that it might or might not explode through internal combustion, meaning that it would explode if certain things happened inside it, and that otherwise it would not. The accuracy of such statements depends upon the fact that our knowledge of the agent is merely general and incomplete. Some things of that kind do, and some things don't. Plainly, our knowledge both of ourselves and of our fellows is, in general, far too slender and far too general to enable us to say more of a given agent than that one or other of a few alternative reactions is, humanly speaking, certain to occur; and so far as I can see, this interpretation of the meaning of possible alternatives in human conduct is amply sufficient for legal and other practice in this matter of responsibility. It is also consistent, as we have seen, with a great mass of evidence. Still, it is not the straightforward meaning of a "genuine alternative" in action, for the straightforward meaning is tychistic.

I believe this circumstance to be decisive. Tychism, of the type which inclines without necessitating, is logically possible, both as a general theory of nature and as a particular theory of human nature; and, this being so, I am myself inclined to accept it, precisely because it seems more congruent with the moral fact than any other, and because the moral fact is more stubborn than most. However carefully we phrase our determinism, it seems in the end to evade a certain portion of the moral issue. If this question were one of language only, the resources of language would doubtless be sufficient to overcome the obstacle. It seems, however, to be more than verbal, and therefore we cannot afford to leave the question open.

CHAPTER IX

A SURVEY CONCERNING IMPERATIVES

AT the cost of some repetition it seems advisable to recall our discussion from these ampler reaches to something indubitably central.

Up to the present we have attempted to explore two themes, the first of them being the analysis or anatomy of moral conceptions, the second the character of psychological fact to which these conceptions apply.

From the standpoint of moral analysis (by which I mean analysis proper, and not the palpable evasion of the moral problem set forth in spurious moral doctrines which are content with plausible accounts of the origin and growth of social customs) two principal theories contend for the mastery. These are the attempts to interpret morality in terms of value on the one hand, or of obligation upon the other. Of these, the former, by itself, seems insufficient; the latter, when justified by the former, to be the proper object of moral study.

Pure axiology (or the science of all values) cannot be the same thing as ethics. In the first place, it is far too wide. The values of truth, beauty and happiness would be included in this science, each on its own merits; and these taken *simpliciter* (or without addition and qualification) are not what we mean by morals. These values are relevant to morality only when they carry with them a certain authority for action and direct or prescribe what *ought* to come about.

I have argued that there *is* such a science of pure axiology, although its exactitude needs a debate. Its existence, however, does not show its sufficiency for moral theory, or even tend to do so ; and other interpretations which renounce this science of axiology are also insufficient.

A very ancient theory identifies value with attractiveness. What we take to be good is that which attracts us; what we mean by goodness is just the capacity for attracting.

This theory, while inadequate, may readily disguise its insufficiency. The good does attract us (at least in a measure), and anything which attracts us is probably *speciously* good, at any rate in some of its aspects. On the other hand, much that is attractive should often be relinquished for something more valuable but much less attractive ; the discipline of our preferences may have a very faint and remote attraction, and we may like what on the whole we know to be bad (although to us attractively so) and continue to dislike what (again upon the whole) is to us unattractively good. Furthermore, the objections which show the insufficiency of pure axiology for moral theory, also demonstrate the insufficiency of this merely sensitive axiology in a moral regard. The sensitive theory also is far too wide, since it includes æsthetic and other attractions for their sensitive, not for their moral sake. And mere attractions do not govern. They do not decree our duty. Duty, to be sure, need not be distasteful, but it may be ; and, when it is, we have to go through with it. Indeed, this doctrine of mere attractiveness is in the end an account of play and not an account of what should be done with our might. It is the essence of play to pursue an activity only so long as it attracts, and to stop when the amusement ceases. In short, this sweet and gentle theory is better fitted for Lotos-eaters than for men.

A third theory, which also has many supporters, successfully avoids many of the pitfalls which entrap the two former by basing itself entirely upon action and active disposition. The good, on this view, is that which we seek and struggle for, and it rests upon our impulses and instincts. In general it is attractive, since we are attracted by what we want and by what we need. Sometimes, however, we are inclined and impelled towards that which we do not like. Obligation itself, according to this theory, is simply a particular form of human forcefulness, a summons and decree of our own strength. This may be rational, for there are impulses towards thought and reflection, and in any case it is not too wide for morality. While the enjoyment of beauty, for example, is not necessarily moral, the search for it and the attempt to bring it into being are always moral pursuits. Certainly some part of the force that is in us (say, the strength of our corporeal tissues) is not usually supposed to pertain to ethics, but this, in its turn, may be a mistake. All these forces are requisite to our efficiency, and if it is usual to limit the scope of ethics to certain psychological forces and to these only, this limitation need not touch the essence of the theory.

Nevertheless, this doctrine also is insufficient. Might is not right, even if the autocrats (and Carlyle with them) tell us so. What we crave and seek and strive for need not be morally good, and the strength of our impulses bears no evident proportion to their moral worth. We ask, in a word, for authority, and are told to be content with power. This is to cheat us. While authority cannot be powerless, it is not naked strength; and obligation is not moral simply because it is tense and forceful. The theory, indeed, does not begin to

discriminate between the right and the wrong use of
our forces, and even if it were true (as, in fact, is most
disputable) that the moral course is always the strongest
in our power, this simple-minded statement of a correla-
tion would not be an ethical discussion.   In ethical
reasoning it is necessary to *show* that the best must always
be the strongest, and nothing could show this except
an argument based upon good and evil themselves.
Certainly it is astonishing how frequently this simple
necessity of the argument is ignored or forgotten.   We
are told, for example, that the greatest possible harmony
of our impulses (this being our greatest strength) is also
the moral ideal.   But what sort of harmony ?   Would
Napoleon's life have been more of a harmony if he
had had more of a conscience ?   If moral scruples
wreck our peace, is there no relevant difference between
this discord and the jangled nerves of a pleasure-seeker
who has sought his delights unwisely ?

When we turn to moral obligation we see that its
standpoint may also be misinterpreted.   When duty
is regarded simply as the residue of archaic fear, the
legacy of custom and *tabu*—in short, as a superstition
psychologically explicable—a serious mistake is made,
and doubly.   The psychology is a partial and negligent
explanation of the facts as we find them, and the type
of explanation is inadequate since it does not ask or
discuss whether our imperatives are justified, but merely
supplies them with a pedigree.   Assuming, then, that
our enquiry is critical and not historical, we are bound
to discuss the logic of this criticism, and are sometimes
presented with the theory that moral imperatives are
ultimate, and therefore forbid all further discussion.
We have no business, it is said, to ask why anyone should
be moral.   On the contrary, knowing that a man should
be moral, we have only to criticize his actions *within*

the moral field.   There should be no question of finding a reason for morality outside morality itself.

This view has been expounded in many forms, but
may be said, on the whole, to have three prime divisions.
These are, firstly, that some one or a very few supreme
commandments, like the Golden Rule, are ultimate
and self-justifying ; secondly, that a number of commandments (indeed, the ordinary moral rules) are of this
order ; thirdly, that our conscience is such as to perceive
(if we do not try to puzzle it) that particular injunctions
are mandatory for particular occasions as they arise.
This ought to be done, and there's an end on't.   It
would be logically consistent to hold all these three
opinions together, and therefore it is easy, with or without
a change of emphasis, to combine them.

On the surface it seems evident that some theory of
this type might possibly be true.   Somewhere we must
run upon the ultimate, and when we find it we have to
stop.   In the given case, however, all these theories
are shattered on a rock which is quite sufficiently charted.
The truth is that a reason *may* be given for these imperatives, and that no imperative is justified *unless* this reason
is given.   It is self-evident that anyone ought to do the
best he is able to do, and that, if any given action is not
the best he can do, then it cannot be his duty to do it.
Actions, in short, are justified if they work for the
best, and otherwise they are not justified at all.   When
we say, as we often do, that such and such a commandment is self-justifying, we should mean that it contains
its proper reason wholly within itself, and it may be
doubted whether this can ever be.   Certainly we may
trust very firmly to the authority of certain commandments ; but, morally speaking, it is always relevant to
ask whether some other mode of action might not be
better than they.   If so, no commandment justifies of

itself alone, but each must vindicate itself after criticism and comparison with other alternatives.

This general contention, if true, is sufficient. Believing it to be true, therefore, we should not labour the point any further. If confirmation were needed, however, it would be amply supplied (I think) by the arguments set forth in our second and third chapters.

Our obligations, therefore, are justified in terms of the *best*, and we have to consider the way in which this principle applies to moral agents.

Here we may say with some confidence that a being who has knowledge of good and evil is aware that good and evil pertain to his own actions, and that such a being admits his obligation to pursue the best in so far as he believes that his actions may be guided and controlled by the knowledge of it. In its turn, however, this admission of obligation on our own part seems to presuppose, firstly, that the authority of con-science depends upon the possession of a certain species of knowledge (viz. a comparative knowledge of what is better or worse, good or not so good, best and worst); secondly, that these beliefs concerning good and evil (while not infallible) are not inadequate to the requirements of our action in a given situation, in so far as moral considerations really are binding; and thirdly, that these beliefs must be capable of effective influence upon our conduct (since, if they were not, they could not guide us in the moral way.)

These assumptions are taken to be true of human nature, and therefore to be applicable psychologically, in the ordinary sense of psychology. A great part of our psychological enquiry, therefore, was concerned with a defence of the truth of them. The authority of our beliefs concerning good and evil I believe to be self-evident; and I take the serviceableness and the genuine efficacy of these beliefs to be vindicated, on the whole, by an empirical survey of human action. Certainly these beliefs vary very considerably in point of adequacy. The moral beliefs of children and of the stage of " innocence " which is sometimes alleged to precede the possibility of virtue are not very adequate, and " practical sagacity," as I have called it, has vastly different levels and directions. For the most part we attempt to convince ourselves that the most important moral duties are known to all, and moralists concentrate their attention upon these. Plainly, however, certain moral duties really do depend upon special knowledge— e.g. professional duties and the peculiar responsibilities of the most skilful members of some particular profession. More generally, since all do not have either the same capacities or the same opportunities, duty cannot be the same for all (if duty means the actions which ought to be done), and this difference is connected with the adequacy of our beliefs concerning the good or the evil we are fitted to achieve. The third point (which has to do not with the correctness of our beliefs concerning good and evil, but with their capacity for influencing our conduct) is the most hotly debated of all, and it is entirely fundamental. Knowledge is certainly not the only regulative influence in our constitution, and when it regulates, it may guide and control forces and organizations much stronger than itself. Nevertheless it may effectively guide them, and so it has power as well as mere nominal authority. It is the habit of rulers to control forces in comparison with which their own strength seems miserable weakness ; and knowledge, despite its detractors, is really most puissant.

Summing up, then, we conclude that moral obligation, as it affects human beings, has a double implication. A moral self is capable of possessing, admiring and pursuing values, but furthermore it is conscious (often self-conscious) and intentional in its use of these capacities. This double implication leads to serious and yet inevitable difficulties which must now be considered.

Plainly, there may be a very manifest and quite inescapable difference between what really is the best that some given agent can do and what that agent *takes* to be best. Certainly we may maintain with a good deal of reason that what anyone *can* do is, in the most important case, what he can do *intentionally* (on the ground that, psychologically speaking, this conscious direction of conduct is the normal and fundamental governance of human action). To this much may be added. It is to be remembered, for example, that one of the things which a moral agent usually *can* do, and *ought* to do, is to inform himself, not without adequacy, concerning his resources and opportunities. Again, since the conscious enjoyment of good things seems to be an essential ingredient in most that is to be accounted welfare, there is a strong presumption in favour of the view that our conscious experience is concerned not merely with the direction, but also with the sustenance and, indeed, with the very tissue and substance of attainable human good. Thirdly, and perhaps still more importantly, it is necessary to observe that praise and blame, exhortation, the fear of punishment, the searching of our own hearts, and such-like matters are conscious motives and employments; so that, while it is just conceivable that a greater moral improvement might be effected by other means (e.g. by sanitation and increased medical skill), it is natural that the majority of moralists should concentrate their attention upon these manifestly important questions.

Nevertheless, honest and conscientious mistakes concerning the best actions are not merely possible, but very frequent ; and therefore there is a difference between what we take to be the best use of ourselves and what really is the best. Where this exists, we commonly hold that, *although* a man is mistaken, he still *ought* to follow his honest beliefs. *He* has this obligation. To be sure we endeavour to soften the discrepancy wherever we can. There is so much uncertainty concerning human conduct, we say, that even the plainest error (to all seeming) may sometimes be truth after all, or a smaller error than the plainer " duty." We may not know all the circumstances which the agent knows. It is well for us, so far as possible, to refrain from judging our fellows, and to let them follow their own determinations. Indeed, since the only species of morality that is truly practicable or inherently sound demands, in the last instance, that each man is the final judge of his own obligations, it is necessary, if not quite accurate, to speak always as if the obligations which any man, after due consideration, takes to be his, really are his from a moral standpoint. In the end, however, when the discrepancy becomes palpable, we usually contend that a man's own conscience finally decides what the man's duty is. In short, the question is not simply whether a man is the vehicle and the instrument of excellence, but, still more importantly, whether he directs himself, and consciously, towards this end as well as he may.

When we address ourselves, however, to consider the relevance, worth and efficacy of this intentional self-direction and self-regulation, we find ourselves enmeshed in a labyrinth of problems, and the purposes of this retrospect may perhaps be best served by a freer discussion than that which has hitherto been given in the present retrospect. At this point, therefore, I propose to offer a compact and reminiscent, but still a relatively independent, treatment of some of the principal ethical problems that concern volition. We can hardly avoid the conclusion, I think, that the " will," as it is interpreted by Puritan common sense, is frequently far too much of a wizard and far too little of an authentic reality. The perplexities which invest it, however, are plainly the same as those with which *any* theory of imperatives has to reckon—that is to say, they are our perplexities ; and if, as I have argued, imperatives are truly the pivot and focus of moral theory, it is necessary, at the least, to explain the meaning of this statement as fully as is reasonable, and to defend it, if the thing is possible, not only against misconceptions, but against the serious and persistent objections that may be brought against it.

According to Sidgwick, " If, then, we ask in what phenomena Virtuous character is manifested, the obvious answer is that it is manifested in voluntary actions so far as intentional ; or, more briefly, in volitions. And many, perhaps most, moralists would give this as a complete answer." [1]

It is likely, I think, that this usual opinion is held so frequently, not because it is really thought to be sufficient, but because it is plainly perceived to be essential. The omission of this standpoint of intentional control would run counter to all our beliefs upon moral matters, since it would seem to imply that anything capable of achieving good would therefore be a moral agent. Showers and sunshine, on this view, being beneficent, would also be moral things. This we do not believe, although sometimes, by metaphor, we speak as if we did. " How these people who would

[1] *The Methods of Ethics*, 7th edition, p. 222.

moralize Nature hate Nature," Mr. Santayana tells us;
" and if they loved Nature, how sweetly and firmly
would morality take its human place there without all
this delusion and bluster." [1]   Morality has a human
place in Nature, and some of the animals may show
the rudiments of it in an infra-human way; but if we
suppose this to be possible, we must also credit these
animals with righteous intentions.

On the other hand, certain moralists express themselves very differently.   " I shall define as virtues,"
Mr. (or Mrs.) Russell says, " those mental and physical
habits which tend to produce a good community, and
as vicious those that tend to produce a bad one." [2]
This definition, to be sure, is concerned ostensibly
with " habits," but the principle of it might surely be
applied to *all* actions (whether or not they had become
habitual), and if it were applied in this way we should
reach the conclusion that all moral standards are simply
concerned with the question whether or not any given
actions, irrespective of consciousness or intention, do
or do not tend towards the welfare or improvement of
the community.   (The chief ingredients of this welfare
are stated to be happiness, friendship, enjoyment of
beauty, and love of knowledge.[3])   It is likely, again,
that the principle of " most moralists " (as described by
Sidgwick) is expressed, on the whole, without due
reflection.   " The morality of conscience," Troeltsch
tells us, " for us Europeans has its principal foundations
in the Stoic-Christian ideas " [4]—but many may think
it more Stoic than Christian.   The ideal of Christian
ethics seems to be very largely a subconscious condition
of the spirit and heart—not perhaps with the logic,

---

[1] *Soliloquies in England*, p. 232.
[2] *The Prospects of Industrial Civilization*, p. 162.
[3] *Ibid.*, p. 163.   [4] *Christian Thought*, p. 103.

emphasis and rigidity of Couéism or of Christian Science, but pretty plainly notwithstanding; and even the Greeks, it is agreed, were inclined to put a lesser reliance upon the individual mind and conscience than was done in the later European tradition. When they spoke of reason (as they did) they thought, on the whole, of *de facto* conformity with the True and the Good. The Socratic dictum itself that Virtue is Knowledge may be supposed to have meant for many Socratic interpreters rather a right and true condition of the soul than the rectitude of explicit volition. Aristotle spoke of the good man being good when asleep; and he also said that the good was that at which everything aims. If so, *our* good is only a special form of that which all Nature strives after. Again, when he says that the good life consists in the due performance of function, or that it is a disposition of the soul which is praised there seems to be no particular occasion for making very much of consciousness or intention.

Indeed, on any theory, it has to be admitted that moral excellence may be largely un-self-conscious, and that a great part of it must be held to consist of dispositions and settled qualities of the character which show themselves only intermittently in conscious intentions and volitions. The first point is illustrated by the " paradox of hedonism," and compactly expressed in the epigram that to *get* pleasure you must *for*get it. This paradox, however, is not confined to the pursuit of pleasure. In its more general aspect it is the paradox of all morality. To get virtue, too, you must forget it very often; and although you should think very hard about the rightness or excellence of what you set out to do, you should not, in general, think much of your own excellence in doing it. Sometimes, to be sure, you may. A man may ask himself, and quite rightly,

whether the doing of a certain action would or would
not cost him his self-respect.   But even this is dangerous.
The virtue which proceeds from the self is centrifugal
rather than centripetal, and the " inward " contemplation
of it (as all experience proves) may tend towards a sort
of moral Narcissism, like Eastern sages contemplating
their own navels.   Too much inwardness quite certainly
impairs " outward " efficiency, and certain good things
lose their savour when we persist in asking ourselves
whether we possess them.

Again, it is clear that a great part of what we mean
by character, disposition and habit (all of which pertain
to virtue) is not continuously willed or conscious.
While it may be too much to say, as Landor did of the
poet, that " he is not aware of all that he knows, and
seems at last to know as little about it as a silkworm
knows about the fineness of her thread," there is need
at least for drawing the distinction which Plato drew
long ago when he told us how Socrates explained to
Theætetus the image of the *columbarium*.   I quote the
passage with the briefest comment [1] :

Soc.   I should distinguish "having" from "possessing" ; for example, a man may buy and keep under
his control a garment which he does not wear ; and
then we should say, not that he has, but that he possesses
the garment.

Theæt.   It would be the correct expression.

Soc.   Well, may not a man "possess" and yet not
"have" knowledge in the sense of which I am speaking?
As you may suppose a man to have caught wild birds
—doves or any other birds—and to be keeping them
in an aviary which he has constructed at home ; we
might say of him in one sense, that he always has them
because he possesses them, might we not ?

[1] *Theætetus,* 197 (Jowett's translation).

THEÆT. Yes.

Soc. And yet, in another sense, he has none of
them ; but they are in his power, and he has got them
under his hand in an enclosure of his own, and can
take and have them whenever he likes ; he can catch
any which he likes, and let the bird go again, and he
may do so as often as he pleases.

The statement here made concerning knowledge
plainly extends to all moral experience ; and virtue, in
the language of this distinction, cannot be simply a
question of use and intention, but must also include
the wider notion which Plato calls " possession."

When the common opinion is qualified in these
necessary ways, it loses much of its indefensible abrupt-
ness, and invites no serious objections. On the one
hand it insists, and rightly, that an action is not to be
accounted moral simply because it is a constituent of
some species of welfare or because it tends in that
direction. A moral action must also be the act of an
agent capable of appreciating this justification and of
responding to it. His response must be conscious,
and perhaps should even be reflective, but the *capacity*
for consciousness and reflection is sufficient, and this
process, in the full sense at least, need not actually
occur when we act responsibly and yet from habit.
It may be held, indeed (and here I should agree), that
a certain form of consciousness, and even a faint adumbra-
tion of reflection, is present in all moral action. This
is what certain older writers (the " great " Arnauld,
for example) called *réflexion virtuelle*, and opposed to
réflexion expresse. Obviously, however, express volition
does not encompass the whole of moral action.

In short, there is no sufficient reason for departing
from the analysis given in the earlier chapters of our
enquiry, according to which imperatives consciously

accepted as such are the central theme of moral enquiry. It is probable, however, that imperatives do not exhaust the moral characteristics of righteous action, and the reasons for this must now be considered.

As we have seen, it is clear that no one can be commanded to do anything unless he can understand the command (at least, if he tries), and unless he is capable of responding to it. The fact that moral commandments are self-accepted (although they may be suggested and influenced by anything in the world) does not affect the truth of this statement; and, on the whole, it seems plain that there are moral distinctions which cannot be exhausted by these requirements.

In the first place, as we have had to notice so very frequently, the capacity for understanding the good differs in different people. Some, as we say, are more finely touched than others. Undeveloped peoples, we believe, have a feebler sensitivity in these matters than more developed ones, not merely in respect of " cultural values " (as they are sometimes called), but over the whole range of moral enterprise. Children have to *learn* about values, and before they learn cannot be supposed to have adequate moral discrimination. If moral perceptions can be improved, then, it is not plain that some of them are better than others, and is not this improvement itself moral ? If so, the moral superiority of certain ethical perceptions affects the worth of the imperatives, since the nature of the imperative must be consciously perceived. Again, of two honest men, one of whom is mistaken and the other not, although both have done their best to understand, is it not reasonable to suppose that the one who is not mistaken is morally the better in this thing ? Certainly the prime consideration is to act according to the best of our conscience and belief, and this requirement is too high for most of us. It is not to be denied, however, that this very conscience and belief is morally finer in some than in others.

As a rude and over-simplified example, let us consider the attitude of certain Christians towards the greater pagans of more than two millennia ago. On this view, the Christian ethic is final truth, and therefore superior to any other. While true, however, it could not have been known in its depth and scope before Christ's coming, any more than the existence of Neptune, although entirely true, could have been known before there were means for discovering the planet. If so, many pre-Christian pagans might be better than many Christians (when the former are faithful to their ideals and the latter not), but the good Christians, notwithstanding, would be morally better than the good pagans. On the hypothesis, I think, the inference must be granted ; and it answers our question, very definitely, in a certain way. The principle is the same when we apply it, not to the heroes of antiquity, but to any comparison between men and women who follow, conscientiously, a different moral code.

The same verity holds, more generally, of all our capacities. " This low man with a little thing to do sees it and does it." Such scorn of the lowly is perhaps unjust, for everyone, even in a short life, may have infinite moral capacities. Yet infinities themselves differ, some being greater and some less, and the duties of mediocrity, although they be so great, are not the greatest. Here also there is room for a significant moral distinction.

Perhaps, indeed (although this is much more doubtful), something of the kind should also be said of opportunities, in so far as these are distinguished from luck and good fortune. To be sure, the good things which simply fall to us are not morally good, but our opportunities—anything which we may use, including the making of further opportunities through our use of it—do not seem to be morally irrelevant. Certainly, we may concede the probability that a great many moralists have made too much of " external goods." Length of days, health and physique, the absence of egregious ugliness or a menacing deformity, security and the means of livelihood, the good opinion of our friends (not for merit's sake, but from simple good-heartedness) are perhaps not strictly moral goods in any sense, and it may be irrelevant to consider what would happen if a man had no opportunities, since in that case he could not have any moral problems to confront him. Yet when we read, for example, of strange abnormal creatures like the " elephant man " of Sir Frederick Treves's reminiscences, what are we to say ? The " elephant man " was not unmoral or unintelligent, yet he was so incredibly repulsive to look upon that no one without practice and warning could so much as glance at him without manifest horror. Nevertheless, the man lived without rancour, and when his condition was made tolerable he was even serene. His moral achievement, therefore, was worthy of the highest praise. It is hard to deny, however, that the deprivation of so many moral opportunities was a moral loss and an ethical calamity.

In the second place, the perennial conflict between the " head " and the " heart " has certain plain implications in this matter. Indeed, if imperatives could be nothing but settled, frigid, steely determinations of the will—the monitors of conduct and not of the spirit of conduct—it would be entirely evident that they are insufficient for moral theory. As we have already seen, a great part of what we mean by virtue consists, quite precisely, of certain emotions and sentiments arising on appropriate occasions. Chastity, in the end, is purity, not simply the discipline of certain impulses and imaginings (although discipline also is needed since promiscuity and joyful freedom are insufficiently restrained by the proviso that they should not be lascivious). Love remains a sentiment wherever it is bestowed. Generosity, while it prompts to action, is fundamentally an emotion. Sweetness, serenity and compassion are moral qualities, and yet emotional through and through, and these are not merely the grace and the bloom of virtue, but part of its life. There is not even an excuse for neglecting these manifest truths.

What should be urged is something quite different. It is false, in fact, that these sentiments and emotions are wholly or mainly beyond our control, and misleading to aver without further explanation that they may not be commanded. The governance and direction of them *is* commanded, and the sentiments, as we have seen, while capable of independent growth, are necessarily allied with thought and intelligence, and in moral matters properly subordinate to the authority of the good as we see it. This direction and this control, as we have also seen, are not merely negative ; and even if the commands of this sort which we can respond to *immediately* are largely restraining if not bluntly inhibitory, a remoter and very positive commandment may be, and is, enjoined. We may not like to think so, but it is true. Suspicious of a " forced " and " unnatural " and " artificial " compliance, reluctant to admit that even the best things may be cultivated, we decline very often to see ourselves as we are, and ascribe to an inborn temperament, or to chance, or to a gracious dispensation excellences which we are able to improve and defects which it is our business at least to mitigate. Our practice, however, belies these opinions, and rightly, since the truth is with it. We do enjoin ourselves and others to hope and not to despair, to pluck up heart and not to faint, to be patient and not merely to endure, to love as well as to cherish, to pity as well as to succour. These are positive commandments addressed to the sentiments, and it is nonsense to say that they are always and necessarily useless. Like "spirit," or τὸ θυμοειδὲς in Plato's psychology, the moral sentiments in their own way may be commanded.

Nevertheless, Nature treats us very unequally in this affair. The steadfastness, generosity and compassion, which in some are as spontaneous as breathing is, must for others be always cramped and tended things. We may all improve ourselves, but not in the same degree, and the differences which remain are moral differences, impervious to any commandment. In the end, therefore, there are moral differences here, differences of better and worse in a moral regard, which an ethic of imperatives has simply to accept. While imperatives are the primary stuff of moral doctrine, they are not, in any narrow or even in any usual sense, the whole of it.

CHAPTER X

SELF AND OTHERS

THE marrow of our discussion hitherto, and particularly the crucial question of the justification of imperatives, has been restricted to the standpoint of the individual moral agent. These imperatives, we said, were self-accepted and self-imposed, and although this formula would apply to any moral agent or moral organization capable of regulating and determining itself wittingly, we have occupied ourselves, almost exclusively, with the application of it to responsible human beings—this personal self, or that other.

This was necessary, since individual human beings *are* centres of self-determination, and are capable of responding to the guidance and authority of their beliefs concerning good and evil. On the other hand, it may be maintained that the whole of this argument is, after all, very partial, since the standpoint of the individual conscience is only one of the positions from which moral theory should be envisaged. To meet this contention a further debate is needed, and I intend to divide what I have to say upon this topic into two main sections. In the present chapter I shall try to enlarge, explain and defend the course of argument hitherto pursued, with special reference to the problems which concern a man's duties towards his fellows, and the rights which his fellows should accord him. In other words, I shall try to show (as I have assumed, incidentally, so often) that the duties of a self are not selfish. In the succeeding chapter I shall discuss some of the principal aspects of the thorny but (morally speaking) unavoidable problem which has to do with collective duties, responsibilities, and values.

At the outset a certain explanation seems advisable. A man's self, I have asserted, and the selves of other people do actually exist and are known to exist. Moreover, we know in our own persons that *we* are moral subjects, and we have reason to believe that other people are so also, in the same fundamental sense. This assertion, however, may itself be challenged. According to a small but eminent party among philosophers, what we call the individual " self " or " person " is an idol and fiction and mere appearance, a half-truth and make-believe instead of authentic reality. Consequently, any theory which is based upon its existence is at least half pretence. As Dr. Inge says (dealing, no doubt, with a special problem, but voicing a general opinion which in some form is often asserted) : " Frankly, I see no other road to immortality for the consciousness which we commonly call our self than to condemn to death the false self which clamours for a promise of perpetuity. The soul may, in Biblical phrase, ' lay hold of eternal life ' by identifying itself with the unfailing springs of truth, beauty and goodness ; or it may, in the words of Plotinus, condemn itself to ' live with shadows ' Here and Yonder, now and hereafter. I think the ' consciousness of self ' has been made far too much of in modern philosophy. I am never ' conscious of myself ' without being very unhappy ; and, so far as I can analyse my feelings, that unhappy consciousness is precisely a feeling of isolation and imprisonment. Self-consciousness is in my experience only another name for acute psychalgia. I can entirely understand what the author of the *Theologia Germanica* meant when he said, 'Nothing burneth in hell but self-will.'" [1]   And again: "The stream of life, of which we are a ripple, flows on and on. We may look upon our lives as a temporary bubble in the water. But *we* are the river, not the bubble." [2]   And yet again: "We may then say with confidence that the self or soul, of which some people would like to be assured that it will live for ever, does not exist even now." [3]

The force of these arguments is diminished by the intrusion of certain misconceptions and irrelevancies into the statement of them. There is no reason why the fact of our existence shou be peculiarly allied with loneliness. On the contrary the joys of friendship are felt by individual friends Similarly, he kind of self-will which "burneth in h ll " need nc be the only species. Self-devotion is equally possible, and might be a credential to another place. And we may exist, although we are unhappy when we take note of it.

The Dean's principal contention, however, might be freed from these weaknesses. I do not believe, indeed, that the problem whether " we " are bubble or river—whether the essential *we* is not ourselves but some impersonal or super-personal Life—is really so very formidable, for it cannot be shown, I think, that, if there are these alternatives, they are mutually exclusive. On this I shall touch in the sequel, although, for the most part, indirectly. On the other hand, there are certainly problems of a less metaphysical, but not of a less serious, kind concerning the strength of our evidence for the social assumption and the usual belief

[1] " Platonism and Human Immortality," *Proceedings of the Aristotelian Society*, 1918–19, p. 277.
[2] *Ibid.*, p. 283.   [3] *Ibid.*, p. 287.

in the unity, continuity and substantial integrity of what we commonly call an individual self or person. It is easy to show that from many points of view we are wayward, disintegrable things at the mercy of a blow or of a drug, intermittent in our consciousness, non-existent, perhaps, during sleep and trances, losing every trace (in our own opinion) of our early childhood, developing constantly into something new and amazing. To resolve these perplexities (if the thing were possible) would demand, at the least, a very prolonged discussion, and this is not the place for it. We may say, however, with great confidence that the psychological and other evidence for our usual opinion is far too strong to be dismissed, and that in the main it should be accepted. As James puts it : " Whether anywhere in the room there be a mere thought, which is nobody's thought, we have no means of ascertaining, for we have no experience of its like. The only states of consciousness that we naturally deal with are found in personal consciousnesses, minds, selves, particular I's and you's. . . . Everyone will recognize this to be true, so long as the existence of *something* corresponding to the term ' personal mind ' is all that is insisted on without any particular view of its nature being implied. On these terms the personal self rather than the thought might be treated as the immediate datum in psychology. The universal conscious fact is not ' feelings and thoughts exist,' but ' I think ' and ' I feel.' " [1] Evidence of this sort is far too strong to be overborne. I, who think now, am the same person who remembers how he began to ponder these things. If I show signs of being educated, it is *I* who was trained. If I come to a conclusion for certain reasons, *I* must hold the reasons together in my mind in order to be able to infer from them. If I am

[1] *Principles of Psychology*, vol. i, p. 226.

disappointed at my indifferent success, *I* must have hoped for better things. Theories of the self are another matter, but the fact of personal existence should not be in dispute. We may argue, indeed, that we do not fully understand the fact, that it is a problem and an enigma ; and the like. But we should not aver that we do not know it at all, or (by an odd relinquishment) maintain that we believe it to be make-believe.

While these things have to be said, however, it is also most necessary to beware of accepting them uncritically and too easily. Both the fact of personal selfhood and its extreme relevance to ethical enquiry are matters that deserve careful discussion ; and no one has any business to assume them glibly and unthinkingly, as if the consideration and interpretation of them were topics fit for Bedlam and for no other place. A sufficient reason for this caution (if there were not a hundred other reasons) would be established by the truly appalling levity with which certain authors are accustomed to pass from the inescapable and highly significant fact of selfhood, in this our world and in society as we find it, to the assertion of sounding mockeries that have little except a specious dogmatism to recommend them. Slovenly nonsense here masquerades in the guise of principle and of profundity ; and even among writers of deserved repute the weakest and flimsiest assertions of this variety are allowed, not infrequently, to accept the accolade that ought to be reserved for robust and effective verities. When it is said, for example (as, in fact, it *is* said all too frequently), that individual selves, simply because they are " unique," or (by a variant) " uniquely creative," are manifestly the fundamental units for the sake of which all association, community or sovereignty exist, we are given an impossibly empty reason for what may, after all, be a true and important conclusion. None of us, I suppose, would wish to deny a place in the sun or any other modest perquisite to the Fattest Girl in the World or to General Tom Thumb, but it is nonsense to assert that the mere singularity or even the literal uniqueness of the midget, or, again, the unique abnormality of the maiden's pituitary body, affords anything like a metaphysical, or even a sensible, reason for anything at all; and if it is creativeness that is in question (whatever creativeness may mean, and passing the point that societies may be both singular and creative if, in fact, they have an over-individual efficacy), the moral question is surely whether this creativeness is good or bad, and not whether it is singular.

In short, the truth of these conclusions (if, indeed, they *are* true) depends upon quite different reasons. They are records of the empirical circumstance (supposing it to be a circumstance) that, so far as we can see, individual selves are the most important entities in social theory, and that their " creativeness " describes their nature and potential functions. On the other hand, we have reason to complain of a writer who, like Mr. Laski, informs us on one and the same page [1] that " we have rights to safeguard our uniqueness in the vast pressure of social forces," and that " rights are imposed upon the condition that in seeking to be the best self of which I am capable I seek, in virtue of the common end I share with others, their well-being in my own," and leaves us to make what we can of it. Again, the following statement of M. Duguit's, which I translate freely, seems even more indefensible as it stands, and is promptly contradicted by M. Duguit himself, although he gives no sign of appreciating the contradiction.

---

[1] *A Grammar of Politics*, p. 94.

" The individual man," he says, " is by himself a value, a force, a reality, existing in himself and for himself, *anterior* to society, and *independent* of it. Just because he is a man he has a predominating dignity . . . and in consequence his personality imposes itself as such upon every society politically organized. Individual autonomy may be contrasted with national sovereignty, and in case of conflict it is the sovereignty of the nation that ought to give way. Individual autonomy is anterior and superior to national sovereignty and limits it. Political power, even, has no other *raison d'être* than to protect this autonomy. It may limit the liberty of each, but only in so far as this is necessary for protecting the liberty of all." [1]

Granting, however, that we *are* selves, it is plain that there may be problems concerning the moral relation of *each* to others ; and we know, in fact, that such problems have been raised concerning selfishness, self-love, self-interest and self-sacrifice.

Each self, it is clear, is in a certain sense in an egocentric predicament. It is *our* agency that is in question ; and this, being self-directed, may be said to proceed from an inner spring. On the other hand, it does not at all follow that the actions of each man are necessarily directed towards himself. On the contrary, in so far as the action is an adjustment to its environment, spiritual or physical, it is unlikely that it should, in this way, be completely reflected back upon itself.

Putting the matter otherwise, we may speak of the " inward " and " outward " direction, and the " inward " and " outward " effects of any agency, and include under " outward " the direction of action towards others, or its effect upon them. In this language, it is entirely evident that an action which proceeds from

[1] *Souveraineté et liberté*, pp. 8–9. [Italics mine.]

within need not terminate upon itself. On the contrary, *every* action is both inward and outward. An action must have inward effects, since by the mere doing of it we affect the subsequent course of our own biography. We may not mean to do so, but we do ; and if we prevent any further biography by putting an end to ourselves, this plainly makes the greatest possible inward difference. Similarly, every action has outward effects, at least indirectly. Although we may not intend it, the thing is so. When we devote ourselves, for example, to inward contemplation and mere self-improvement, although we might be up and doing, there are at least the outward effects of this absence and withdrawal ; there is also an outward bodily withdrawal which has its physical effect ; there may be an example to others, and the hint of a principle which, if followed out, would people the world with monasteries. Some such effects therefore must actually occur.

In our intentions, indeed, we may neglect much that in reality is bound to happen. This, however, cuts both ways. We may neglect every consideration save what we take to be our own advantage, and so act in utter selfishness. We may also, however, think of nothing but the benefit we hope to bestow upon some other person, or the good, not our own, whose coming we hope to facilitate. Psychologically both courses are possible, and it is a common observation that a great part of our action is at least un-self-conscious.

More generally, there is no sufficient reason why an action performed *by* a self, and even pursuant to the purposes *of* a self, should be performed *for the sake of* that self, either in part or altogether. On the contrary, a great many of our actions are in this sense unselfish. In doing them, our attention may be entirely devoted towards what we are trying to effect outside our own selves. In the usual case we do not begin by " invading our secret souls," and thereafter " rush out again to the world, to see A saner multiplicity." We are concerned with this multiplicity all the time.

I suggest that this is the truth of the question, and that the principle of it needs no very minute enquiry. The point, however, has been discussed so much that courtesy seems to demand a certain concession, and so we may address ourselves to the consideration of some further arguments that are commonly adduced. What is asserted, then, is that, psychologically speaking, we are naturally, if not invincibly, selfish, and consequently that the only reasonable ethic is that which restricts itself to rights and duties which are consistent with this fundamental selfishness.

Now if this means, quite simply, that most of us are pretty selfish creatures in most of our actions, there seems to be no occasion for a serious debate upon principle, although the matter of fact may be more doubtful than many suppose. A cool and calculating self-interest, indeed, combined with a cynical refusal to consider the interest of any other person except in so far as our own turn is served by making use of their goodwill, is, we believe, comparatively rare ; and, in exaggerated instances, it may be thought to be even monstrous. The reason for this, however, may be, not that egregious selfishness is uncommon, but that coolness and calculation are. It is plain that most of us, very often at least, do not act for what, on reflection, we would admit to be our own interest, but succumb to rage or spite or even goodheartedness instead. For the most part, however, we may be selfish notwithstanding, just as children or savages, without reflecting, may nevertheless be greedy and prone to snatch at what they want for themselves alone. Against this we have to set many impulses which are unreflectively generous. The giving of gifts, even from a very slender store, is one of the most primitive impulses (as we see in little children), and the impulse to help or to pity is neither sophisticated nor rare. Very often, indeed, when we speak of selfishness we mean restriction of outlook. A man seeing things from his own point of view should take pains to enlarge it, and he need not do so. He is properly responsible for his own concerns, but he may not have imagination enough to get very far beyond his own skin. In particular, it is very hard for anyone, even taking his fill of thought, to put himself in another's place. This inconsiderateness and comparative blindness, however, are not the same thing as blatant selfishness, and may be very different indeed. To be troubled and obsessed with fear about one's wages, for example, may not be an altruistic moral attitude, but need not imply any neglect of one's dependents or fellow-workmen. To be sure, the scales may incline towards simple selfishness, but there is something ponderable on the other arm.

Invincible selfishness, then, is something very different indeed from this prevalent narrowmindedness, and the principal psychological argument which is used in support of it is as follows: In our actions, it may be agreed, we may be largely occupied with "outward" matters, but the ultimate question is *why* any agent acts as he does; and the contention of egoistic psychology is that a man acts because he wants to satisfy himself. It is *his own* satisfaction, therefore, which governs his action. Consequently his ego-centric predicament is necessarily and essentially egoistic.

This statement may mean at least two different things. In the first place, it may mean that a man acts because he expects satisfaction in the future as a result

of the course of action which, in the present, he is about
to begin. If so, it is plain that not all action is of this
kind. We expect satisfaction only when we have
learned, by hearsay or from personal experience, that
some particular action is likely to yield satisfaction. In
the beginning we try first and learn about satisfaction
afterwards. Accordingly, unless the past deeds of our
ancestors are supposed to endow us with a truly miracu-
lous prescience, it is necessary to maintain that we
frequently act adventurously without any genuine
expectations at all.

The statement thus interpreted, consequently, cannot
describe all our actions, and it does not seem to give
an impartial account of those which it might describe.
It is surely plain that we may try to regulate our actions
with respect to expectations of a future which we know
will not be ours. This happens, for instance, whenever
a man makes his will. He does not expect to participate
in the distribution of his own property, and many of us,
at least, do not expect disquietude in our graves on
account of any frustration of our present purposes.

On the other hand, what may be meant is a statement,
not about the future, but about the present. We must
be satisfied, it is alleged, concerning the course we are
about to pursue at the time when we resolve upon it.
This satisfaction, being an affair of the feelings of the
agent, must plainly be ascribed to him. It follows (we
are told) that all our action is in this sense egoistic.

If this is what is meant, it is badly expressed.
" Satisfaction " is a term appropriate to a certain degree
of fulfilment, and is misapplied when it is antedated
in this fashion. All that is declared, in reality, is that
we must be attracted or inclined towards that which we
begin to do. This contention, as we have seen, is
dubious. Action " in the line of greatest resistance,"

16

action from duty when it is opposed to inclination, is *sometimes* possible in any reasonable sense of the phrase. We may act, that is to say, for a purpose which, if it attracts us, does not, in any ordinary sense, attract us as much as the solicitation which we reject.

Let us assume, however, that we are always, in fact, drawn and inclined towards anything which we begin to do. On this assumption, it does not at all follow that we are necessarily, or even predominantly, attracted by some state of ourselves. We may be attracted, so to speak, as builders or surveyors, and not as occupiers, and attempt to contribute towards a certain state of affairs in which we do not enter at all. This happens, in the extreme case, when a man gives up his life for the sake of a cause, and it happens every day in cases that are much less extreme. Whenever, indeed, we employ ourselves for the good of others, we devote ourselves, not to ourselves, but to an achievement which is brought about, in part, by ourselves, but is our *private* contribution for a *public* end.

I conclude, then, that egoism, as a psychological theory, is *not* invincible. We have next to ask whether there are ethical reasons which constrain it, and, despite the paradox, these are sometimes urged. A man, we are told, can only justify his actions *to* himself if he sees them to be directed towards *his own* greatest good.

This seems erroneous. The truth, I suggest, is that a man should so direct his actions as to achieve the best that he may effect, and that, if this conflicts with his private good, he ought, nevertheless, to pursue it. Instances of the sort seem to abound. If a man at the cost of his own ease and pleasure gives ease and pleasure to others, and if their pleasure is greater than his loss, his action would seem to be completely justified *in point of pleasure*. There is no need for maintaining that the action is unjustified hedonically unless the man obtains a greater, if a more subtle, pleasure for himself by this action than by a more selfish course. Such conflicts, however, are not confined to pleasure, and the logic and the ethics of them seem in all cases to be the same. A statesman, for example, may know that he could be elected Prime Minister if he used his influence and called attention to his seniority, and yet he may yield to a junior whom he believes to be better fitted for the task, not from lack of ambition or from unreadiness to undertake any duty that may fall to him, but because he believes that his own withdrawal is for the good of the State. In doing so he diminishes his chances of personal fame, and much of the opportunity for signal personal service. And yet he may be justified. A small community, similarly, may sacrifice its own advantage, power and utility for the needs of an empire. As we all know, it is often asked to do so, and sometimes, perhaps, rightly.

This problem of self-sacrifice, however, is sometimes, supposed to be so very perplexing and so exceedingly intricate that a much more discriminating treatment of it is required. Let us consider it, then, in greater detail. It is clear that there is no sacrifice at all unless a real good is relinquished, and that no sacrifice is justified unless it achieves, or is a means towards achieving, some better thing. The first of these conditions, the relinquishment of a real good, very commonly occurs, but it need not involve self-sacrifice. Even a man who puts his money to usury relinquishes for a stated time and for a sufficient consideration many of the uses to which this money could be immediately put. And yet he hopes to gain. In the same way, a professional man who resigns from a position that suits him in one place in order to occupy a better position in another place forgoes an authentic good.   He abandons the amenities, and much of the honour and the friendship he has built up for himself in his first position, hoping for greater things in the other.   Such ambition, however, although it does forgo a good, is obviously not a sacrifice in its intention.   There would be self-sacrifice, however, and the sacrifice would be morally justified if a man chose a lesser good for himself in order that other people might enjoy a greater, and I have argued that such cases frequently arise, although we may hope that there is no antipathy, in general, between a man's own good and that of his fellows.

It may be maintained, however, that this analysis is superficial, on the ground that when a man forgoes an authentic good of his own for the sake of other people, he must nevertheless, by this very action, do what is morally right, and therefore attain what is morally best so far as he may.   If, then (as is hard to deny), his own moral excellence is his own greatest good, he *must* make the best of himself by doing the best.   Even the voluntary submission, for conscience' sake, to a martyr's death without hope of immortal reward or existence, might be held to conform to this doctrine, for it might be argued that the making, through poltroonery, of some great refusal, always poisons the springs of subsequent existence, and therefore that it is better for a man not to live at such a price, even if he strives ever afterwards to make amends, by good will and good works, for the cowardice of his surrender.

Obviously, this argument is mistaken, if it is based, as sometimes it seems to be, upon the satisfaction or self-appraising excellence of a good conscience.   In certain men, it is true, the memory and belief that they have sullied themselves, even if others do not know it, by some disgraceful surrender, is an abiding and an intolerable wretchedness. In most, however, it is not. The penalties that are felt are visited upon others more commonly than upon ourselves. The sinner himself either forgets or persuades himself that his lapse was not a lapse at all. Moreover, many who have acted as they thought to be right are accustomed to grumble, afterwards, at the hardness of their fate. They are misunderstood; they are passed over; their fellows do not respect them. And yet, if the truth were only known, they have endeavoured to act for righteousness' sake. For this reason they sometimes suppose that a Righteous Controller of the universe will somehow compensate them (as if a real injustice could subsequently be annulled by a gratuity, and virtue were a mockery unless it were repaid not in its own coin, but in some other).

Accordingly, it is not the appearance of righteousness —righteousness appraising and congratulating itself— that should be intended by arguments of this order. Indeed, it may be doubted whether this should ever be sought. To look for a gratified conscience may be the destruction of conscientious action. If, on the other hand, it is the reality of a good conscience that is meant (whatever we may think about it), the argument would seem to be sound. If we *are* what is best by honestly seeking the best, there seems no room for maintaining that the sacrifice of *this* excellence can ever be demanded of us. Certainly there is a difficulty concerning a man's moral good at one time, and this good during the whole of his life. It seems possible, at least, that a man should think it his duty to pursue a course which is likely, at a later date, to involve his own moral degradation. To imperil one's health for a good cause with the strong probability of a subsequent breakdown; to submit to obloquy and social ostracism despite the probability that we shall succumb to the bitterness we shall have to suffer, would seem to be possible examples. Anyone who, like the hero of *Old Mortality*, allies himself with rebels and murderers for the good of the people, takes the risk, at least, of becoming, from circumstance and association, very much as they are, and might know in his heart that he is very unlikely to escape from contamination. According to many accounts, the certainty of losing one's artistic ideals is the chief penalty for deserting art, and (let us say) supporting a family. Yet this sacrifice may be demanded, and it *might*, at least, involve a moral loss. These difficulties, however, depend in their turn upon the difference between life as a whole, and particular actions ; and so they may be intricate rather than essentially insoluble. While it is not entirely evident, then, that a man, at any given time, himself attains the greatest excellence possible for his whole subsequent existence by endeavouring to accomplish what at the time seems to be the best for all, it seems clear that his greatest moral excellence is thereby attained at the time in question. And, as has been said, most of us would assert that a man's moral excellence is better than any other nobility he can achieve.

It may be true, therefore, that every instance in which a man, for the greater good of others, relinquishes an authentic good of his own is an instance in which the agent is bound to attain the highest excellence of his own soul. If so, morality can never demand the surrender of that which is best in any man. This reservation, however, does not affect our previous argument. It is often our duty to sacrifice real goods of our own in order that others may enjoy goods of that very kind in a greater degree.

To be brief, then, actions *may* be other-directed (that is to say, this is psychologically possible), and they

should be other-directed in so far as they affect the welfare
of others. The ethical standards which conform to
these requirements are the very substance of justice
and of equity as regards both rights and duties. The
proper application of equity, it is true, is extraordinarily
hard to discern, for human beings, and even the animals,
are exceptionally complex, their potencies equally so,
and their interlacing relationships more entangled still.
In view of this, the bare enunciation of a formal, naked
principle is obviously inadequate and may seem to be
even trifling. Yet it is essential, and there really would
be intolerable levity in attempting to discuss in a few
pages what manifestly demands a treatise. Our study,
therefore, must remain quite abstract here, and the
abstract principle should not, I think, be disputed.
This is that value should be sought wherever it may
be achieved—in ourselves, in our fellows, in the other
animals. Justice is not simple equality, for it is not true
that all are (or could be) equal, even in their opportunities;
and it is unjust to treat as equal that which is not equal.
What justice enjoins is, negatively, the absence of any
regard for *arbitrary* inequalities, and the effective removal
of these in so far as such removal is possible ; positively
the promotion of values, strictly and solely on account
of their value, wherever such promotion may occur.
In this an agent's self counts for no more than any other
self unless there is a relevant difference in point of value.

This is not to say that an agent may not properly
be concerned with his own affairs in a sense in which
he is not concerned with the affairs of any other being.
For this, on the contrary, there is an inevitable and a
sufficient reason. Except for the reservations which
have been noted in a previous part of the discussion,
a man, from the moral standpoint, is in charge of his
own life, and responsible for that in his own conduct

which he is able to control. He may also, to be sure, control the lives of others—their liberties, the conditions of their existence, and even that existence itself—as parents may, or employers, or statesmen. For the most part, however, we influence rather than control the action of others ; and we may not even influence these others very much. Ourselves we influence a great deal. In short, in so far as a man is accountable for himself he should take account of himself ; and although he is accountable for the effects of his actions (and not on himself alone), he may still, in many obvious ways, be concerned primarily with his own good and with his own future. In so far, indeed, as he has greater mastery over his own ways than over the ways of others, he has a more urgent duty concerning his own.

Again, this ultimate responsibility of a man for his own actions, while it should never impel him towards mere opinionated obstinacy, or to a simple insensitivity towards the beliefs and the wishes of others, may direct and indeed compel a course of action which is not merely distasteful or painful to his fellows, but may be a reproach to their moral convictions. This clash of moral opinions, this war of conscience within a man and with the conscience of his fellows, cannot be avoided always when conscience (as we know) is swayed by so many forces. What is more, it could not be avoided even if tradition and the more obvious forms of prejudice could be set aside, and everyone thought for himself as candidly and as clearly as he might. It may be mitigated, indeed, by the sedulous remembrance of the right and the duty of tolerance. No one should claim the right of final and profound disagreement on his own part without admitting the same right to others ; and humanity, we may fairly concede, has advanced some little way along these tolerant paths. It is quite false, however, to suppose that toleration can or should always be the last word in this important matter. Conscience does not consist simply in the holding of opinions. It also enjoins the translation of these opinions into appropriate action, and this action may have the widest social effects. To hold, for example, that troops should throw down their arms rather than use them in an industrial dispute or for the coercion of a body which proclaims itself loyal, is not simply a pious, an impious, or a private opinion, but one which affects vast social arrangements; and those who take action, on either side, in accordance with their opinions on this question, cannot avoid conflict, however anxious they may be for toleration. Life, indeed, would be an easy thing if conscience were only a matter of private beliefs, or if it affected ourselves alone.

I cannot think, indeed, of any general principle of equity which approaches in certainty, clearness, or accuracy this formal principle that value alone justifies action, and that it justifies wheresoever and in whomsoever it may be achieved. At any rate, this seems to me a truer maxim than the more celebrated one which Kant laid down, and so many have accepted from him whether they follow the sage of Königsberg in other things or do not. " So act as to treat humanity," Kant says, " whether in thine own person or in that of any other, in every case as an end withal, never as a means only." Kant's reason was that every moral person is an autonomous moral will; but even if the ground be accepted, the maxim itself seems incomplete and dubious in other ways.

It is incomplete because the principle of equity applies to everything that may have independent value, not simply to beings who are morally autonomous. The happiness of a dog, as we have seen, if it is worth considering at all for any moral reason, is worth considering for the dog's sake, not simply for some man's; and if it is right for us, in fact, to use the dog for some human purpose —as guarding the home or guiding the sheep—the dog's good is surely to be accounted a part of the total value which justifies (if it does justify) this employment of him. If the dog is a loser and his master the gainer, the man's action is justified, not because the man is a moral being and the dog not, but because the dog's loss has been made as small as may be, and because the man's purposes are more important than the dog's. This may be true, even when man is the judge, but in many ways we ought rather to be more careful than less so, of the interests of those who are not, so to say, our equals; and we admit the fact when we have to deal with the custodians of those who are weak, or helpless, or very young.

The difficulties concerning ends and means, more-over, make this Kantian *dictum* exceedingly hard to understand or to apply. The injunction *never* to treat ourselves or our fellows as mere instruments would seem to be hopelessly impracticable. When I send letters by the post, letter-sorters and engine-drivers *are* mere instruments so far as I am concerned, and similarly I may make a mere instrument of myself. Again, if the statement means only that whenever we use a human being as an instrument we should remember that he (or she) is a creature who has rights and an independent standing, the application of this principle to our practice may be very hard to interpret. It is often maintained, for example, that it is vicious and unprincipled to treat labour as a commodity, and the practice of certain employers in this affair is sometimes even contrasted unfavourably with the familiar (and perhaps too familiar) regime of master and slave. Many, however, would prefer to barter their labour as a commodity. There is nothing servile in this action in itself, and the grievance is that the bargain is forced and unequal, not that it is making a tool of oneself for stated periods and in a covenanted fashion. Finally, if the statement means, as some have supposed it to mean, that we should always regard ourselves and our fellows as ends altogether and not as means at all, it seems obviously inconsistent with any instrumental function. It is better if we are willing instruments, but instruments we must certainly be, and it may be a duty to compel the unwilling.

It is even contended by certain authors that all human beings are the chattels of a community in whose interests, if need be, any member should be plucked out and cast aside whether or not he has become an offence. Kant's moral democracy is a protest against the extremer forms of this communal solidarity, and in this very possibly he was right. It will repay us, now, to consider this intricate question.

CHAPTER XI

THE ETHICS OF COLLECTIVE ACTION

We are sometimes informed that moral values—and indeed all values—are essentially and (so to say) constitutionally social, with the consequence that a solitary person, if there were one, could have no duties at all; and that the mutual relations between different members of a society are not as they seem to be, but, on the contrary, are a forlorn and sapless effigy of the ultimate moral fact which is collective willing itself. This opinion is different from any of the views we have hitherto advanced, and opposed in its principle to some of them. It is necessary, therefore, to give reasons for dissenting from it, or else to admit our failure.

Among recent writers, Mr. Alexander, I think, has given the most weighty support to the collective theory, and there may be a certain gain in clearness if we confine ourselves to his statements.[1] "Values, then," he concludes, "or tertiary qualities of things involve relation to the collective mind, and what is true, good, or beautiful is not true, good, or beautiful except as so combined with the collective mind." The steps which lead up to this conclusion are principally that values imply the amalgamation of the object with the human appreciation of it, and that they arise out of intercourse between minds. "The rose," we are told, "is red whether we see it or not, and a man dies whether naturally or by our act. But the redness of the rose is judged true,

[1] *Space, Time and Deity*, vol. ii, pp. 240–1 and 274–7.

and the dying of the man by our act is judged a wrong only through the clashing and confirmation of these judgments." And on the moral issue we read at greater length : " Morality arises out of human affections and desires which we seek to satisfy. Some of these are self-regarding, others are natural affections for others. In willing the realization of these desires, we come into partnership with others, partly by way of co-operation and partly by way of rivalry. We sympathize or dis-sympathize, according to Adam Smith's doctrine, with certain impulses or tendencies of others. Morality represents the solution of the problem set by this state of affairs. The good wills are those which cohere with each other ; the bad ones are those which fail to fit into the system thus arrived at, and are excluded." " By the phrase ' coherence amongst wills ' we are but expressing in a more scholastic and technical manner the social character of morality." " The good is thus the system of satisfactions of persons which is effected by right willing. Mere satisfactions, such as possession of wealth, or pleasure, or, in general, happiness, or having good looks, or an even temper, are not of them-selves good in the moral sense, though they are good in the general sense of bringing pleasure. What makes them morally good is that these satisfactions of persons should be organized and made coherent within the individual, and in the relations of individuals to one another within the social group, and thus ' maximized ' or made as great as possible consistently with the conditions of social life."

This is partly argument and partly assertion. As argument we have, firstly, the contention that our ideas of values are evolved, tested and elaborated in a social atmosphere ; secondly, that our appreciations of value could not occur except as a social achievement ; thirdly, that it is the social organization of values that makes their binding, objective character; fourthly, that the social 'maximization' of satisfactions is precisely what distinguishes good in the moral sense from any more general meaning of goodness. In addition to these arguments we have the assertion that 'coherence of willing' constitutes goodness.

I shall endeavour to show that the arguments are insufficient and the assertion false.

It is true that we come to appreciate moral distinctions in a social environment, and that we are guided by example, precept, tradition, sympathy and rivalry. The same thing, however, would be true, in its principle, of the way in which we come to learn arithmetic; and numbers, surely, do not depend upon our ability to count them. The way in which we come to appreciate values, therefore, tells us nothing essential concerning their constitution.

The second argument seems highly dubious. Who *told* Mr. Alexander that no one could understand what value means except through the aid of his fellows? If there *are* values they might be known, and the materials for comparison seem to be freely offered in a man's own private disappointments, memories and expectations. The supposed impossibility, in a word, is pure speculation. Even if values and their appreciation were really the same thing, all that would be proved would be that values are mental, not that they are collectively so.

The third argument, I think, is not even plausible. That which is best ought to be done simply because it is the best. It is not made best by being socialized. Indeed, things which are socialized may nevertheless be very bad indeed.

To the fourth argument I venture to oppose the

analysis already given of the distinction between value in general and moral value (pp. 54 *sqq.*).

Finally, I submit that the assertion concerning "coherence" is false, and that it may even be wickedly so. While lack of coherence usually entails pain, inefficiency, distraction and the like (and so may contain the seeds of much that is evil), coherence or organization need not be a good at all, and may even be an added reproach. Despite such maxims as *Pecca fortiter*, it seems plain that a coherent scoundrel is the worse for the very organization of his villainy. It is possible, to be sure, that evil can never be completely organized, and that a perfect devil could never exist. Something pretty near to deviltry may exist however, and be a devilish coherence. More generally, it is obvious that coherence of a society may be achieved in various ways —by military or economic oppression, for example, as well as by good fellowship—and it is manifest that the excellence of the society is not at all proportionate to the excellence of its organization. In short, we may always ask (and should always ask) whether the organization is a good one ; and the mere fact that we ought to ask this question shows that we have no right to maintain that anything is good just because it is organized.

I think we should infer, then, that this line of argument is not at all convincing ; and although the application of this conclusion to some mythically "solitary" individual is of no great consequence under actual human conditions,[1] there are (as we shall shortly see) very noteworthy differences between the duties of each

---

[1] Even if some think otherwise, as Blake did :

> The angel who presided at my birth
> Said "Little creature formed of joy and mirth,
> Go, love without the help of anything on earth."

Sir Edmund Gosse is obviously right in calling this stubbornness and lack of logic.

of us severally (or in regard to each several neighbour) and duties which are collective. It may be just worth noting, however, that "solitary" individuals *would* have duties towards their solitary selves, irrespective of the rest of mankind. If we suppose a Robinson Crusoe stranded, without hope of deliverance, upon his desert island, it is plain that he has at least the alternative of cutting his throat or of endeavouring to make his lonely existence tolerable. That this is a moral alternative cannot, I think, be denied, and although the absence of any possible difference to any other human creature (for we may suppose, in addition, that no one will ever find out about our Crusoe) would probably affect our hero's moral action, it could not convert his problem into something entirely unmoral. Thus, if the main reason against suicide is really that it should not be *general*, and if Crusoe's action, under the circumstances, could have *no* general effect, his moral problem would be thoroughly different from that of other people— a point, by the way, which may be commended to the attention of those who hold, with Kant, that the test of a man's duty is always whether the course he pursues could be universally prescribed. The grief and pain, again, which suicide usually entails upon relatives and friends could not be relevant to Crusoe's problem under the conditions we have stated. He would have nothing to fear on that account. Yet if his solitary existence were better than none at all, it would clearly be his duty not to put an end to it ; and since this duty has to do with his future and not with his past, it is obviously irrelevant to argue, as Mr. Burns does, for example, that "even one who was a Robinson Crusoe from his birth would have had parents, and the mother-mind at least would have come into contact with his mind before birth." [1]

[1] C. Delisle Burns, *The Contact between Minds*, p. 97.

Immensely the more important point, however, is the distinction between several and collective welfare. This is sometimes obscured by the things that are said about the Common Good. When moralists assure us, as they often do, that the Common Good is the end and dictator of all our duty, we are apt to accept the statement as something axiomatic and even sacrosanct, because we read into it an effective denial of the sufficiency of egotism and a concise expression for the most inclusive point of view which seems adequate in moral affairs. The phrase, however, is radically ambiguous, since it may mean either the good which is common to each (or at least to a majority which takes heed of the minority's interests as well as of its own), or the good of the community organized as a whole. These need not be the same, and the difference between them, so far from being a mere logical subtlety, may be profoundly active in our everyday lives.

Suppose, for example, a warlike State, organized for the glory of its arms, and allow, as many assert, that this bellicose efficiency may really be a good. If so, and if military aims have precedence in time of peace as well as in time of war, it is plain that the women of the community are to be regarded essentially as the mothers of warriors ; that the boys are fighting-men *in posse* ; that civilians are the tools of the body militant, gathering its supplies, manufacturing lint and uniforms and poison-gas. The old and useless strictly exist upon sufferance, and in time of stress should be exterminated. Is there any military reason, then, under these conditions, why the private welfare of any member of the community should be considered except in so far as a diffused discontent is a source of military weakness ? In a modern regime, it is true, a vast industrial organization is necessary for any considerable military strength upon

17

a wide scale. There may be military reasons, therefore, for bowing to the demands of a Trade Union. Nevertheless a comparatively small group of rulers in a military empire may control an immense warlike organization at the price of very widespread discontent. The subject peoples of the empire may be forced to fight the battles of their masters, and millions may endure a service which they abominate for the sake of the thousands who rule. Even the rulers, moreover, may serve the war machine and not themselves or their fellow-slaves, so that, in the end, there may be no private welfare, but only Bellona's good.

With equal plainness, the material prosperity of some vast economic organization is compatible with the greatest inequalities of distribution, and even with the economic serfdom of the majority of the workers. Indeed, if economic solidarity and aggrandizement come about most easily in a system where the rich, out of their superfluity, can support enterprises whose returns are slow and not immediate (while the poor, although rich enough to keep their health, have to work because they cannot afford to wait), and where the many are forced to work, it would seem that there is a natural antithesis between labour and the possession of capital. The system, indeed, may afford a livelihood to many millions who could not exist under any other, but this may be only if the vast majority have a status of economic inferiority. It is manifest, therefore, that the economic prosperity of a community need bear no simple or direct relationship to the prosperity of its several members.

The good of the community, accordingly, need not be the same as the good of each, and the more we pursue the point the more clearly we perceive the distinction. It may be argued, indeed, that these illustrations are really exceptional, or even that the " goods " of which they speak are spurious in the end. There is little force, however, in these objections. Military ends, indeed, may never be truly good. They may be nobody's benefit, and only the pomp of a machine ; and economics may be held to be filthy as well as dismal. This, however, is false. Even if wealth itself be dross, the comfort, leisure and opportunity which it brings may be good, and very good. Our distinction, consequently, embraces something that is not an illusion, and it has a very wide range. In the opinion of many, the greatest triumphs of the human spirit in literature and in the arts occurred when the many toiled in dreary drudgery, while the few had leisure to create and to enjoy. This may not be inevitable, but it was not and is not an accident. It is the ambiguity of the Common Good appearing in another form.

Accepting the difference, therefore, we have to explore the more important of the implications that are wrapped up in it, and of the consequences to which it leads. Of the implications the most fundamental is that these social collectivities really do exist with a distinctive individuality of their own, and that value (or disvalue) really does apply to them as collective entities. On logical grounds, of course, it is entirely possible that this should be true. The properties of the part *need* not be applicable to the whole (as the dog's tail may wag, but not the dog), but they *may* be applicable (as a book may be precious, and a library too). This second possibility seems the truth concerning societies and their members. The value of a society, indeed, may be different from the value of its members, but in both cases there may truly be value, just as a book and a library may both be well arranged, although the book is arranged in a bookish fashion and the library in a

librarian's.   So here we are not concerned with the
lawyer's question whether a corporation should or
should not be treated as a legally responsible person, or
with the fantastic verbiage which proclaims it to *be* a
person.   Our statement is only that societies, in their
collectivity—the college, the regiment, England, or the
League of Nations—really are distinctive things, and,
again in their collectivity, truly may be either good
or bad.

The truth of this implication, I think, cannot be a
matter of serious dispute, although it may slip away
from our attention because of the bewildering intricacies
towards which it points.   When the good of " the "
community is set before us and proclaimed to be the
consummation of all our loyalties, it is reasonable to
ask, *What* community? And even without the aid of Mr.
Cole, or Mr. Laski, or M. Duguit we might perhaps be
able to see that this simple question is as perplexing as
it is pertinent.[1]   With their assistance we cannot avoid
admitting it. We may hold, indeed, that the rights
and the duties of some minor association, formed for
a special purpose, are properly subordinated to the
corporate organization of a wider community organized
for all the purposes of all its members living within
certain admitted geographical frontiers.   This opinion

----

[1] " Your first duties," Mazzini said—" first, at least, in importance—are, as I have told you, to Humanity.   You are *men* before
you are *citizens* or *fathers*.   But what can *each* of you, with his
isolated powers, *do* for the moral improvement, for the progress
of Humanity . . . if no means is found of multiplying your
forces and your powers of action indefinitely?   But God gave you
this means when He gave you a country, when, like a wise over-
seer of labour, who distributes the different parts of the work
according to the capacity of the workmen, He divided Humanity
into distinct groups upon the face of our globe, and thus planted
the seeds of nations."   Even in Mazzini's times this may have
seemed just a little naïve.

yields a certain plausibility to the doctrine of an omnicompetent State, and the claim of States to the supreme and unquestioned exercise of power, together with their readiness to undertake almost any function, and their reluctance to accord a legal autonomous status to associations within their borders, may increase the plausibility so long as this claim is accepted. The realities of political life, however, quickly give us pause. When Governments bargain with groups of their own members, when they are influenced, in fact, by stresses and strains arising from associations within themselves, we begin to ask whether they are the sole repositories either of power or of sovereignty, and whether they ought not to consider the interests of groups within themselves as well as "the" General Good. Does government cease when an association is allowed to coerce its own members or to interfere with the actions of competitors who do not belong to the association? If it does, where is the reality of its sovereignty to be found? If it does not, what is it at the best but *primus inter pares*?

There is a world of problems here, and others press at their heels. The age-old conflict between allegiance to the temporal or to the spiritual power has often been chosen to show (because it does show so very clearly) how dividing and ambiguous the "good of the community" has proved itself to be in practice. If the "things that are Cæsar's" were sharply sundered from the things that are God's in all our communal life, or if the incursions of the Church into temporal affairs (as to-day, perhaps, in divorce, or formerly in the activities of cardinal-princes and warrior baron-bishops) were plainly intrusion and nothing else, it would be possible to maintain that although the Christian community was Christendom itself, not the territorial perquisite of a heaven-sent monarch, there were still no problems of allegiance. The realities of our existence, however, both in mediæval times and later, denied this easy subterfuge. When the Church claims the direction of all man's life as living unto God, and the State claims the whole of a man too, a compromise may be achieved, but the sovereignties are incongruous. The principles themselves are the seed-plots of conflicts. *The* common good cannot command when, in fact, there are many and discrepant ones. And so of our present perplexities. The *principle* of seeking the community's good cannot tell us whether nationalism is a dangerous, heady superstition or a moral commandment; whether cosmopolitanism should or should not be preferred to internationalism; whether a scientific fraternity, with its far-flung observatories and seats of learning, should or should not give place to territorial units. These cross-divisions, so untidy for many of our theories, actually do describe collective social entities, and the members of each such entity owe it their loyalty, although they also belong to other societies which lay claim to their allegiance too.

This tension and turmoil of our loyalties, therefore, are very far from being things we can hope to escape from, and the incidence of them in our souls is not eradicable by any summary simplification. Certainly there are proportion and subordination in all these matters. A temporary association for a narrow purpose is only temporary and only narrow (unless, indeed, it outgrows itself), and it should retain this small proportion in our thoughts so long as it really has it. Wider ends imply firmer loyalties. Our own lives, again, and the existence of all societies, compel us to distinguish very often between what is subordinate and what is super-ordinate, between what is permitted and what controls, between delegated and governing organization. With this to help us we should not, perhaps, be for ever forlorn, and, tentatively at least, we have the right to expect a greater clearness and understanding to emerge from reflection and active experiment in these important affairs. In all these experiments, however, and in all these reflections we ought to confess that our loyalties should respond to *any* value, wherever it may be found, and that nothing but a greater value should displace it. Against this, facile monisms and undisciplined pluralisms should not be allowed to prevail.

Here, then, is one side of the question, and I propose to leave it for the moment. Another side of it (which is not, perhaps, less difficult) concerns the duties and responsibilities of these social groups. From the moral standpoint societies are to be considered not as ends only, but also as agents. We consider their good, but we also treat of their corporate action and call it right or wrong. What we mean by this may not, indeed, be easy to decipher, as is acutely evident from recent events in which the conquerors, reprobating their enemies on moral grounds, maintained (apparently) that the rulers of the vanquished should be punished for an ethical reason while the conquered people should only be compelled to make reparation for the material losses they helped to inflict. Still, we do mean something, and sometimes we praise or blame a whole people for its virtue or its vices.

Very often, it is true, when we say "the people" we mean the members. When we speak of a people, for example, as dirty, lascivious, malicious, kindly, cultured or cheerful, we commonly think of the prevalence of these qualities among its nationals; and our logic is the same when we are treating of societies which are not peoples. We may, however, mean something more, and refer when we speak, say, of an uneducated people, not simply to the prevalence of illiteracy within it, but to the absence of organized measures to prevent general illiteracy. Again, we may mean something less explicit, but still collective. We *might* call a people irreligious on the ground that it gave no official Established sanction to religious institutions, but we might mean (more vaguely, but still with a meaning) that it paid no unofficial, but public and corporate deference to these beliefs and practices. On the other hand, our meaning may be entirely and most manifestly corporate, and be consistent, on its surface at least, with the sharpest moral difference between the qualities of the people and of its individual members. Thus Albion may be thought perfidious, or Persia false, although individual Englishmen or Persians were noteworthy for their veracity. A wasteful people, similarly, may be composed of frugal folk, a group be short-sighted although its members are not, and a society be undignified or cruel in its corporate action although its members and constituent societies do not deserve the reproach.

An active group, therefore, may have different moral qualities from those of its members, yet be manifestly a moral agent; and this conclusion seems thoroughly congruent with the analysis of moral agency previously set forth in these pages. The kernel of this question is to be found in the fact of obligation, and there is obligation wherever an agent is responsible as well as imputable.[1] If a group were merely imputable—that is

[1] An action is " imputable " to any agent when that agent is the cause of it. This agent, however, owing to ignorance or to a thousand other reasons, may not be " responsible " in any significant sense. In the case of the action of individuals, for example, anyone who, without knowing it, carries the germs of an infectious disease, may be the cause of widespread pestilence without being morally responsible for the pestilence. " Typhoid

to say, only the proximate cause of its collective behaviour
—I do not think we should have the right to praise or
blame it in a moral sense. In this case it might be an
irresponsible agent, achieving good or evil indeed, but
not accountable for the same ; and this, in fact, is the
position of those who withheld their censure from the
German people for the mischief they declared them to
have caused. Collective action, however, may also be
responsible—chosen, that is to say, and self-determined
for a purpose which is admitted to be good or bad ;
and therefore it is a thing which is either morally
justifiable or subject to moral condemnation. The
sense, indeed, in which these moral obligations are
self-accepted and self-imposed *collectively* may be something more entangled than what we take to be the
more straightforward interpretation which applies to
individual human beings ; but there *is* collective control
and collective direction for an object of intended value
or disvalue, and there is moral accountability wherever
this occurs.

This identity of principle, indeed, and its necessary
application to a situation of the same order, compel a
distinction where there is relevant difference in the
agent. Just as one man's duty differs from another
man's when there is a relevant difference in the capacities
or in the opportunities of each, so collective duties differ
from personal ones when something may be attempted
collectively which could not be attempted by individual
agents. Thus, if we select a State as our instance of a
collective agent, and compare the duties of the State
with the duties of men and women (as Plato and so

Mary," when no one knew that there were disease-carriers of her
description, is an instance. Wittingly to convey disease (as to
the enemy in war), or carelessly to allow its spreading, is obviously
very different indeed. Similarly an irresponsible agent (e.g. an
idiot or young child) may very well be " imputable."

many other moralists have done), we see that these duties are only analogous, not identical, or even homologous (in the sense in which the wings of a bat are the homologues of the fore-limbs of a mouse). Our problem, in other words, is to apply *the same* principle to a different moral case, and not to conceal the difference, or to suppose, as some say unthinkingly, that *different* canons should be applied.

The truth of this is indeed apparent. The duties of a human being, living amongst his fellows, are self-directed or other-directed. The duties of a State are towards other States and towards itself. The absence of an international police, or any other reason of the same type, does not show, and does not begin to show, that States are in any degree exempt from the duty of being just and honourable towards one another, or that cruelty and greed are in any way ennobled when they are the cruelty and the greed of political communities. It is not to be supposed, however, that these other-directed actions are necessarily the same. Drake singed the king's beard by attacking Cadiz. And similarly of self-directed actions. The duties of a State towards itself are chiefly a matter of general internal self-regulation —enforcing the peace within its borders or taking organized measures for the prevention of pestilence, a pauper's old-age, or a prevalent inability to read or to write. A man's own care for the peace of his soul, (or his health or his culture), is characteristically different, because he himself is characteristically different. The same virtue, indeed, is required of both, if it applies to both, and is not like chastity, an individual affair, or like taxation, an affair of State. The principle again is the same. But the application to different agents is necessarily a different application, and the respects in which these differences may reveal themselves are almost endless. The State's control may be far more effective than any man's control over himself or over anyone else. If so, there is proportionately a moral difference. The contrast between the self-sufficiency of States and the insufficiency of human beings for their own needs may sound very oddly in our ears in these days when we are all forced to feel that we are at least Europeans, but it may have been both true and natural-sounding to an Athenian before and during the days of Pericles, or perhaps to a Florentine during the rule of Cosimo dei Medici.

Granting, then, that societies are distinctive entities, and that they have duties, responsibilities, and other moral characteristics, we have to ask where precisely these responsibilities lie, who or what has them, and in what sense, and how this department of ethical enquiry is related to our other problems. About this, as we know, very various opinions are given, most of them plausible, yet many, notwithstanding, partial, tendencious or downright confused. No attempted solution, therefore, can hope to win general assent, yet every investigator should explain and defend his opinion on the question.

All human societies, it is plain, are composed of individual human beings, and it is equally plain that the fact, formally and in its logical skeleton, may be quite negligible, since the properties of the units which compose an organized entity need not belong to the entity which is organized. This cuts both ways. It forbids us to assert that the properties we assign to a society can be nothing but a summary of the properties we assign to its members, but it also forbids us to assert, for example, that a *group of minds* must necessarily be a *group-mind*, or even that an organization of mental units must itself be a mental unity. This species of argument, we have been taught, was employed by the philosopher Hui Tzŭ, who alleged that "a bay horse and a dun cow are three, because taken separately they are two, and taken together they are one, two and one make three." [1] And its conclusion is not to be accepted, although it is precisely what is said by those who tell us that where two or three minds are gathered together, a third or fourth mind, the collective one, is always and necessarily in their midst.

Accordingly we have to appeal, not to formal argument, but to descriptive interpretation; and here we are told that the critical question is one of appropriate definition. "We may fairly define a mind," Mr. McDougall says, "as an organized system of mental or purposive forces; and in the sense so defined every highly organized human society may properly be said to possess a collective mind. For the collective actions which constitute the history of any such society are conditioned by an organization which can only be described in terms of mind, and which yet is not comprised within the mind of any individual; the society is rather constituted by the system of relations obtaining between the individual minds which are its units of composition." [2] The question here, of course, is whether this definition really is commensurate with the term defined. Our minds, we may agree for argument's sake at least, *are* organizations of mental processes, but they are also highly distinctive, and, as we think, quite peculiar organizations. To say, then, that *any* organization, or any "high degree" of organization, of thoughts and purposes, is *this* distinctive and peculiar organization, is a mere *non sequitur*, and we are justified, I think, in saying (as we did) that it is fantastic. A society may be a "mental" organization,

[1] Russell's *External World*, p. 206, quoting from Giles's *The Civilization of China*.
[2] *The Group Mind*, p. 9.

but it is not *a* mind in the sense in which the minds of its members are.[1]

If the whole of this debate be considered fine-spun and derogatively scholastic, I can only say that I do not think so. Social theories, understood or misunderstood, are at least effective. We are foolish, not practical or hard-headed, if we treat them as wordy, academic things, and allow them to be used for the vital purposes of social regulation without addressing ourselves to the question whether their intellectual substance entitles them to be used at all. Their ethical incidence, moreover, seems plainly of the first importance. As we have seen, it is not enough for moral theory to consider, quite simply, whether some particular agent brings good and evil about. If this were all, these questions *might* be academic, since States or societies do achieve good things and bad things as well as individuals, and since the difference between collective and private influence is usually pretty clear. The moral question, however, is that of the control over good and evil through the knowledge of them, the love that the good inspires, the authority it is admitted to impose. Now human beings know and love and admit the authority of the right, but it is not evident that communities can be said to do these things in any strict and proper sense ; and this is not a scholastic quibble. There is no more and no less scholasticism in it than in the question whether a king should go to the scaffold because he has confused his private interests with the nation's, whether the Cabinet binds the nation, or whether Cabinet responsibility ties the tongues of those of its ministers who dissent.

The moral question, therefore—the question of responsibility for actions which are (or, at least, might

[1] See note at end of chapter.

be) striven for, meant and intended—seems to demand
a genuine effort towards finding out where the responsibility rests ; and it is trifling with the problem merely
to say what it is, and to leave it there. This may answer
some other question, but not the one before us. When we
are told, for example, that societies, being *moral* organisms,
are peculiar because they are composed of self-conscious
beings (so that the duties of the whole may somehow
be found in the duties of the parts), we are informed
of something which may distinguish an " organism "
of this kind from a merely biological organism
(although it may be replied, quite effectively, that an
animal organism is composed of cells which are also
alive), but are left to interpret the difference for ourselves. The proper interpretation is just what we want
to know ; and since very few philosophers suppose
that a society is self-conscious precisely in the sense
in which its members are, or that it is ever self-conscious
except by the metaphor which transfers to the society
as a whole the traditions of integration and the desire
for concerted action which are felt by the members
severally, it is at least worth enquiring whether anything
is meant by collective responsibility that is other than
the responsibility, accepted by the members, of acting
in concert with their fellows and in accordance with
their sense of tradition and intention to bequeath to
posterity that which, as they suppose, has been committed
to them.

For my own part, I believe that the implications of
acting in concert answer all the legitimate questions that
concern collective responsibility, and so that there is no
occasion for demanding any other solution. Before
attempting to defend this opinion, however, I shall
endeavour to prepare the soil by explaining one of the
things I do *not* mean, and certain other things which,

although I do mean them, are insufficient, by themselves, for the burden of the argument. I do *not* mean, then, that collective action is to be resolved into the actions of " individuals taken as a mere aggregate." This criticism, reiterated with all the tedium that its authors are disposed to bestow upon the infinite, may be summed up as the obstinate foolishness which informs us that anyone who maintains that there is no action of a collective whole other than the conjoint actions of its several members is logically committed to the absurdity of treating " as a mere aggregate " that which by definition (and for common sense, too) is *not* a mere aggregate. There is no such logic except in the minds of those who reveal the condition of their intelligence by attempting to use it as a weapon. They are willing to kill with it, but it cannot strike.

Ignoring this toothless and impotent gesture, therefore, we may turn to certain social facts which, although relevant, do not show the distinctive meaning of co-operation or acting in concert. One of these is the prevalent similarity of aims and intentions within a given society. This shows only that the members of the society have similar wants and similar ideas, and although agreement in these matters may be an aid to concerted action, it may also hinder it when different people, for example, want the same thing. Again, the mere influence of the members one upon another is not the whole of what is meant. Any given human being exists in an environment. He lives and continues his life by adjustment to it. And this environment is partly social, each of us being the companion of books and people as well as of berries and roots, each of us drawing his nourishment from institutions and historical memories as well as from sunshine or protein. These influences may certainly unify, and they always make a difference, but they are not concerted action. The rain that drives a crowd to shelter does not transform it into a co-operative agency.

The essence of acting in concert, on the other hand, is that each of the agents resolves to pursue an end (which may or may not be common) by joining his forces with those of the others. What A does, is done with the object of pursuing what A and B have together agreed upon; and although the elaboration of this principle in complicated societies may involve an immense apparatus of tricks and social fictions, it is agreed on all hands that the fundamental principles of social combination must reveal themselves even upon a tiny scale. We may study it therefore in its simpler manifestations, and select the procedure of a small committee as a sufficiently instructive illustration.

The members of this body, we may suppose, meet for the purpose of reaching a decision which concerns action, and has, in consequence, certain effects which are active. Its existence, therefore, may be properly described as an instance of collective deliberation or collective willing, and it has also a collective responsibility. All these facts, however, may be adequately explained without the tiniest remainder in terms of the intentions and volitions of the members. There is not the smallest excuse for employing Hui Tzŭ's logic and adding another will to the wills which act in concert.[1] The members assemble with the purpose of reaching a decision, and nothing can happen which is not an event in the lives of the members. If they are all agreed in advance, and so have no need for discussion, the sole new fact that emerges is that each to the knowledge of the others has asserted his agreement with them, and pledged himself to the consequences. If

[1] See note at end of chapter.

any or all of them modify their views as a result of the discussion (either for the unusual reason that they discover themselves to be mistaken, or for the commoner reason that without " give and take " there is likely to be no agreement at all), we have only a further elaboration of the same essential principle. It may happen, indeed, that each of them knows that the decision is a bad one—for joint decisions very often are less intelligent and less consistent than the considered judgment of the individual members, and groups may select mediocre people to lead them principally because they cannot agree upon the strong ones. Such decisions, however, even if they are indefensible in themselves, may be expedient and even necessary in view of the urgency of obtaining a decision. When concert is wanted, all that is relevant is the best that can be obtained *in concert*, and this, being admitted by each, has the weight and the authority of all. It is needless, surely, to elaborate further. There is no difference in the principle if the committee is only nominally unanimous, although some have expressed disapproval ; or if the dissentients nevertheless agree to be bound by the general decision ; or if they modify their subsequent action because the decision has become accomplished fact. And in other cases there is not even the shadow of concerted action, but continued disagreement in its stead. Revolt, to be sure, has its own code and its own problems, but these, in their turn, show the negative side of the same situation.

From this simple instance, therefore, it would appear that the agreement and collective responsibility of the committee may be resolved without any residue into the admission by each member of his responsibilities as a party to the agreement. There is no additional collective fact, any more than a nation (as Caligula wished) has a single neck which could be severed at a single stroke. We have to ask, therefore, whether there is any cardinal difference in principle when we have to treat, not of a small and temporary group like a committee, but of a larger, more permanent, more subtly unified society. I cannot see that there is. Mere size, of course, is irrelevant. What holds of a council of five holds also of a council of five hundred, and of an Ecclesia, too. Permanent concerted action, again, is similar in kind to temporary, and requires no special analysis. A difficulty *appears* to arise, indeed, when we contrast the tenacity of groups and institutions with the fleeting participation of their members, and from this point of view it is natural to speak of great enduring social structures on the one hand, and of tiny transient mortals on the other. We have to die while England lives. The fallacy here, however, is readily shown. England at the present time is just what present English-men make of her. This is her life *now*, and England, throughout her history is what Englishmen have made of her at every time. The contrast, in a word, is only between total and temporary existence.

Of subtleties, to be sure, there is no end in these affairs. A small group taking counsel together for a special purpose and according to an agreed rule of procedure is scarcely a token even of the tangled, luxuriant, untidy conformation of many societies or of the elaborate organization of others. Representation, delegation, and implied consent; dumb acquiescence and strident unreal authority; mandates, fictions, obstructions and the countless devices of electioneering; concert unsought and impulsive, as well as planned and deliberate union—all these and a host of others belong to the standing perplexities of social organisation, and the wonder is not that they puzzle, and dishearten, and amaze us so much, but that the human species ever

approaches an approximately workable solution.   The
principle, however, of the incidence of responsibility
seems to show itself in little things as well as in big ones,
and on the same general lines.   Even in a small group
the consent that is given may be implied rather than
expressed, and the dominance of a leader may thrust a
responsibility upon the group which should chiefly be
imputed to him and not to them, although in a degree
of precedence that defies any indubitable (perhaps, even,
any rational) computation.   Even in a small group the
nominal freedom of election may, in fact, be a shadow
only, the consultation itself a pretence, and the circumstance of belonging to the group at all and acting along
with others, due to unavoidable causes whose origin
is often obscure, and whose effects are both repugnant
and overwhelming.   It is the same with those societies
into which we are born or propelled.

Accordingly there are very cogent and quite inescapable reasons why a responsibility which devolves,
in some measure, upon all who act in concert is apportioned very variously, and in a measure both confused
and superficially capricious, among the several actors.
Other things being equal, the clearer the intention, the
stricter the responsibility.   An implied consent, from
the nature of things, is more dubious than express
agreement, unless indeed it is but a lazy acquiescence
when explicit and deliberate acceptance is possible and
properly to be desired.   The greater the influence,
again, the greater the responsibility.   But who is to tell
with precision, either before the event or in the light of
after-knowledge, what the apportionment of influence
properly is?   Sometimes, indeed, we *know*; and sometimes we may arrange our affairs so that the immediate
responsibility for the conduct of the affairs of a group
falls upon a determinate person in certain determinate

respects. Even in this case, however, the question of ultimate responsibility may also be raised; and this, in the general case, must always be doubtful. The Cabinet decides upon war, but with the backing of the party, a former assent of the electorate, and the stimulus (or incubus) of a series of historical actions which have made and hardened the conditions under which wars may occur. The responsibility, it is clear, falls somewhere and upon actual people alive and dead; but Where? and Upon whom? and How much? are questions that we cannot pretend to answer in detail.

When Mr. Churchill, for example, stated in 1914 that the *Audacious* had not been lost, although many thousands in the country knew that she had been, and all must know of it within a very short time, he was not, of course, responsible, *in foro conscientiæ*, for the dubious course he adopted in Parliament. There he was only the spokesman for the Cabinet decision, and his sole responsibility was to mislead as convincingly as possible. As a member of the Cabinet, however, he had a partial responsibility for deciding upon this justifiable (or unjustifiable) deception. And so in other cases. In a sense it is Society which hangs a murderer, but the judge and the jury have a special responsibility, although they act for the community and are parties to an act which, in an entangled fashion, is collectively sanctioned. The hangman, again, properly regards himself as a mere instrument, although he acts with his own consent, and may even be a volunteer (as recently happened in the Canton of Uri).

In point of fact, therefore, the responsibility for collective action is very unequally apportioned among those who act in concert, and the degree of apportionment must often remain indeterminate. What is more, there is no single moral principle which explains, with self-luminous clarity, how it *ought* to be apportioned, but, on the contrary, a variable set of these, each having a claim to moral hegemony. To Plato it seemed that the sages should rule and bear the culminating, if not the sole, responsibility for their ruling. Since Nature is niggardly in her supply of sages, and since wisdom has to be developed through discipline and much service, he inferred that the responsible portion of the body politic should, in proportion, be very small. "For the other occupations it matters less." To others a eugenic aristocracy, instructed by a long family tradition of public service, has seemed the best; to a third party an aristocracy of push and mere business which has hustled itself to the top and is perched there like a kitten afraid to come down. As against these ideals we have the ideal of a democracy of participation. Everyone, we say (although we may whisper "every Nordic" or "every white-skinned Christian"), is fitted by Nature to take an effective, although not perhaps a prominent, part in the collective enterprise of his society. We should therefore "maximize" the opportunities of each for witting responsible co-operation, renouncing a responsibility which ends with the polling-booth or is sucked upwards into the circulating surface of *soi-disant* "representatives" who, once they are elected, transform themselves into a despotic caste. At the worst, if this is not the truth, it is a politic belief. The trouble about an aristocracy is that it has to evince its superiority continuously, and the task, for the most part, is too hard for it. If the plebs does not admit its own inferior capacity, it must be placated with the illusion at least of its power; and the illusion cannot be indefinitely sustained without something (perhaps much) that is not shadow, but substance.

These questions, however, are too large for our

present study, and so must be abandoned. In its stead, let us return to the standpoint of an earlier portion of this chapter, and consider once more how far and in what sense the Common Good should be the ethical end of every society. This earlier standpoint, to be sure, is not *toto genere* divided from the later. If the good of a community were indeed a divisible commodity to be distributed, like sugar, with a ration for each, and if the actions of those who pull together were simply means to this extrinsic end, there *would* be a great gulf between them. Our lives, however, and the existence of our societies, are rather a doing than a getting, and we have already noticed the perils of sundering means from end, except in special cases and for just reasons duly set forth. None the less, there is a difference here, at least of aspect, and a distinguishably different direction of theoretical interest. A democracy (although of another species) is at least conceivable in which the few bear all the responsibilities of collective action in order that all may enjoy the result. This might occur under the banner of socialism, or under many other banners.

Here, again, I do not see that any single *application* of ethical principle is luminously evident. The value of an organized society, as we have seen, may be very considerable without being a "Common Good" in the distributive sense. If it be maintained, indeed (as most of us, I think, would maintain upon reflection), that the most considerable at least of the values pertaining to humanity must be consciously enjoyed or achieved by individual human beings, the difficulty may be appreciably lessened ; for it would not be probable that the splendour and beauty of a social body, achieved at the price of a prevalent condition among the members very much worse than their individual condition under a drab and clumsy regime, would be worth what it costs. A certain possible discrepancy of this kind, however, would still remain ; and the final principle in the problem can only be that the greater good must always outweigh the less, wherever it may apply. This may not be very helpful, and even if the principle of the common good were held to predominate over every other principle of social excellence in case a conflict arose, we might still be very much at a loss. The principle tells us that all should combine for the good of each ; but if the goods that are possible to each differ greatly in value (on the ground, say, of ineradicable differences of capacity), the application of the principle may prove itself highly tortuous and obscure. Many of us hold, indeed, that the greater values of our living are values which are possible to all, and approximately in an equal degree ; but some deny this, and others doubt. It would be safer, perhaps, to say that the burden of proof rests with those who maintain the contrary, and that most of their contentions are suspect —safer, but perhaps false. In most of our pleadings (whatever may be true of our practice) we attribute to psychic individual existence, for its own sake, a value which is very hard to justify. This is natural, since most of us see values there, and perhaps there only ; but the logic of it is often peculiar. We are reluctant to admit that *anyone* should be sacrificed deliberately in order that others may gain, and when we are compelled to act in this fashion we do not care to think of it. On the other hand we praise, with very occasional reserve, anyone who sacrifices himself for such an end. To hold, as is not unreasonable, that communities, being prone to these sacrifices, should warn themselves of the danger n them, while men and women need no such restraint, s partially to remove the difficulty—partially, but not

entirely. There remains the question whether this
seeming inconsistency in the ordinary moral attitude
is not final. If there is a final problem here, we
cannot solve it *ambulando*, for our ambulatory morality
is not the best.

NOTE TO P. 253.

Mr. McDougall's hesitations upon this subject are
not a little instructive. While he does not appear to
hold that *any* group of human beings has a group-mind,
he maintains that certain groups have. The logic here
appears to be that a certain degree of organization of
mental constituents makes *a* mind, and that a lesser
degree does not. We are led accordingly to suppose
that armies are group-minds, and that nations very
certainly are. The plight of Oxford colleges and of
the Church militant seems more doubtful. No serious
attempt is made to show, however, that these mental
organizations, although sufficient to make a " mind,"
have the same type of organization as Mr. McDougall's
own mind or as the mind of Mr. McIver, his opponent.
Yet this, surely, is just what has to be shown. What is
more, Mr. McDougall either rejects or expresses his
doubts concerning most of the important conclusions
which theories of this type are usually supposed to entail,
with rather important social and political consequences.
Admitting the existence of " collective mental life,"
he " holds in reserve " his opinions concerning the
possibility of a collective consciousness until social
psychology shall be enormously more advanced than
it is at present.[1] In short, he does not seem to assert
more than Renan did in the motto Mr. McDougall

[1] *The Group Mind*, p. 39.

chose for his book—a common heritage from the past, and a desire on the part of the members of the group to continue and to develop this group tradition and loyalty. This enormously important truism needs no theory of a group-mind to help it in its great uses.

We may regret, indeed, that Mr. McDougall did not consider the relations of his theory towards what appear to be the essentially different conception of collectivity given, say, by Durkheim. For this was not metaphysical, but methodological and empirical. With his wide acquaintance with social fact, Mr. McDougall might have helped us very much to make up our minds whether collectivity in the sense of " a psychic individuality of a new order " is truly a serious and an illuminating principle in social theory.[1]

NOTE TO P. 256.

Miss Follett, it appears, thinks otherwise, for she says : " The object of a committee meeting is first of all to create a common idea.   I do not go to a committee meeting merely to give my own ideas.   If that were all, I might write my fellow-members a letter.   But neither do I go to learn other people's ideas.   If that were all, I might ask each to write me a letter.   I go to a committee meeting in order that all together we may create a group idea—an idea which will be better than any one of our ideas alone, moreover which will be better than all of our ideas added together.   For this group idea will not be produced by any process of addition, but by the interpenetration of us all.   This subtle psychic process by which the resulting idea shapes itself is the

[1] Cf. W. R. Dennes, *The Method and Presupposition of Group Psychology*, chap. iii. § 2.   University of California Press, 1924.

process we want to study." [1]   The reader must decide for himself whether a "collective idea" is needed in any other sense than the one I have explained, but I cannot think he will be impressed by the remarks about writing a letter.   Does the collective idea, then, require to be generated by animal proximity, and is it impervious to a written discussion?   The logic here, however, seems essentially similar to the rest that Miss Follett employs.

[1] *The New State*, p. 24.

CHAPTER XII

MORAL PHILOSOPHY

THE greater part of moral theory has to treat of ethical science, and this science, like any other, is in the first place highly specialized, and in the second place limited by the purpose of its own pursuits. Ethical science, as we have seen, is concerned with investigations into a certain entirely specific set of questions which are forced upon us whenever we attempt to justify our ways of living, and its sanest policy is to stop at the point at which it is able to evolve an intelligible answer, not to every problem that it meets with, but to the central issues with which it has to do. In these respects a science differs from philosophy, and moral science from moral philosophy. For philosophy is the attempt to approach the ultimate so far as the human understanding may, both analytically and synthetically.

From the analytical standpoint, therefore, the business of moral philosophy is to endeavour to defend the fundamental conceptions of the science against all logical criticisms (or, at least, against the most searching among them), whether or not these logical criticisms are, with their own venom, manifest gadflies, harassing the science in its daily business. Synthetically, again, moral philosophy attempts the attainment of a resolutely catholic perspective. While value and obligation may indeed be ultimates, they should at least be capable of vindicating and exhibiting their ultimacy in the panoply and panorama of all existence.

Philosophy's office, therefore, does not lack in magnificence; and it is not presumptuous simply because it is ineluctable. We *have* to ask these questions, and therefore we should be as philosophical as we can. In the end, it is true, we may have to be content with " ultimates " that are premature, and with a perspective more than half in blinkers. And yet we must continue to try. If anything, after the most strenuous effort towards resolving it *seems* to be final, we may have serious grounds for believing that it really *is* final. In so far, again, as we can correct and make proper allowances for the partial angle from which we see things, we have the right to believe in our approach towards an œcumenical perspective.

Ceteris paribus, the better developed a science is, the more adequate it is in its analytical aspect; and in this respect, at least, ethics, I think, must be accounted a highly developed science. Long ago it put on its analytical spectacles, and it has busied itself with self-criticism of its foundations since the time of the Greeks. So many of the great moralists, indeed, have also been philosophers *pur sang* that nothing else could be expected. Consequently it is a fair inference that the analytical foundations of ethics have already been pretty fully explored. In any case the philosophical enquiry could, at its best, only pursue, with still greater resolution, the type of enquiry towards which our earlier chapters were addressed; and, having expended so much space upon this, I could not easily be pardoned if I beat the coverts again. What we found in these earlier chapters was the necessity for a general axiology, or science of values, together with the understanding of the connection between this axiology and the obligation to pursue the good; and after scrutiny we concluded that we do have knowledge of values and of their relations of sub- and super-ordination, as also that there is a synthetic and governing relation between these and conduct—the relation, namely, that the best is always enjoined, not for some extrinsic reason, but because this government is, in its own right, entirely self-justifying. Here, then, is a claim to ultimacy, and if, after enquiry, it does not show any inherent tendencies towards its own dissolution, I do not think it need fear any onslaughts from without. Discussions concerning the adequacy of logic and the imbecilities of human faculty affect it, to be sure, as they affect everything else; but, as the insight of human faculty into logical truth seems, as it grows, to vindicate that truth, so here. Analysis works from the inside, and I do not propose to carry the internal analysis further than I have already done.

Assuming, then, that this portion of our work is completed—not well, perhaps, but as well as we can —we have to turn to the aspect of comprehensiveness. And first its relation to our analytical studies.

When we analyse into elements, we aim, of course, at the discovery of *different* elements, and when we investigate different provinces of reality we may easily run upon certain wholly recalcitrant differences in the end. Indeed, unless all distinctions are only *prima facie* and provisional, this conclusion is not antecedently unlikely, and is not to be routed by any *a priori* dogmatics concerning the unity of things. In a sense, we may say (especially having regard to the limitations of our point of view, and to the caprice and mere hazard that frequently arouse our interest or our attention) that it may truly be more reasonable to expect to find unanalysable singularities, and unique irreducible principles, scattered broadcast throughout the visible universe (as certain of our modern philosophers so complacently maintain) than to run upon a dead uniformity, or the mere modulation within some simple and entirely inescapable rhythm. Nevertheless, even the most pluralistically minded among us, granting that he takes the universe (or multiverse) to be an archipelago of mere singularities, cannot well avoid looking for consistency, and indeed a certain order, in the archipelago; and others expect a more continental pattern. In short, every one of the analysts has to ask comprehensive questions. Having sifted his conceptions, he also expects these conceptions to play their proper parts with consistency, and with some mutual aid, in a wide, but not in a sagging and anarchic, framework.

This necessity is perhaps peculiarly constraining in the case of the conceptions of value. In the descriptive sciences, and again in the severely mathematical ones, singular and revolutionary ideas do indeed arise; and these, like the discontinuities of the Quantum Theory, may call for a radical revision of scientific outlook in some great department. Singularities of this description, however, are at least as disturbing within these sciences as outside them, and, in general, if they can be made to work (and if they are not absurd) in any one science they may fruitfully be applied by analogy to other neighbouring disciplines. In the sciences which have to do with value, however, we appear to have an entirely new order of predicates, with a visible and quite peculiar autonomy. Indeed, the main thing about them seems often to be that they are so radically different from all other predicates. In particular, they seem to differ from the predicates that merely describe existence with an ultimate difference just to be taken or left. Yet also they apply to existence, and enjoin an altering and a refashioning of something real, or rather of a part of it.

Simply to assert an ultimate difference, therefore, may not seem to take us as far as we have to go.

When we face this problem squarely, it seems unlikely that a mere analysis or mere comparison of *conceptions* could bring us to the core of it. Certain writers, indeed, maintain that value-predicates, whatever else they may be, are at least existential predicates. This, as I gather, is what Mr. Sorley says in his *Moral Values*.[1] A possible value is a possible existent, and an actual value is an actual existent. There is no sense in regarding values in ways more abstruse or less matter-of-fact. Even if this be true, however (and I cannot stay to debate a topic which might easily become very big), it seems tolerably certain that there is no direct or simple connection between the conception of value and the facts of existence. To be sure, certain philosophers appear to assert that there is. " Value," they say, " determines existence "; and they appear to hold that this terse, quintessential formula is the supreme canon of ultimate metaphysics. It may be doubted, however, whether any such formula, either from inspection of it or in any other way in which formulæ may legitimately be thrust upon us, is so much as plausible. When we think of the things that we take to be good, and again of the things we believe to exist, we do not (do we ?) find any visible link of this variety. Things indifferent and neither worthy nor evil, like stars and grains of sand, nevertheless appear to exist. Events may be monstrous, and yet may happen, as war and pestilence so often do. In any ordinary sense, in short, value or disvalue pertains only to certain things (for the most part, indeed, to conscious entities) and not at all to other things. Accordingly, if the value that is supposed to *determine* existence means excellence or

[1] See pp. 81 *sqq.*, and again 138 *sqq.*

goodness as we mean and intend these words, *any* general formula of the type here debated is not only false but positively mischievous.   Our proper endeavour in these affairs is quite precisely to distinguish the good things that exist from the bad ones, and to separate both from that in existence which is indifferent.   If we really do believe that there is a soul of good in things evil, or a righteous purpose in things that seem utterly indifferent, we ought to vindicate our confidence, not in terms of spurious maxims that are neither tough nor plausible, but by a steeper and more hazardous road.

In a word, when we attend simply to the meaning of the conceptions, it is not inconceivable that there might be a valueless universe, and in any survey of the values that actually exist or seem likely to come after us, there appears to be so definite a precariousness in the tenure of the higher values within the universe that many of us are filled with grim foreboding.   If values, in their higher forms, are truly the exclusive possession of conscious beings, and if conscious beings are truly such as we seem to find them, the impermanence of all values is an inference as legitimate as (to many) it is perplexing.   To say, "Let there be righteousness," if the righteous perish, and if their seed may perish also in some cooling or cataclysm of their planet, has seemed to certain minds a truly deplorable commandment and forcibly futile.   And if the only righteous beings exist on the earth's crust when temperature and atmosphere permit (or there and in a few other planets, quite as fragile, in the solar or in some other system), there would seem to be a reason for the profoundest diffidence concerning the power of the good.

Conjoined with this concern over the apparent fragility of excellent things, however, there commonly goes an invincible belief that at least they are not accidental. Value and existence are different concepts. *Soit*. Valuable things *may* perish, or perhaps may exist, even now, through a sort of toleration upon Nature's part. This also may be granted. But at any rate there must be *some* connection. These different things are somehow allied in fact, and our thirst after comprehensiveness asks, for its slaking, some account of the character of this alliance. From this source, therefore, as from so many others, we are induced to make an attempt at the *placing* of values in some more general scheme of reality.

If we set out upon this enterprise, we naturally ask ourselves what plan we are to go on; and there are many for our choosing. Let us keep, then, to one at a time.

The oldest, and perhaps not the least honourable plan is the method of stringently *a priori* metaphysics. According to this belief, the whole task, promise and possibility of philosophy are comprised in the use of certain categorial (or entirely fundamental) principles. These determine everything, and there are not too many of them for the human mind to grasp very firmly. In outline, therefore, at all events, our intellects are capable of understanding the plan and pattern of all existence, and so, by means of a strenuous attention to these fundamental principles and to the manner of their deployments, we may reasonably expect to be able to show the place of values in the scheme of things, and, in principle, to solve all our perplexities.

At various epochs in human enquiry confidence has been proclaimed in these high metaphysical methods, and results have been said to be assured. Most philosophers at most times, however, have been, or have become, convinced that it is hopeless, or at least inexpedient, to expect this kind of result from general metaphysical argument. For this there are stronger reasons than diffidence and lack of faith. It is hard, in the first place, to find any grounds for reasonable assurance that the number of these categories is manageably small, and if we consider, not what might be held in the impalpable void, but what actually has been held even by the most eminent of philosophers who are loyal to this method, we find, for the most part, that the chief of their categories, like Hegel's definition of The Absolute Idea or like the late Mr. McTaggart's definition of Determining Correspondence, are in themselves so tenuous and so abstruse that there is no way of deciding, even by the closest inspection, whether these governing principles are themselves to be accepted or not. Our belief in them, accordingly (if we have it), must, for the most part, be borrowed. We accept them because, if they were true, they would justify, by the rules of logic, most that we already take for certain; and this, in its turn, is rather an empirical and inductive than a stringently metaphysical method in the "high priori" style.

Even the most metaphysical of arguments, indeed (in this sense of metaphysics), are accustomed to proceed, rather swiftly and, indeed, at a gulp, from their "categories" to the "concrete" examples of these in life and the world. This they are entitled to do, but they are also in a hurry to do it. Thus Mr. Bosanquet held that "the things which are most important in man's experience are also the things which are most certain to his thought, because importance and reality are sides of the same characteristic."[1] Mr. McTaggart, again, in his *Hegelian Cosmology* (although he argued the point much more scrupulously than most other philosophers), has to rest a great part of his case upon the fortunate

[1] *The Principle of Individuality and Value*, Preface.

circumstance that our conscious experience admirably exemplifies the nature of his governing category. " It is possible," he even says, " that we might never have thought of such a category at all if we had not had such an example of it so clearly offered us." [1] According to the same authority, again (this time in his *Hegelian Dialectic*), " The basis of the dialectic process is the nature of experience, in so far as the nature of pure thought is contained in it." [2] And again : " Since we cannot observe pure thought at all, except in experience, it is clear that it is only in experience that we can observe the change from the less to the more adequate form which thought undergoes in the dialectic process." [3] Moreover, whatever may be true of Hegel's logic (or of his consistency), it is plain that a great and not the least effective part of his many-sided philosophy was concerned with life, and man, and the State. Lesser philosophers, who believe in his methods and are less scrupulous arguers than Mr. McTaggart was, are accustomed to flit very nimbly from the rarefied essence of " pure " dialectic to something frankly psychic and preposterously mundane.

These remarks, it may be objected, are entirely *ad homines* ; and this, in a sense, may be granted. If values, however, from the standpoint of analysis are ultimate and self-vindicating, it is clear that no *other* category could possibly govern them. Again, since they are found in experience, it seems best to elicit them from the tidings that experience gives—in short, like so many of the philosophers I have mentioned, to choose a metaphysico-experiential method. Let us consider, then, what may be gained by this means.

In general, the method is employed to show that reality is either composed of spirits or, more broadly,

[1] P. 15. [2] P. 20. [3] P. 18.

that it is spiritual in its essence—that is to say, that, despite so many contrary appearances, spiritual meaning may suffuse the whole cosmos, and spiritual aspirations be the final clue to our understanding of its nature.

If so, the possibility of a metaphysical status for values clearly begins to emerge. The question may indeed be argued wrongly as by those who maintain that values, instead of being *sui generis*, are identical, conceptually and in fact, with harmony, say, or " individuality." The trouble here, as we have seen already, is that they are not the same. In a more reasonable and more general way, however, a definite connection might certainly be looked for, supposing that these principles could be proved. As was formerly said, it is nonsense to repeat an empty formula to the effect that value determines existence, but it is very good sense to say that our spirits regulate themselves in terms at least of some specious value. Values *count* in spiritual regions, and therefore if the cosmos itself is a spiritual region, values may surely be supposed to have a most cardinal office within it.

The principal difficulties in the way of all such theories are twofold. In the first place, of course, there is the difficulty of proving the fundamental proposition that all is spirit or spiritually ordered. Secondly, there is the difficulty, at least equally troublesome, of determining the relations between the spiritual beings or the spiritual orders which are said to constitute reality and the spirits that we take ourselves to know.

The latter type of difficulty (although it is minor, being consequential upon the former) is very far from being negligible. If *everything*, for example, be truly spirit, and if, as must be granted, most of the things we encounter in the world do not seem to be spirits, where precisely does our metaphysics take us ? If the action of things which seem wholly unspiritual, like the rain that falls indifferently upon the just and upon the unjust, or the stolid behaviour of fossils or granite, are spiritual notwithstanding, it is not at all apparent what " spiritual " action is. Spirit, in this case, becomes a name for everything, and so is contrasted with nothing. If a thing is to be labelled " spiritual " whatever it does, this interpretation of spiritual should have very little connection with value in any intelligible sense of that term ; for the qualities and properties that we deem to be excellent are contrasted in our minds with much that is not. Again, if the vaguer opinion be held, and all we assert is that somehow reality is spiritually determined, it is still a delicate question how this general determination is related to the determinations of any struggling soul at all similar to the souls we take ourselves to know. To suggest, even, that this our planet is, has been, or ever will be, determined by *human* spirits seems manifestly preposterous. There was a time, we believe, in which these spirits, or anything like to them, did not exist upon earth ; and even at present they are the retainers of warm fires and of green vegetables. Again, the innumerable company of our animal companions (whether vastly unlike us or, as the penguins are, bipeds and erect in stature) do not suffice to control a planet, but on any ordinary theory do their best to extract a living from one. All such theories, indeed, must look upon the universe with very different eyes from the ordinary if they are to become even remotely plausible ; and if we are to alter our opinions so radically about things that we know pretty well, is it altogether absurd to suppose that we should also have to alter our opinion about spirits and righteousness in such a fashion that our beliefs about them are stripped of *everything* that formerly seemed to be true ?

The greater difficulty, however, is the former, or the proof that all is spiritually determined.

In general, as we all know, the aim of post-Kantian metaphysics in the grand manner has been to show that Nature somehow depends upon mind, so that logical, æsthetical or moral values, being the clue to the mind's organization, are also the clue to Nature's secrets. This opinion is usually based upon a theory of knowledge, and we are told, alternatively, that *our* worlds are fabrications of our knowing faculties, or that all we may take ourselves to know is in reality a demand that we make both upon ourselves and upon that which is not ourselves. These contentions are certainly not absurd, and a distinguished company of thinkers, in all probability, will continue to uphold them in a more plausible and far more adequate form than these dry set phrases may have suggested. They are not, however, indisputable. Knowledge may be finding, not making ; or, again, that which it makes may nevertheless be a finding in the end. Furthermore, our demands are also beliefs in that which *is* ; and it is at least doubtful whether we should ever dream of demanding anything in which we could not rationally believe.

The theory of knowledge, then, does not speak with an undivided voice, and these interpretations of it, as recent philosophy has shown, are not to be mistaken for axioms. It may be better, then, to hold ourselves aloof from them ; and in any case it is not apparent where precisely they carry us in the fundamental issue with which we have now to deal. On any theory, *our* environment is not simply the handiwork of our own particular mind. On the contrary, our own minds have to conform to it ; and if we are told that at least it is the product of and conforms to *some* mind, this apparently momentous assertion is really an added entanglement. I do not say, as a *pronunciamento* of indisputable metaphysic, that each individual mind is necessarily an indiscerptible privacy wholly shut off from every other mind, but I do say that the stubborn particularity of individual minds, and the difficulty of their commingling and interpenetration in any plain or literal sense, seems, if not quite certain, to be one of the most characteristic things we can say of them. It is at least a very cogent objection, say, to Berkeley's theophany, that if *my* ideas are never literally *your* ideas, there is little of substance to be expected from the assurance that all our ideas are also, most literally, God's ; and the moral argument, to say the least, is nothing easier than this one. If you insist, let the world, somehow and in some guarded sense, be our idea. If so, this idea contains what our idea of the world expresses. It therefore contains earthquakes and tedious distances, and the conditions which, as we say, wring sweat from our brows. From the moral aspect, therefore, these tedious or terrible or onerous ideas have precisely the opposition to our moral purposes that the *things* would have ; and they have not a whit more of conformity. If these ideas are also the ideas of a great opportunity, so the things would be a great opportunity. In short, although your language seems odd, your difficulties seem to remain.

If we have the right to insist that what is central in minds as we know them is also central in the universe (and this is what the argument is all about), we have surely to show that the human mind, or the human mind " at its best," shows the essential features which, on a vaster scale, are also exhibited in its universe. While the problems and the partial successes of particular minds differ notably in scale and in range from those of the cosmos, a certain clear analogy must exist, or we have not advanced a single step. Are we justified, then, in maintaining that the universe as a whole is visibly ordered as a mind, at all analogous to the best we can conceive a human mind to be, would order it if it had the power? Is it making for justice, beauty and truth, and if so, why does it falter or even tarry? Or did it try once, and now is tired or careless, or on a holiday? Apart from revealed vision, can anyone answer these questions with even a shadow of confidence? We may think, to be sure, too much of our mere humanity when we explore these analogies; yet if we shed our humanity for the argument's sake, we may well be doubtful whether anything distinctive is left, and be totally unable to say whether a magnified version of this purified remnant could or could not control the All. These problems of evil and of the indifference of so many things (for, on these premises, they *are* problems) surely imply the most desperate hazards. There is no question of a difficulty here or there, scarcely discernible by a man of good moral character and born in the years of grace. Instead, there is an immense and dateless enigma. Again, if we quail before the idea that the universe is a private mind writ large, are we any the better if we think of it as a communal mind upon a gigantic scale, or regard the poor State as a cosmos *in petto*? The universe is not like a political organization, nor is the State morally better than private persons, although it is better in some ways and worse in others.

The metaphysico-experiential method, to be precise, owes indefinitely less than is often supposed to these premises from metaphysics, or from the theory of knowledge. It has to vindicate its assertions by a broad and (in a sense) by an empirical survey of those central features in the world and in life which, as it avers, tally with its fundamental tenets. And this review may be undertaken independently of the method ; indeed, even for the method's sake, it is better that such a review should be independent. What is needed is verification—that is to say, independent evidence. Again, apart from the method, an independent review is altogether an advantage, for it is free from some of the more onerous complications that beset the method. Unlike the method, it need not, furtively but continuously, cast its side-glances upon its conformity with prior suppositions or their stringent implications in logic.

Let us not assume, then, that mind constitutes or governs the whole of Nature, but in the first instance at least (with a greater caution, perhaps, than is altogether just) that it constitutes nothing but those mental units that we see to pertain to it, and governs nothing except what is clearly governed by these ostensibly mental entities. This yields the result that mind is manifestly to be found among human beings, and that it has a certain power and governance in *their* pursuits. Something similar, although of lesser force and complexity, also exists among many of the animals.

The most critical step in our discussion, so regarded, is the problem of the relations between Nature and the mental or spiritual aspects of human nature, and especially Nature's relation to those purposes which are aimed at the betterment of conscious living.

In modern terminology, we have to discuss the theory of Naturalism, and since Naturalism is a vague word, having several possible meanings, we must try to define it in order to know where we are.

The marrow of all Naturalism, speaking generally, is its decree that human nature, in all its aspects, is nothing but a department of Nature in general. Hence the conclusion is drawn that the principles we use in interpreting Nature are also the principles fitted to interpret human nature in all its guises, or, again, that since the "natural sciences" are the only sciences, every statement that pretends to describe anything in human nature must be either a logical consequence from these sciences, or else a lunatic folly. Such reflections, we are told, put the moralities in their proper place.

These generalities, however, need not be very much to the purpose, and may easily become a piece of verbal conjuring. Their plausibility (if indeed they are ever plausible) depends upon the apparent truism that Nature, in strictness, means all that there is. Nevertheless, we *also* contrast human with non-human nature, or the "natural" and the "spiritual" within human nature, or the "natural" with the "supernatural." It is most *un*natural, surely, to suppose that everything in human nature *must* be explicable in terms of something inhuman, and it is equally apparent that if the spiritual part of man is not identical with the "natural," and if he really has a spiritual part, then this spiritual part is something that *is*. And so of the supernatural, if there is a supernatural. In other words, if Nature means quite simply all that there is, the theory of Naturalism may not tell us more than the undeniable certainty that whatever exists, does exist; and this is not a theory. On the other hand, if Nature and Naturalism are used as contrast-terms, then there is *something* (viz. that with which they are contrasted) that they do not include. Moreover, the realm of morals is very often contrasted with Nature in this way. Thus, according to Mill, Nature, considered as a guide, is "immoral, because the course of natural phenomena being replete with everything which, when committed by human beings, is most worthy of abhorrence, anyone who endeavoured in his actions to imitate the natural course of things would be universally seen and acknowledged to be the wickedest of men." [1]

Keeping to morals, therefore, we must try to state the issue in real, not in verbal, terms. Moral commandments claim to legislate autonomously with a view to the maximization of values, and if anything in Nature seems an obstacle in the way of this maximizing of values, it may be, and in the usual opinion very frequently *is*, our duty to remove such an obstacle if we may. This is the essential predicament that sets our problem ; and so if it is held that these moral standards are themselves " natural," we have to ask very carefully what the meaning of this " naturalism " is.

For this reason, certain entirely legitimate uses of the adjective " natural " must clearly be set aside. When we speak of a " natural " process we often think of that which is usual and oppose it to that which is rare ; or, again, we oppose nature to artifice.[2] Neither of these senses, however, is appropriate here. Beautiful and excellent things are rare indeed, but their rarity is no proof that it is not good to seek them. We cannot show saints to be villains because they are not so very common. Similarly, man is a born artificer, and our lives would be intolerable without sagacious artifice in industry, trade and politics. The moral question is always whether the artifice is good or bad, and never whether it is or is not an artifice. To follow Nature, yet not to alter her, although our very being is to effect an alteration, is too shoddy a maxim to be worth the briefest glance.

[1] *Three Essays on Religion*, p. 65.
[2] I omit the absurdity which identifies " natural " with " primitive " and professes an allegiance to standards that know nothing of soap or of dentists.

Accordingly, if Naturalism is not to be an empty babbler or flatly to deny the plainest truths, it must in some way throw light upon the moral predicament whose outlines have been suggested above; and, to do it justice, this is exactly what it tries to do. Our ordinary moral theories, it suggests, are based, for the most part, upon a mischievous misapprehension of our place in the universe. In reality we are the children of our Mother Earth, not lordlings over her or beings apart. As Spinoza said, we are only members within an empire, not an *imperium in imperio*. Nature, indeed, permits the milder of our conceits, and follies, and vagaries, for she does not crush them out. It is not wise in us, however, to accept her partial permissions, and the reason why it is not wise is just that we are her children.

The sting of the argument here is the reason alleged. If all that were meant were that a certain attitude towards Nature proves also upon examination to be the sweetest and the wisest that reflection upon true values can show, the naturalistic thesis, while disputable, would at least be to the point. And very often this is all that is meant. All of us, in certain moods at least, are able to find a brooding peace in solitary wastes and spaces, in the ocean, in great naked mountains, in the wide, arid sweep of the desert, with nothing but sage and twisted cactus-trees to arrest the wanderings of the eye, in the sheen of the firmament on a cloudless evening. Nature in this sense, to be sure, is very probably sentimentalized. Its cruelties and brutalities are hidden, its ugliness blotted out; and it cannot give us truly determinate direction or any specific solution of our perplexities. Nevertheless it may yield a certain serenity of temper, together with something, at least, of reverence, humility and devotion. This is the mood in which we pray that the earth may not become man-sick, and in which, renouncing our customary arrogant pose, we treat ourselves after a creaturely fashion and not as those who have complete and irresponsible dominion over all that they touch. Or, again, we may remember Meredith's lines :

> For love we earth, then serve we all ;
> Her mystic secret then is ours :
> We fall, or view our treasures fall,
> Unclouded, as beholds her flowers
>
> Earth, from a night of frosty wreck,
> Enrobed in morning's mounting fire,
> When lowly, with a broken neck,
> The crocus lays her cheek to mire.

Our attitude in these moods, however, is wholly and entirely ethical. We find a value in Nature which, on reflection, we pronounce to be supreme, and on account of this value find the ordinary moralities thin and barbarous and utterly sour. This is a question for ethical argument of the ordinary type, and it does not demand any serious alteration of fundamental principle. It would be otherwise, however, if blatant and dogmatic naturalism had its say ; for then we should have to hold, not that " natural " values govern all the others, but that all values are empty names for the necessities of " natural " history, and that the physical sciences, when they have an hour or two to spare, may settle, as a sort of recreation and harmless amusement, all the perplexities which attend the critical examination of worth and dignity and excellence. It is this blatant and exuberant thesis that is totally opposed to all the contentions of the greater moralists. I shall try to show, therefore, that the greater moralists have been right, and that all naturalistic arguments in ethics either covertly presuppose a certain *value* in " Nature," or else fail utterly to substantiate their assertions.

Let us suppose, then, that " Nature " is intended to describe that general order of existence of which our most adequate knowledge is afforded by the " natural " sciences. If so, what has ethics to learn from these sciences ?

The answer, I suggest, is not doubtful. If these sciences, in their own proper principle, contain no mention of value, nothing concerning value can directly be extracted out of them. If, on the other hand, value is assigned to the lessons from them, it must really be assumed within them, and their argument becomes ethical only because ethics has been wrapped up in them all the time.

To clarify the point, let us consider certain questions that have to do with conscious existence, the organic and the inorganic. The consideration of these questions is necessary in any case, since the higher values are associated with consciousness, consciousness as we find it is associated with life, and life, in its turn, is manifestly beholden to its inorganic environment in many obvious ways.

The origin of life is still a highly speculative question ; but life, as we know it, seems to flourish only within a certain range of temperature, and to require nourishment from very special things. It follows, therefore, when we consider the probable history of the material universe, that, even if something life-like has always existed, life as we know it has not ; and, again, that even if something life-like is very widely distributed throughout the universe, life as we know it exists only in a very few regions.

Granting, then, that life as we know it, is a highly specialized phenomenon within (at the most) a few pockets of the stellar universe, we have clearly to ask why the whole (or the rest) of the material universe should be expected to prescribe to, or to strive after, the animate portion of things. Here the answer would seem to be that general physics, for example, might reasonably be supposed to explain those features of organisms which they share with inorganic things, and that, if and when biological events can be shown to be direct consequences of the distribution of physical and chemical facts, together with the ascertained laws of physics and of chemistry, then, although there can be no question of *prescribing* behaviour, there would be, of course, all these consequences. For the time being, however, we do not have this knowledge, and have to treat the behaviour of living things as truly distinctive and as explicable by quite special canons. It is only these special canons that have *any* ethical relevance; and since many different speculative theses may be held concerning them without any interference with the ascertained message of physics (if, indeed, in these days of revolutionary theory, we are entitled to speak of *any* ascertained message), it is clear that we have to treat biological categories as if they were *sui generis* for the purpose of any effective argument upon these questions.

When we reach biological phenomena we have not, indeed, reached the level of values, still less of right or of wrong. We have, however, the fact of teleology, and this brings us near to values. Organisms, without any confusion, may be said to be actively selective for a purpose (although they may not in any intelligible sense either know or accept the purpose); and manifestly they sustain themselves during life and reproduce their kind. Here we seem to have the beginnings, at least, of something which may approach a definite part of our moral problem. For we, on this earth, are mind-body systems, a great part of whose endeavours are necessarily bound up with the search for food and warmth and shelter, to say nothing of the urgency of sex.

The distinctive laws of biology are the laws of self-assertion, either of individuals or of groups, and these *must* have a distinctive province, for the sufficient reason that this self-assertiveness, by its definition, is the assertiveness of something distinctive setting about *its own* ends.   It is the preferring of oneself, or of one's group, to all others, and if necessary against all others, the preserving of one's own existence in spite of the rest of the world.   It is quite unreasonable, therefore, to expect the general synthesis of physics or of chemistry to show any such preferences for these tiny portions within their domain, or to speak as if matter had the special purpose of bringing organic beings into existence, or of sustaining some species of these in its struggles with the others. Yet this is the implication of those who say (with all the solemnity that becomes a cardinal principle) that we or the higher animals are the bloom and reward of physical Nature, as if this Nature were a plant that, unlike other plants, instead of using its beauty as a tool for organic ends, sets out with delight to be lovely. In any serious sense we have to suppose, on the contrary, that according to these principles certain physical conditions bring life about, permit the relative (if precarious) dominance of certain species for a certain space of time, and then in their sightless course may render the existence, to say nothing of the dominance, of this species utterly impossible.   How far the life of any species might conceivably be prolonged, what chance any species has to draw life from its roots in the earth, or how long any life is likely to endure, are from this point of view mere problems in physical science concerning which we have some of the relevant data in our possession, and a strong propensity for making guesses.

From the self-assertive biological point of view, however, it is these parochial and transient possibilities that
really matter.

A *general* Naturalism, in a word, cannot be said to
have a biological end, or to teach or to preach one.
On the contrary, biological self-assertiveness, if it cannot
use other things, must fight with them or be destroyed.
The ethics of Naturalism, however, if it is plausible at
all, must rest its case chiefly upon its biological basis.
We have to pass, therefore, to the question whether
biological principles determine ethical ones, and whether
ethics, in consequence, is ultimately but a department
of general biological theory.

The principal arguments which may be brought
forward in order to prove this contention appear to be
the following : Firstly, it is said that we are mind-bodies,
and that our bodies are biological things, subject to
biological conditions, and acting according to the laws
of biological behaviour; secondly, that everything
within us that is alleged to be non-bodily proves itself,
when it is carefully examined, to be very distinctively
carnal ; and therefore, thirdly, that bodily laws (which
are biological) ultimately determine all that we call
spiritual, and include all our spiritual values.[1]

Of these arguments, the first is undeniable, for we
are body-minds. What we have to do, however, is
to interpret the implications of this circumstance, and
principally to consider the interpretation given in the
second of these arguments.

And so we come to it. When we oppose the flesh
to the spirit, or endeavour to mortify the flesh, we
commonly speak of the flesh as mere brutal appetite,

---

[1] As Democritus said : " Nature and culture are akin ; for
culture transforms man, but in doing so it only continues the
work of Nature."

and, indeed, as something worse than brutal. For the brutes, we may suppose, go about their affairs in their own way, often with a certain dignity, whereas, when we speak of the beast in mankind, we think of behaviour stripped of everything that might dignify it in a beast, and without any of the dignities that men may achieve when they act in their own kind. Manifestly, however, a great deal in this way of speaking is most thoroughly perverted. The anchorite does not scourge himself into a pure spirit. When he is most successful (and still alive) he makes a bleeding body, which may not be better than the body he had before ; and, as history shows, he may very readily substitute one sort of carnal existence for another, not nearly so wholesome as the first. Similarly, it is unnecessary to do more than mention the notorious circumstance that it is not the simple brutishness of certain actions (that is to say, the qualities which these actions have in common with those that a brute, supposedly unintelligent and quite without ideals, would achieve) that excite what we consider an unworthy curiosity, or, when they are talked about, are deemed, by the purists, a danger to morals. Brutal murders and the ugliest sins do not so much as excite a paragraph in the yellowest and in the dirtiest Press. The murder that attracts almost universal human interest is one that has some element of surprise about it, some ingenuity required for its detection, some flavour of romance, however sickly, some singularity and resource in the mode of its accomplishment. And so of the recent alphabet of A's and X's. Instead of mere bestiality, we want our palates tickled by an intriguing human quality.

For reasons of this type, therefore, there are very strong grounds for saying that, instead of attempting to widen the difference between a spirituality that can

never be really discarnate and processes plainly bodily,
we should set ourselves to consider the sweetness and
the dignity that the flesh may assume. If we do so,
the argument runs, our difficulties in the end disappear ;
for in truth they are the products of long-standing
misdirection. This is true of the greatest things as well
as of lesser ones. To speak of love between the sexes,
for example, as if it had nothing to do with the body,
and were either invariant or only accidentally affected
when the lovers are aged, or children, or infirm, is to
use a language totally removed from the realities of
human existence. It would be matched by the absurdity
of maintaining that a mother's affection for her children
is wholly disconnected with the physical basis of mater-
nity. What we ought to do, we are informed, is
neither to abolish animality nor to forget it, but to
consider instead the heights to which animality may
rise. On an animal basis a world of duties may be
built, and fragrance may be scattered around it. Beauty
itself is not incorporeal. On the contrary, the graces
of form and of feature, the cleanliness of uninhabited
spaces, the very rhythm of a sonnet or the proportions
of some great cathedral, belong to what is sensuous and
material, yet are fair and finely wrought. Indeed, is
there anything splendid we can conceive which may not,
at least, be the splendour of a sensuous thing ? Pride
of intellect itself would be something strange and only
half-alive if there were no possibility of physical utterance and no relation of any authentic kind to the
physical conditions of a social habitat.

Even supposing, however, what is most highly to
be questioned, and accepting arguments of this second
species as final and beyond dispute, the inference from
them to the third and critical step is still exceedingly
precarious. What has been asserted above is that

bodily facts may achieve the highest dignity, and that it must be doubtful whether there is anything else that could achieve it. This is very different indeed from the assertion that biological principles determine moral ones, and it is the latter assertion that requires to be proved. Biological categories, in a certain sense, may, indeed, be purposive; but what is the relation of biological purpose to moral endeavour? It is surely quite insufficient to maintain that the beings who profess moral purposes are themselves biological creatures; and even if it is urged in a broad way that our consciousness and all the values that pertain to it are themselves continuations and refinements of an infra-conscious biological adaptation, the argument remains inconclusive. We have still to ask, independently, what these biological purposes are, and how they are related to moral commandments.

In general, we are told that the biological purpose of any individual or species is sustenance for as long a time as possible and in as great numbers as possible. Furthermore, that complexity of development or organization is also such a purpose. The creature, as Ward said, by filling its skin well, gets a better skin to fill.

The mere duration and fecundity of animal existence, however, is very far indeed from determining the true ends of moral conduct. It has relevance, and that is all. Granting that ethics has to do with the conduct of life, the ethical question proper depends upon the distinction between living well or ill. Both of these are instances of living. Therefore life is pre-supposed in both and in a certain quantity. Hence the relevance of its duration and fecundity. The critical question, however, is quality, not quantity. A species better adapted for survival or multiplication need not therefore be the better species. If it were so, then, if the conditions of our environment altered and a world of lichens replaced the world we live in, the lichens would have to be finer beings than the races they supplanted. And so wherever we look. The relinquishment of life itself may be a moral duty, and apart from this extreme instance there is a host of duties that could not possibly be justified from the standpoint of simple health or longevity. It is not obvious, even, that if our present human species learned to live as long as oaks or parrots do, it would therefore be the better. It might only be more tenacious of its existence. Similarly, if medical skill learned how to make our last illnesses endure for many years, it would not follow that this was one of the major advantages we owe to a noble profession. And if industrialism has made the population of Europe immensely greater than it was, does it stand to reason that Europe must have gained in consequence?

Accordingly, if this biological hegemony over moral principles were to be established by reasons that are not merely relevant, but sufficient, biology itself would have to offer an adequate basis for the qualitative differences in living, and here (as in Ward's *mot* quoted above) it has only complexity to offer. This increase in organic complexity, however, is itself neither a biological necessity nor a manifest token of excellence. It is not a necessity, as we have seen, because a less complex mode of existence (as in the hypothetical survival of the lichens) might come to be decreed by the environment; and, again, because certain species may never become more complex, and may retain their station in the world, not by developing further, but by using the complexities they have attained. In passing, we may say, indeed, that this is the common conception of human nature ; for we hold that in essentials it is always the same, and we may even build our hopes of progress upon this foundation, and at any rate be confident that we are not in a stage of transition and on the way to becoming strange and inhuman supermen. We prefer to consider ourselves super-anthropoids. Similarly, complexity need not bespeak excellence, although excellent things are usually, and perhaps must be, complex. For complexity may nevertheless be bad. The truth is that evolutionary theories in the past have assumed quite uncritically some biological necessity for progress, and that Darwin *substituted* a natural for a theological account of perfecti-bility. This may have been a reasonable description of historical process in Nature for very lengthy periods, but it might all be reversed or made to falter, and so need not be more than contingent. The dogma of inexorable improvement can never be a lesson from evolution.

These general arguments, therefore, force us back upon ethics. When we ask to be shown what is good we need not expect anything except the good itself to instruct us. This revelation of the good is axiology, and the use of it is ethics. There is no other monitor. Instead, then, of attempting to determine ethics from the outside we have to work from within ; and if biological principles are to help us as much as is claimed they must vindicate themselves by their ethical merits. This, however, is also claimed, and so we must examine the pretension.

If the biological principles in question are admitted to be the " self-assertion, the unscrupulous seizing upon all that can be grasped, the tenacious holding of all that can be kept," of which Huxley spoke in his famous Romanes Lecture, it is manifest that these standards, when applied to individual conduct, are, as Huxley said, " the headquarters of the enemy of ethical nature." Even Machiavelli supposed these maxims appropriate to the ways of princes only, not at all to private citizens.   It is unnecessary, however, to maintain that these biological standards should be applied directly and without qualification to individual behaviour, for to do so would be to misread the biological situation. Animal species, very frequently, could not continue unless the parents showed solicitude for their broods, educating and protecting their offspring ; and the care of hens or of insects over their egg-laying, the rotation of family duties among mating ostriches, and the like, are matters of common knowledge.   An extension of these principles, then, it is claimed, yields the moral commandments.   Human beings, delicate and often help-less in their lonely powers, become great by co-opera-tion only.   First the family ;   then the clan ;   then the nation ;   then, if we are wise, humanity itself.   It is the paramount biological duty of acting in concert for the ends of the human species that determines all our defensible codes, and this for the general advantage of individual human beings as well as for the strength of the race.

This is a serious argument, strong at the first look, and perhaps stronger still.   It tallies with much in our current practice which we do not take to be morally indefensible—indeed, this should almost go without the saying.   Take, for example, our ordinary attitude towards the resources of the world.   In a small degree, it is true, we protest rather fitfully against the devastation of natural loveliness, but we do so from the standpoint of human enjoyment, and most of us are rather tepid in our protests.   On the whole, we have enormously increased the sum of terrestrial ugliness, and are con-tent to suggest plaintively that some of our slag-heaps might be made green again.   Or take the crucial example to which moralists, as we have seen, should return far more frequently than they do. According to Mill and to many other moralists, it is true, we ought to strive for the happiness of all sentient creatures; but we do not consult the salmon and the turkeys and the rest, and most of us would admit, I think, that there is an unconscious but highly significant hypocrisy in the way in which we single out certain of the animals for special praise, not because they make a stand for their own ends, but because they are faithful to *us*. The best that can be said here is that, while we might vastly improve our practice in these matters, we could not afford to make it radically different from what it is; and that, after all, we *are* superior to the other animals. This may be enough, but it is an odd way of denying that our standards here are completely ruthless in their essence, and very thoroughly self-assertive.

Even within our own species, again, certain parts of our code do not seem to be distinguishably different from predatory force. When all is said, we have a somewhat watery regard for humanity as a whole. International relations, class-warfare, the attitude of white-skinned people to the coloured races when the whites want oil or copra or ivory and the others have it, seems to indicate sufficiently what we really believe. To be sure, we claim, very often, that we are as unselfish as our means allow, and that out of dubious motives we have often succeeded in achieving a greater welfare for the majority. After all, Britain abolished the slave trade. Again, even a vehement moralist might be constrained to admit that it would be very difficult indeed to explain in detail how our practice in these matters could be fundamentally improved with immediate beneficial results. All this may be true, and yet we must say one or other of two things. Either our practice here is wholly indefensible in a moral regard (as is held, for example, by those who maintain that the experiments of Christianity or of Socialism have never been tried), or else, being on the whole defensible, it is not entirely opposed to the law of force and self-assertion.

Laying hold on these admissions, therefore, our biological moralists proceed to assert that the primary law of all living is just tenacity and security of existence, and that the way in which human beings actually contrive to secure a firm and tenacious existence governs and compels the moral order itself. The ordinary moralist, they go on to tell us, unless like Hobbes or ourselves, he is shaken out of his sheltered complacency by the bitter ferments of political unrest, forgets that there are problems concerning the possibility of existence, and is absurdly preoccupied with cloistered excellences. He forgets, in fact, that a great part of our conduct *is* concerned with the bare possibility of living— with health and the means for health, with protection and security for the employment of any of our capacities. If it be true (as I dare say it is true) that the " naturalization " of disease and its separation from the idea of a penalty for sinning is one of the greatest achievements of the science of medicine, it might similarly be contended, we are informed, that a sane, natural and purely physical regard for the health and longevity of our species is the finest, not the most despicable, means for attempting to lay the foundations of a Moral Ideal. Our moral theories should not be unbiological ; on the contrary, we should endeavour to make them less ignorantly biological. If we knew enough, we should see that our duties towards the unborn are at least as great as any others, and might learn more from medicine than from superstition and *tabu*. We might also find that sanitation is more useful than mere high-mindedness, and hospitals more splendid than naval predominance. When we have learnt these lessons our morality will have come near to vindicating itself.

In short, according to the argument, the moral virtues are precisely (and only) those qualities of character which make for social solidarity, and therefore, in the large, for social strength. Truthfulness and the keeping of covenants are the foundations of trust and credit in any society which co-operates through language and writing. Hence their moral importance. Love, benevolence, generosity, sympathy are the very cement of corporate existence. Of obedience, tolerance, discipline, courage and the rest, the same may be said; and the defence may penetrate even further. Obstinacy and opinionatedness prevent the smoother workings of social life, but a society, nevertheless, may be all the stronger if its members are rather tough-minded and even opinionated. The reference to social solidarity, therefore, cuts both ways; and this, as we all know, is exactly the difficulty of our moralists concerning these qualities of character. Mere docility, similarly, and the trooping of the herd, although they may be useful, need not be the strongest social bond. Hence, again, our perplexities concerning valour and humility, and the whole " reversal of values " in the Sermon on the Mount. In short, it is only anti-social qualities that are morally vicious, and by these are meant, not rebellion against the established social order in some given society (since rebellion itself may aim at and possibly achieve some better thing for the society), but qualities which are a source of weakness to *any* society, wheresoever and whensoever they exist.

It would not be possible, of course, to vindicate all our values, or to justify all the injunctions of our reigning codes in terms of this principle, but then it is extraordinarily unlikely that any principle can prove itself able to bring definitive and impeccable order into the labile entanglement of our living. What is claimed, then, according to this principle, is only that these biological necessities always furnish a governing canon which should never be flagrantly violated and cannot be ignored in the smallest degree without raising serious difficulties in any honest mind. And this, we are told, is enough.

Even a doubtful instance may strongly support the contention, and we may select an illustration from Mr. Hobhouse. " On a torpedoed ship," he remarks in his *Social Justice*, " if the last boat will only take twenty of the thirty that remain, it is better that twenty should be saved than that none should be saved. Justice can show itself only in the selection; and, so far as they can, men choose (1) those who can manage the boat (i.e. by function); (2) those who have the greatest claim upon life, e.g. married people or mothers and children. In general, women and children are preferred partly because men (in accordance with a race-preserving instinct) place a higher value upon their lives than upon the lives of other men, partly because they are more helpless, and in preferring them men have the compensation of death with honour; (3) the feeble generally. In their case a sentiment of justice operates, even if it be not easy to validate in its particular application; for, as a matter of justice, it is a general function of the strong to protect the weak; and though in the case contemplated weak and strong are much on a level, the sentiment holds, and is backed perhaps by the feeling that the strong have more endurance." [1]

Assuming, as I think we may assume, that these principles are a fair statement of the code we actually

[1] Pp. 118–19.

follow in such matters, it is plain that even the most
arbitrary portions of the code have a colourable pretext,
at least, of tending towards social solidarity. Social
efficiency, however, is much more doubtfully obeyed.
From this point of view, any race-preserving measures
should extend, not to all women, but only to the younger
ones ; it is quaint to argue that the married have a
greater claim to life than the unmarried, or that death
with honour should be a compensation for men only ;
and the protection of those who must always be feeble
is at least as much a burden as an aid to society, even
granting that the assurance of a provision for old age
is an encouragement to those who are still very far
from having reached the years of superannuation.
Accordingly, there seems a pretty definite contrast
between the law of the strongest society and certain
portions of our ordinary code ; yet even here we may
say that, precisely where the conflict is at all acute, we
wonder most frequently whether the law of the strongest
society is not, after all, the saner and the better justified.
In general, it includes the protection of the weak by
the strong, the taking of risks and responsibilities in
dangerous callings like a seaman's, the setting of an
example by responsible officers to their less responsible
subordinates ; and even when we turn to special cases
which, as Mr. Hobhouse says, are " very hard to
validate," we have at least the truth to confront us that
difficulties thicken for us precisely at the point where
a marked loss of social efficiency seems to occur (for
instance, in the protection of the feeble). It is obviously
disputable what proportion of a limited revenue should
be devoted to the education of the young as compared
with provision for the widowed, the infirm, and the
old ; and all of us, I think, are profoundly impressed
by the pity of the world when we think of young people

devoting themselves, even with the sincerest affection and gratitude, to the care of some helpless invalid.

This attempt, therefore, to show from within that animate creatures, for their moral purposes, find biological conditions present at every turn, and that the dominant part of their duty consists simply in endeavouring to find that social solidarity which is essential to their security and continuance, is impressive because of its wide and subtle range. Nevertheless it fails in the end. The argument from within, as we have seen, is necessarily an ethical argument—that is to say, its business is to justify conduct in terms of achievable values. It has shown, let us grant, that, in an indirect but very puissant and pervasive fashion, the fundamental necessities of biological existence, and the mere strength and efficiency of the community can seldom, if ever, be safely neglected. But security for what end, and efficiency for what purpose? To these questions neither security nor efficiency can supply any answer, for the former is not enough and the latter may be abused. Despite the seeming strength of the argument, it has left huge gaps vacant. It has shown that love brings strength, but not that the grace and sweetness which love may attain are necessarily stronger than love of a coarser fibre; that truth is strong as a means to social confidence, not that, apart from and in addition to this, the truth claims our allegiance; that beauty, perhaps, gladdens and rejoices us (being, therefore, strong), not that the beauty which is, biologically speaking, a luxury and a partial enemy to sterner things may not be a worthy end notwithstanding. In short, when we consider the whole range of values from within we are led into a discussion indefinitely wider than the important but limited question of the relations between value and strength. The mere reminder, indeed, that, as we saw in the last chapter, might need not be right even if it is the efficiency of a powerful people, is enough of itself to overthrow the contention ; but it seemed better to give the argument a freer range.

Among further reasons, then, against this omnipotence of social solidarity in an ethical regard, one which seems strangely alien to many of the best of our contemporary thinkers, is in reality entirely conclusive. If the argument we have been engaged in considering were sound, it would prove that values are not, authentically speaking, *values* at all, but, on the contrary, completely relative to the human species, the mere perquisite of one particular anthropoid herd. Even the mediæval cosmologists made no such error as this. They were mistaken, no doubt, in assigning to man's Earth a privileged station of geo-centrality, but they also took the Earth to be the Lord's, and instead of regarding man as the aim of all things, or the only arbiter of his own or of any values, they asserted him to be the servant of the highest. This was the salt of their other-worldliness.[1] Renouncing his dream of a spatial privilege, man, in these modern times, is apt to assume to himself a moral finality which, if it were true, would be the destruction of all his ethics. Even our theologians to-day are apt to speak as if a mere description of man's " religious psychology " were an adequate substitute for the study of *theology*. Yet if values are not absolute, they are nothing. As we have seen already more than once, we all admit the fact when we admit that we owe anything to any of the other animals for their own sakes, or even that it is wrong in principle to torture them. It is not simply the evil effects of cruelty upon humanity that makes the torturer what he is. The suffering of his victims who are

[1] See Appendix IV.

not men is its chief condemnation. Therefore human values are not the only ones with which man is concerned, and if they were, since values are absolute, the circumstance would be an accident, not a thing of principle. On the question of policy it is true, this modern outlook may conceivably have proved itself the wiser. It is an illogical conclusion from the sense of our loneliness and helplessness in these cosmic immensities, but it may be salutary all the same. We have to cultivate our gardens, and we have not, as yet, learned to cultivate them nearly well enough. Therefore, perhaps, it is possible to think too much of heaven. Nevertheless, if our convictions are not shams, all our directions in terms of value must have an absolute, not a relative, basis. We must seek them, not because *we* are men, but because *they* have dominion within man and over him. On any other theory there are *no* values, but only certain anthropomorphic tendencies and satisfactions. This justifies nothing; and therefore it cannot be the basis of morals.

Accordingly, an ethical naturalism, like any other theory that is truly ethical, leads us straight and sure to the absolute sovereignty of commandments grounded upon the best we may achieve. The truth of " naturalism " in this regard, if even here it is true, is that we have to employ our natural talents by natural means for a natural end ; but it is the good in our nature and environment we have thus to develop, and this goodness is determined by its own standards, and is never a good simply because it is natural. The same holds if we have supernatural assistance. If finite creatures, through the imperfections of their imaginations, are unable to see God's purposes as God Himself does, they must at least believe that goodness in its fundamental character is the same in God as it is for us, and that God's very being is the pure essence of this sovereignty of the best. In this, we must admit, Mill's argument was final when he prevailed over Mansel's "Unconditioned." "If," he said, " instead of the ' glad tidings ' that there exists a Being in whom all the excellences which the highest human mind can conceive, exist in a degree inconceivable to us, I am informed that the world is ruled by a Being whose attributes are infinite, but what they are we cannot learn, nor what are the principles of his government, except that ' the highest human morality which we are capable of conceiving ' does not sanction them ; convince me of it, and I will bear my fate as I may. But when I am told that I must believe this, and at the same time call this Being by the names which express and affirm the highest human morality, I say in plain terms that I will not. Whatever power such a Being may have over me, there is one thing which He shall not do ; He shall not compel me to worship Him. I will call no Being good, who is not what I mean when I apply that epithet to my fellow-creatures ; and if such a Being can sentence me to hell for not so calling Him, to hell I will go." [1]

The meaning, indeed, of our convictions upon this matter is so thoroughly plain that nothing but sophistry, or a finicking distrust in visible things just because they are visible, can be set in the scales against it. As we all know, every sensible man comes of himself to this conclusion. He may not appreciate, indeed, how hard it often is to discern the good, but he never falters in his belief that if he sees the straight and the decent thing to do, it is his duty to do it, irrespective of all other considerations. In these islands, to be sure, unless it is wartime, we do not talk overmuch of duty, and one

[1] *An Examination of Sir William Hamilton's Philosophy*, 4th edition, pp. 128-9.

of the reasons is its entire finality. To perceive a duty is to put a stop to all else, and because it is so manifestly final we are chary, when in our right minds, of thrusting it in anyone's face, or of proclaiming to anyone that we ourselves are obeying it. The appeal to duty should therefore be reserved for the greatest occasions. Nevertheless, it is ultimate ; and if we do not say very much about it, we are fully aware of the fact.

Certainly, the spirit (although not the essence, and perhaps not often the letter) of moral direction would properly be altered if we knew certain other things and were assured of the substance of what we may hope for. If we were assured that right must prevail in the end, or that we put on immortality if we do not destroy ourselves by our continuance in evil, then, although the details of moral conduct might not be appreciably affected, the spirit and tenor of it very properly might. For in this case our opportunities, capacities, and environment would be greater things than, without this assurance, they now might seem to be. The greater historical religions, indeed, have been far from content with this general reference to the spirit of our action, and have sought to deduce certain alterations in our practical codes. They have enjoined fasting, or prayer, or the avoidance of certain contaminations, and since these means to salvation depend upon a theological assurance concerning the divinity that surrounds our living, these practical consequences very logically follow from the general theological outlook. The principles of morals, however, do not stand or fall with the possibility of revelation or any similar assurance. Given this assurance, what we have to do is to apply our moral principles in the light of it. Without it, we have to apply these same principles to that which, apart from revelation, appears to be our station.

These questions, in a word, concern the power of the good and not its essential character or the basis of our allegiance to it.   That which I ought to do is not logically dependent upon that which I hope for except in so far as the things I may reasonably hope for affect the use of my capacities that I take to be possible ; and this is the fundamental question of the relation of moral principles to God and freedom and immortality.   As I have suggested, indeed, at an earlier stage of the argument, a part of the problem of freedom may have a different place from the others, for if a certain kind and degree of freedom is implied, not, indeed, in the character of values, but in the possibility of any moral regulation in terms of them, it follows that this degree of freedom must be taken to be of the essence of morality, and so to be different from the rest.   For this degree of freedom, however, no profounder metaphysic is required than that given in outline at the close of our chapter on freedom, and it is notorious that God's foreknowledge and omnipotence rather complicate than alleviate the perplexities of the special question.   Concerning the " conservation " and progressive triumph of values, however, and concerning immortality, the relation is the one stated above.

It is well that it is so, for these latter questions are of the utmost difficulty, as we may readily see when we take them in turn.

The progressive evolution of values, for reasons we have already noted, is perhaps the hardest of them all. Passing over the more empirical reasons, however, we have to remark on more ultimate ones, and these concern time itself.   I do not think, indeed, that time (if there is time) should be accounted a metaphysical evil and the natural enemy of the good.   It implies, indeed, a species of finitude, but finitude need not be evil; and we need not hold, I think, as so many do, that change (and with it time) implies imperfection. There is no manifest inconsistency in supposing the existence of a perfect being who enjoys and exercises his perfections at successive moments, not timelessly, or, again, all at once; for although the changes we desire are often to remove an evil or to attain some better condition (or, in other words, are directed towards the removal of some admitted imperfection), it is possible that they might not be of this order, but, on the contrary, like many others among the changes we desire, a passage from something which would be evil only if we persisted in it too long, to the next subsequent stage in an appropriate rhythm. Changelessness, again, need not be good; and so from this general reasoning nothing whatsoever follows.

When we turn, however, from these abstract proofs to the possibilities open to human agents, the argument does depend upon imperfections. We are arguing here about the conditions of progress and about the grounds for a rational confidence in the emergence of something better. Here the change from our great imperfection to at least a lesser imperfection is the very pulse of the affair, and is undoubtedly relevant to any beliefs we may cherish concerning the supremacy of values. If values are subject to temporal obstructions, they are certainly not omnipotent; and if the obstructions are temporarily overcome, why should they not break out again? A more moderate theory, indeed, may bring the greater comfort. Empirically, we may reasonably expect an ample scope in futurity for this essential betterment; but if we are told that all that we call change is not change at all, neither progress nor retrogression would seem to have any proper meaning. What *could* our morals be if we never are, and never were, in our sins?

The attempt, therefore, to avoid these difficulties by denying the reality of time or of change seems a remedy even more desperate than the disease. If that which seems of all things the most certain is itself to be called an illusion, what greater certainty can we hope to put in its place? Again, time and change seem part of the substance of much that we take to be valuable. When it is right and fitting for an unburdened mortal to fleet the time carelessly, the evanescence of this holiday leisure is an integral part of the duty. The uncertainties of life, and the need to employ ourselves when we may, are bound up with the very being of all our endeavours. And who could preserve a melody if there were no sequence within it?

It may be replied, however, that at least we need some assurance of stability in these affairs; and this, I suppose, is the problem of the " conservation of values."

It is difficult, I think, to give an interpretation of this phrase that is likely both to be true and to be congruent with moral opinion. On these grounds, at any rate, certain possible interpretations should clearly be eliminated. A possible meaning of the phrase, for example, would be the principle that nothing valuable can ever perish. This seems plainly opposed to the fragility of many valuable things, and a denial of the essential connection between uncertainty and the best exercise of many moral qualities. Again, we are tolerably certain both that good may come out of evil and that evil may come out of good, and so are forbidden to hold another possible interpretation, the view, namely, that everything that is good continues to have good effects. This prohibition is no loss in reality, for it would be fully as plausible to hold that everything evil continues to work evilly.

What seems to be meant, rather, is a certain stability in moral opportunity and the continuance of the agents which are capable of laying hold of these opportunities. The point is that radical impermanence, not of this or that in morality, but of all moral opportunity and achievement, is a proof of failure. Moral practice *must* be able to make indefinite drafts upon the future. If the end of all our strivings were silence and utter night, there would be a radical futility in the whole process.

This is true in a sense, but it is important to notice what the true sense is. If the Whole were the subject of our censure or admiration, and if it had the power to continue what it thus permits to lapse, we should have to condemn it on this very account. When the argument, however, applies, not to the universe, but to moral agents within it, the proper conclusion is quite different. Although our works may perish in the end, they were still good works when they were good, and better than no work at all. We are the more powerful if we work for all time, but if we have to work for a short time only, we may still be better or worse, and it is still our business to act as well as we can. Accordingly, we cannot claim perpetuity either for ourselves or for the consequences of our acts, as an essential requirement of the moral life, and if we attempt to apply these conceptions to the universe we seem in the end to be asserting a special, if highly important, consequence of our beliefs concerning the supremacy, or at any rate the power, of values within it. What the argument shows is that if there is this dominion, it must show itself *in sæcula sæculorum*; for its instability, if it need not be unstable, would be a sorry jest and a piece of childish wantonness. A supremacy, however, which governed only in the point of *time* would be an odd sort of supremacy; and it can never be plausible to make an axiom out of the consequence and application of a greater principle.

The application of this demand for continuance, on moral grounds, to the case of our own selves is manifestly still more disputable. Yet the question presses, since we are told both that there are moral proofs which plainly indicate the probability of our personal immortality; and, again, that because we are immortal it behoves us, morally, to order our lives in a different fashion from the lives which are without any hope of it. I shall conclude our study, then, with a brief examination of a few of the chief considerations in this double line of argument.

Among the " moral " proofs of immortality we may mention the following:

(1) That if we did not continue for ever it would be unreasonable for us to try to be good for a time;

(2) That certain things which we must admit to be duties would not be duties if we were not immortal;

(3) That in a short life certain of the consequences intrinsically appropriate to moral or immoral conduct could not be fulfilled;

(4) That immortality, principally for our friends, is the main human hope, so that if we are cheated in this we are robbed of the spirit that makes virtue possible;

(5) That in general moral consequences fall chiefly upon the moral agent himself, and so that, if there is any conservation of values, it is most natural to suppose that the conservation is truly that of these moral agents themselves.

It is evident that the majority of these arguments call upon principles already discussed. Despite this, the wide interest in this particular application of them may excuse a more prolonged attention.

Thus, we have just decided that the principle of
(1) is false, but may remark here that even if the possible
cessation of all values implied an invincible futility in
moral endeavour, scarcely anyone not hopelessly prejudiced or incurably sophisticated by the selfish theories
of certain psychologies, would assent to this argument.
Even although we ourselves may perish, we may surely
still be effective contributors towards a work that is
good, and far greater than ourselves. The very persons
who profess to believe in this monstrous sophism
usually give themselves the lie direct by their further
assertions, for they say that if we are not immortal we
should eat and drink and be merry. This is to admit
that there *are* certain values—namely, fleeting, sensuous,
terrestrial blisses. If so, these values accrue to everyone
who enjoys them, and it is plain that, in the present
world, anyone who toils for the general sensuous
welfare of his friends or of the community is committed
to an enterprise indefinitely wider than his own brief
affairs. In reality, therefore, those who assent to this
contention about eating and being merry, in all essentials hold that nothing but a man's *own* enjoyments
should weigh with him, and that any unselfish action in
this life must either be justified according to what Mr.
Bradley once called the " do it or be damned " theory,
or else compensated by some superior bliss in heaven.
It is unnecessary, surely, to consider at greater length
anything so barbarous, mischievous, and grotesque.

(2) This second argument would have a far stronger
foundation, and might even be conclusive if it could
establish its own truth. I must confess, however, that
I cannot see any instance of a manifest duty, revelation
apart, that in this way presupposes immortality. On
the contrary, I am convinced that the instances, if there
are any, are few and highly dubious. If so, this argu-

ment, while admirably fashioned for its purpose, would seem to be composed of entirely insubstantial material.

(3) The third contention refers to reward and punishment, but these notions, in their turn, do not seem to be able to bear the weight of it. As regards rewards, we are all, I think, very doubtful. We do not want spiritual medals and orders; and although we admit the appropriateness and necessity, in a psychological sense, of certain conditions that may be called rewards (such as the satisfactions of self-respect or the esteem that a man's fellows ought to feel for what is good in his work), we cannot regard immortal bliss, or an immense compensation hereafter for those who have been meek and long-suffering for a few years upon this earth, as in any sense an appropriate reward. We might even think it a better universe if everyone were happy, including the wicked, just as we should not grudge anyone sunlight and food and air. Punishment, again, even if it be a moral as well as a practical and a political necessity, does not seem to yield so momentous a consequence as this. We may believe, indeed, that in shame of conscience and the like there is an appropriate recompense in a moral agent; and we may defend punishment proper (by which I mean punishment as described in the " retributive," although non-vindictive, theory as opposed to the conceptions of deterrence or reformation) in two ways. As against the theory of mere deterrence and social expediency, we may urge that if the infliction of pain or loss or some physical evil is the only way of accomplishing some necessary social defence, we must still have a principle to the effect that it is just and right that this physical or other evil should be inflicted upon the *offender* and not upon others. Without this, there would not be punishment, but a measure as little punitive, say, as rationing in wartime;

and although a punishment visited upon the offender
is doubtless a greater deterrent to actual and would-be
offenders than any other, this is not enough ; for, if it
were, a hostage would be in the same moral position as
a delinquent. As against the reformatory theory,
again, we may urge that reformatory punishment, as
opposed to other forms of compulsory initiation into
well-doing, must be reformation through punishment
proper—that is to say, through the infliction of some pain
or loss which is fitted to arouse the " serve-me-right "
feeling, and to lead to self-accepted improvement.

If we admit, however, that some such theory of
punishment is in the end thoroughly defensible, whether
we like it or not, we cannot surely suppose that *any*
theory of this kind implies an eternity of punishment.
There is, in fact, *no* measure in these things. Political
punishments must be measured by the deterrent theory
and by no other. Society should punish in the smallest
degree necessary to the attainment of the social needs
of punishment, and there seems no good reason why
any *man* should adopt a different principle. More
generally an extrinsic pain does not have any proportion
to the moral gravity of any offence (although, no doubt,
if pain be necessary to deter, in general a greater pain
may have to be inflicted in order to deter from a graver
offence). If there were such a proportion, it may well
be doubted whether *any* sin deserves infinite punishment,
or, again, whether *every* sin does not ; and in the latter
case God's mercy seems at odds with His justice. Certainly the wicked in this life often take their sins very
lightly, and are stricken neither by gods nor by men ;
but if this is an aspersion upon the terrestrial order of
affairs, the same aspersion, for all we can tell, might still
be made if life continued beyond the grave. Why
should this *physical* difference so profoundly affect a

moral order? What right have we to hold that a continuation of our existence is likely to imply a radical discontinuity in the course of moral development?

(4) *Non sequitur*; and the premise is doubtful, although this hope is passionately cherished by a great number.

(5) I have intentionally stated this argument in a form which does not pretend to be conclusive, because there should be no such pretence. Nevertheless, although this argument, at the best, can only " incline without necessitating," it is stronger, I think, than the others and, indeed, should have weight. It is unlikely, indeed, that in any scheme of things everyone would be able to bring all his capacities to all the fruitions of which they are capable. As we saw when we dealt with " self-sacrifice," authentic goods must indeed be relinquished (although only for greater ones); and although a great mind becoming feeble is one of the saddest of mortal things, it is possible that if everyone lived out his days to a ripe old age, or, in general, if the opportunities for moral fulfilment were at all commensurate with moral capacity, we might, on the whole, be less affected by the force of this contention than in fact we are. The waste of great capacity, when it has reached its zenith, would indeed be a terrible thing, and a decade or two of the prime of life is on any theory woefully brief. It is not what we should expect of a moral universe. Still we may toil with greater zest and freshness if the generations work in relays; and this consideration (again on any theory) mitigates the severity of the argument before us. The waste that we find, however, is far greater than this, for disease and death are not even stayed by the greatest capacity or by the finest conscience, and the duration of human existence, as we find it, does not seem to be ordered in the

ways we should naturally take to be appropriate to a moral order. We can scarcely avoid the reflection, therefore, that if death is not the end, the moral government of the universe is the easier to comprehend.

The other set of moral arguments upon this question has the object of showing that the fact of our immortality should profoundly affect the conduct of our lives. This, with an important reservation, is undeniable. Just as, among human beings, it makes a great difference what time a man has to count upon if he is sanely to consider what he ought to do; or, again, just as it should make a great difference to the plans of humanity if we knew for certain that some madman who had learned how to disrupt the atom would also, very shortly, disrupt this pleasant globe and could not be prevented from doing so, so here. We cannot suppose that " business as usual " is the last sane word in any emergency. The reservation, however, is so important that it affects these general truisms very profoundly indeed. We know so very little of a future existence that we have only the vaguest conjecture to go upon. There is no question of Pascal's bet, but, in terms of his arguing, a wagering with an indeterminate number of indeterminate possibilities. There is no use, therefore, in attending to any such wagering; and even if we have a better assurance than this unworthy application of the doctrine of chances, we know that our most reasonable confidence in an endless future is not likely to instruct us overmuch concerning the things which we have now to do.

Therefore, I think, we are bound to infer that neither the more special arguments which concern our immortality, nor the more general arguments that have to do with the stability and the conservation of values have an ethical importance at all comparable to that of the autonomous ethic which this study has attempted to analyse and to defend. Even if we were assured of an abiding spiritual home for our own unending existence, or of a fundamental conformity between the aims of the universe and our own aspirations, the effect of this assurance would be rather to supply information concerning the extent of our opportunities and of the limitless assistance we are entitled to count upon than properly to determine the use we should make of them. Indeed (and going further), it seems unnecessary to concede that a morality that is " fired with religion " is truly to be preferred to one that might conceivably exist without this inspiration. Morality is absolute and autonomous. It is neither cold nor unsubstantial, and its strength, psychologically speaking, is authentic and well attested. Indeed, there are solid reasons for supposing that many religions would be of little account if *they* were not " fired with morality," and that, where the two conflict, it is not morality that should yield.

As we have seen, the autonomy of ethics and the absolute character of values necessarily go together. Ethical premises, and these alone, are able to answer the question, " Why should I, or any other being, be moral ? " and moralists, in the end, have either to show that morality is what it claims to be or else to deny it in principle and explain its pretensions away. In this study the former course has been pursued, and for reasons that seemed truly to be such. Obligation, we have maintained, is a reasonable thing, defensible upon considered reflection, and it is reasonably to be accepted by mankind without any overweening pretensions concerning their singularity or their pre-eminence in the occupations of the universe. " Human affairs," Plato said in his *Laws*, " are hardly worth considering with any great seriousness, and yet we must be in earnest about them " (803*b*). This is perhaps too hard a saying, and may seem even terrible. Yet if it were indeed the truth, we should have to hold fast to that which it is our duty to do. It is our proper and our reasonable business to make ourselves worthy of our undoubted resources and of our many opportunities, however insignificant, in some larger cosmic sense, we might, peradventure, be forced to admit them to be.

ON "MIXED" ETHICAL ARGUMENTS

It may be pointed out that the principles enunciated at the beginning of Chapter II and elsewhere in this book are not inconsistent with the legitimate employment of "mixed" ethical arguments where the term "mixed" has the same meaning as in the "mixed hypothetical arguments" of school logic; and Mr. Broad, in his recent *The Mind and its Place in Nature*, has thought it advisable to show this in detail. "Mixed ethical arguments," he says there on pages 488–9, "can always be put into one of the two forms: "If anything had the ethical characteristic E, it would have the non-ethical characteristic N," or "If anything had the non-ethical characteristic N, it would have the ethical characteristic E." The valid arguments are accordingly: (*a*) If E, then N. But E ∴ N, (*b*) If E, then N. But not N ∴ not E, (*c*) If N, then E. But N ∴ E, and (*d*) If N, then E. But not E ∴ not N (*i.e.* the legitimate affirmation of the antecedent and the legitimate denial of the consequent).

The truths, however, remain (as Mr. Broad fully admits) (1) that no purely factual conclusion can be proved from purely ethical premises; (2) that no purely ethical conclusion can be proved from purely factual premises; and (3) that any "mixed" ethical premise must ultimately depend, for the ethical part of it, upon purely ethical argument or intuition. The obscurity from which so many so-called " ethical " theories suffer is precisely that, while they ought to be set forth as "mixed" ethical arguments, they do not, in fact, distinguish between their ethical and their non-ethical constituents. Accordingly, readers and writers alike fall into quite hopeless confusion.

Sometimes it is well to remind ourselves of Pascal's saying that every universe and every intelligence put together would not be worth a single movement of charity, since the latter is of a different order.

ON "ART FOR ART'S SAKE"

AN important lesson, I think, is conveyed by the ruthless consistency of Mr. Aldous Huxley's hero :

"It's a queer prejudice, this one of ours in favour of
art. Religion, patriotism, the moral order, humani-
tarianism, social reform—we have all of us, I imagine,
dropped all those overboard long ago. But we still
cling pathetically to art. Quite unreasonably ; for the
thing has far less reason for existence than most of the
objects of worship we have got rid of, is utterly senseless,
indeed, without their support and justification. Art for
art's sake—halma for halma's sake. It is time to smash
the last and silliest of the idols. My friends, I adjure
you, put away the ultimate and sweetest of the inebriants
and wake up at last completely sober—among the
dustbins at the bottom of the area steps."—*Those Barren
Leaves*, pp. 84–5.

APPENDIX III

ON THE " CALM PASSIONS "

THE following quotation from J. S. Mill's *The Subjection of Women*, Chapter III, indicates the possibility of a theory much less superficial than Hume's, although in conformity with his general argument: " History and experience prove that the most passionate characters are the most fanatically rigid in their feelings of duty, when their passion has been trained to act in that direction. The judge who gives a just decision where his feelings are intensely interested on the other side derives from that same strength of feeling the determined sense of the obligation of justice which enables him to achieve this victory over himself."

APPENDIX IV

DESCARTES ON MAN'S PLACE IN THE UNIVERSE

AND here is a quotation from the destroyer of mediævalism: "For although, as far as regards morals, it may be a pious thought to believe that God made all things for us, seeing we may thus be incited to greater gratitude and love toward Him, and although it is even in some sense true, because there is no created thing of which we cannot make some use, if it be only that of exercising our mind in considering it, and honouring God on account of it, it is yet by no means probable that all things were created for us in this way that God had no other end in their creation; and this supposition would be plainly ridiculous and inept in physical reasoning, for we do not doubt but that many things exist, or formerly existed and have now ceased to be, which were never seen or known by man, and were never of use to him." [1]

[1] Descartes, *The Principles of Philosophy*, Part III, § iii (Veitch's translation).

INDEX

Absoluteness of values, 302 *sq.*, 316.

Accountability, 37, 72, 185 *sq.*, 232, 248 *n.*, 249 *n.*

Action and morals, 12, 37 *sq.*; conditions of 82 *sq.*

Active disposition and the meaning of good, 198 *sq.*

Aesthetic character of morals 85, 96 *sq.*; æsthetic conscience 30 *sq.*, 54 *sqq.*; æsthetic judgment 104.

Aggregates, "mere," 255.

Alexander, S., 236 *sqq.*

Ambrose, St., 84.

Animals, duties toward xi *sq.*, 120, 296, 302; mental and moral characteristics of, 206, 277, 281.

Approval, characteristics of, 88 *sqq.*

Aristotle, 36, 68, 113, 124 *sqq.*, 135, 137, 140, 165, 207.

Arnauld, A., 209.

Art, as self-complete, 46; for art's sake, 31, 55 *sqq.*, 320 (see also Beauty); of morals, 63.

Audacious, loss of, 260.

Augustine, St., 84.

Authority and power, 121, 198 *sq.*, 202, 305 *sq.*

Autonomy of morals xii, xiv, chaps. ii, iii *passim*, 283 *sqq.*, 316.

Axiology, 33 *sq.*, 196 *sq.*, 268 *sq.*, 294.

Axioms in morals, 18 *sq.*, 80 *sq.*

Bacon, F., 9.

Beauty, authority of, 30, 34 *sq.*; as a dominant good 49 *sq.*; moral, 97; "objectivity" of, and variability, 100 *sqq.*; its carnal character, 291; and biology, 301.

Beccaria, the Marchese, and the Utilitarian formula, 109.

Bergson, H., 176.

Berkeley, Bishop G., 279.

Biology, and "mechanism," 170 *sqq.*, 192; and teleological values, 287 *sqq.*

Blake, W., 239 *n.*

Bradley, F. H., on casuistry, 62 *sq.*; on egoism, 311.

Brentano, F., 92 *sq.*

Broad, C. D., 318 *sq.*

Bosanquet, B., 274.

Bunyan, J., 99.

Burnet, J., 124, 135.

Burns, C. D., 240.

Butler, Bishop J., 72, 76.

Calculus, of goods, 106, 113; of pleasures, 107 *sqq.*; 116 *sqq.*

Caligula, 257.

"Calm passions," 127 *sq.*, 321.

Camelford, Lord, 15 *sq.*, 85.

Carlyle, the surgeon, 15.

Carlyle, T., 198.

Carnal and spiritual, 142, 289 *sqq.*

Casuistry, 62 *sq.*, 76 *sq.*, 86.

Catharsis, implications of, 155.

Change and imperfection, 307 *sq.*

Chicago murderers, 54.

Choice, 19, 35, 122, 138 *sqq.*, 166 *sq.*

Co-consciousness, 144.

Coherence not goodness, 236 *sqq.*

Cole, G. D. H., 244.

Collective control, 249; responsibility, 244, 256 *sqq.*; welfare, 241 *sqq*; willing, 236 *sq*, 256 *sqq.*

Common Good, ambiguity of, 241 *sqq.*, 262 *sq.*

Common sense and moral theory, 6 *sqq.*

Comprehensive aspect of moral philosophy, 269 *sqq.*

Compulsion, sense of, 162 *sq.*; character of, 163 *sqq.*

Concert, action in, 256 *sqq.*

Conclusiveness in moral argument, 2 *sq.*

Conscience, 30 *sq.*; distraction of, 232; psychology of, 120, 130 *sqq.*, 200 *sq.*; qualitative differences in, 210 *sqq.*

GEORGE ALLEN & UNWIN LTD.
LONDON: 40 MUSEUM STREET, W.C.1
CAPE TOWN: 73 ST. GEORGE'S STREET
SYDNEY, N.S.W.: WYNYARD SQUARE
WELLINGTON, N.Z.: 4 WILLIS STREET